# CREATIVE HOMEOWNER

# DECKS

## PLAN · DESIGN · BUILD

CREATIVE HOMEOWNER PRESS®, Upper Saddle River, New Jersey

Editorial Director: Timothy O. Bakke
Art Director: Annie Jeon

Author: Steve Cory
Editor: David Schiff
Copy Editor: Margaret Gallos
Deck Plans: Joe Baker of Decks by Baker, Geneva, Ill.,
        *Low-to-the-Ground Rambler* and
        *Simple Rectangle with Bays*;
        Joe Wood of San Diego,
        *Japanese-Style Covered Deck*

Graphic Designer: Heidi Garner
Illustrators: Ray Skibinski, Craig Franklin
Project Editor/Illustrator: Paul M. Schumm

Cover Design: Annie Jeon
Cover Photo: Ernest Braun, Dr. Robert F. Powers (Design)/
        California Redwood Association, Novato, CA

Photo Researchers: Alexander Samuelson, Georgette Blau


Manufactured in the United States of America
Electronic Prepress: TBC Color Imaging, Inc.
Printed at: Webcrafters, Inc.

Current Printing (last digit)
10 9 8 7 6 5 4 3 2

DECKS: Plan, Design, Build
Library of Congress Catalog Card Number: 96-72417
ISBN: 1-880029-93-6

## Photo Credits

p.1: Maurice Victoria, St. Charles, IL

p.6: Melabee M Miller, Hillside, NJ

p.7: John Schwartz, New York, NY

p.8: Melabee M Miller, Hillside, NJ

p.9: Western Wood Products Association, Portland, OR

p.10: The Flood Company

p.11 (top & bottom): Melabee M Miller, Hillside, NJ

p.12: Western Wood Products Association, Portland, OR

p.14: John Schwartz, New York, NY

p.16 (top): John Schwartz, New York, NY

p.16 (bottom): The Flood Company

p.17 (top): The Flood Company

p.17 (bottom): Southern Forest Products Association, Kenner, LA

p.18 (top & bottom): Western Wood Products Association, Portland, OR

p.19 (top): Western Wood Products Association, Portland, OR

p.19 (bottom l & r): Ernest Braun/California Redwood Association, Novato, CA

p.20 (top): Jessie Walker/ California Redwood Association, Novato, CA

p.20 (bottom): Western Wood Products Association, Portland, OR

p.21 (top): Ernest Braun/California Redwood Association, Novato, CA

p.21 (bottom): Intermatic, Malibu, CA

p.22: Ernest Braun/California Redwood Association, Novato, CA

p.52 & 53: California Redwood Association, Novato, CA

p.153, 154, 159: Maurice Victoria, St. Charles, IL

p.163: Edward Gohlich, Coronado, CA

# SAFETY FIRST

Though all the designs and methods in this book have been tested for safety, it is not possible to overstate the importance of using the safest construction methods possible. What follows are reminders; some do's and don'ts of basic carpentry. They are not substitutes for your own common sense.

- *Always* use caution, care, and good judgment when following the procedures described in this book.

- *Always* be sure that the electrical setup is safe; be sure that no circuit is overloaded, and that all power tools and electrical outlets are properly grounded. Do not use power tools in wet locations.

- *Always* read container labels on paints, solvents, and other products; provide ventilation, and observe all other warnings.

- *Always* read the tool manufacturer's instructions for using a tool—especially the warnings.

- *Always* use holders or pushers to work pieces shorter than 3 inches on a table saw or jointer. Avoid working short pieces if you can.

- *Always* remove the key from any drill chuck (portable or press) before starting the drill.

- *Always* pay deliberate attention to how a tool works so that you can avoid being injured.

- *Always* know the limitations of your tools. Do not try to force them to do what they were not designed to do.

- *Always* make sure that any adjustment is locked before proceeding. For example, always check the rip fence on a table saw or the bevel adjustment on a portable saw before starting to work.

- *Always* clamp small pieces firmly to a bench or another work surface when sawing or drilling.

- *Always* wear the appropriate rubber or work gloves when handling chemicals, doing heavy construction, or sanding.

- *Always* wear a disposable mask when working around odors, dust, or mist. Use a special respirator when working with toxic substances.

- *Always* wear eye protection, especially when using power tools or striking metal on metal or concrete; a chip can fly off, for example, when chiseling concrete.

- *Always* be aware that there is seldom enough time for your body's reflexes to save you from injury from a power tool in a dangerous situation; everything happens too fast. Be *alert!*

- *Always* keep your hands away from the business ends of blades, cutters, and bits.

- *Always* hold a portable circular saw with both hands so that you will know where your hands are.

- *Always* use a drill with an auxiliary handle to control the torque when large-size bits are used.

- *Always* check your local building codes when planning new construction. The codes are intended to protect public safety and should be observed to the letter.

- *Never* work with power tools when you are tired or under the influence of alcohol or drugs.

- *Never* cut very small pieces of wood or pipe. Whenever possible, cut small pieces off larger pieces.

- *Never* change a blade or a bit unless the power cord is unplugged. Do not depend on the switch being off; you might accidentally hit it.

- *Never* work in insufficient lighting.

- *Never* work while wearing loose clothing, hanging hair, open cuffs, or jewelry.

- *Never* work with dull tools. Have them sharpened, or learn how to sharpen them yourself.

- *Never* use a power tool on a work piece that is not firmly supported or clamped.

- *Never* saw a workpiece that spans a large distance between horses without close support on either side of the kerf; the piece can bend, closing the kerf and jamming the blade, causing saw kickback.

- *Never* support a workpiece with your leg or other part of your body when sawing.

- *Never* carry sharp or pointed tools, such as utility knives, awls, or chisels, in your pocket. If you want to carry tools, use a special-purpose tool belt with leather pockets and holders.

# CONTENTS

# PART 1

# DECK DESIGN AND CONSTRUCTION

Picture this: You invite friends over for supper, but instead of spending frantic hours cooking and cleaning, as you would with a dinner party, you just give the deck a quick sweep and fire up the barbecue. As guests arrive, they eagerly dip into the ice-filled cooler for drinks and snack on chips and dip, and nobody fusses over table settings. As the steaks hit the grill, some gather around to offer you encouragement, while others help spin the salad or relax on other parts of your deck, engaging in amiable conversation as the sun sinks over the trees.

Or imagine a lazy Sunday afternoon spent lounging in a hammock or deck chair. The newspaper in your hand holds your attention from time to time; you occasionally take note of the sun's course through the sky; you catch glimpses of birds and squirrels; nobody minds if you doze a bit; and keeping an eye on the kids is a breeze, since you enjoy being outdoors just as much as they do.

Then look ahead to the time when you want to sell your house. The real estate agent takes a look at your well-planned deck and informs you that it will increase the value of your home far beyond what you paid for it.

As you can see, there are mighty good reasons for building a deck. With a deck, you expand your living space and increase your home's value for a tiny fraction of what it would cost to build an addition. And you expand your living style as well, away from the T.V. and out into the open,

where friends naturally feel freer to chat and family members enjoy each other's company more easily than in enclosed spaces.

But for a deck to do all these things, there are many pitfalls to avoid. If attention is not paid to how the deck

relates to the yard and the way it fits with the house; if the deck is not the right size and shape to accommodate your needs; or if traffic and weather conditions are not sufficiently taken into account; then your money and hard work could be wasted. And the posts, beams, and joists must be of

the right size and must be correctly spaced. Even the most skilled carpenter cannot overcome a bad design. This book will help you avoid these problems and build a deck that is as eye-pleasing as it is functional.

A well-designed deck can not only enhance your life once it's built; it can be fun to build as well. Because of its size and importance, building a deck may seem a daunting task. But if you have even modest carpentry skills and are willing to work carefully, then you are up to this task. Deck building is not disruptive of your home life, as is the case with, say, kitchen remodeling. All the mess is kept outdoors, and as long as you have a good place to store materials, the job can stretch from weekend to weekend with no problem. Decks go up quickly, and you will be working in the beautiful out of doors.

*Decks* will show you how to design a deck that will please you and your family, and it will give you the instructions you need to construct a stable structure that will last for years with minimal maintenance. We will first help you to cultivate your dreams and come up with a design that is uniquely yours. For all aspects of the deck—framing, deck patterns, railings, stairways—we will give you a wide variety of options to choose from. Then we will give page after page of solid, easy-to-follow instructions that will enable you to correctly construct every part of your deck.

This book emphasizes designs that are "forgiving." Nobody is perfect, and even journeyman carpenters make mistakes. Wherever possible, we will recommend designs and methods that either will allow for

small mistakes, or that can be easily dismantled and corrected.

The first chapters of this book will show you how to envision and then plan for a deck that fits your home and your lifestyle. Then you will move on to easily followed, step-by-step instructions that will guide you from the bottom of the foundation to the top of the railings. We will give you a number of exciting options for enhancing your deck, and will describe for you how to finish and maintain your deck. The second part of the book presents three specific deck plans with complete drawings. These plans range from the very simple to the elaborate. With the information from the main body of the book, you will be able to modify these designs or come up with a design of your own to perfectly suit your needs.

# Chapter 1

# DESIGNING YOUR DECK

This chapter will help you envision your future deck in general terms; the next chapter is for making the serious drawings. Don't hesitate to do some dreaming as you seek to conjure up the basic idea of your deck—it doesn't cost a penny at this point! And don't rush the process. Your deck will be there a long time, and you are hoping everyone in the family will be happy with it.

## DESIGN CONSIDERATIONS

Many people are reluctant to make design decisions. But if you take the time to think things through carefully and if you enlist the opinions of others, you may be pleasantly surprised at the ideas you come up with. You have memories of pleasant places you have enjoyed, as well as dreams of the ideal place to relax. Of course, dreams can rarely be re-created in the real world. But by letting your imagination run loose and tapping into those images, you can provide yourself with a fund of design concepts that will help you come up with a down-to-earth deck design.

Draw a series of rough sketches as you proceed. Expect to fill a wastebasket or two with these. Don't think of them as actual designs so much as focal points for conversations—it's sometimes easier to point to a place on your drawing than to walk around the house.

Feel free to steal ideas from other people. (The best architects do not hesitate to do so.) When you see a deck that particularly pleases you and seems appropriate for your situation, take a few photos and jot down some notes. Talk to the owners about how their deck works for them. Most people will be flattered that you like their deck and will be more than glad to talk to you about it. You not only learn about pleasing designs and materials, but you can also avoid making mistakes they have made.

You will probably come up with an idea that you later discard, either because you no longer like the way it looks or because you discover that it will not be practical. Don't be discouraged. In fact, *expect* it to happen, and happen several times, before you come up with the best design.

## How You Will Use Your Deck

Call a family meeting to discuss your deck plans. Find out everyone's vision of the deck. What would they like it to look like? Where would they like it to be? Most importantly at this point, what do they expect to use it for? Then take a walk together around your property, examining possible sites. Think about how a deck could enhance the way you use your yard now. Consider new ways to enjoy outdoor living as well. Here are some things to think about:

**Entertaining and barbecuing.** This will be high on many people's list. Plan for a cooking area as well as a place for a good-sized table for seating

*With its built-in grill and hot tub, this deck is ready for barbecuing and entertaining. While the areas of your deck may not be so strictly defined, you'll still want to consider how you entertain when you design your deck.*

smaller groups or for buffet settings if you have large parties. For nighttime entertaining, choose lighting.

**Lounging and sunning.** Pencil in space for a hammock or a swinging chair. Determine the right mixture of shade and sun to suit everyone. Visualize the perfect spot for Sunday brunch, afternoon reading or drinks in the evening.

**Privacy.** Decks are usually raised off the ground, which might mean you and your family will be on display for all the neighborhood to see. Existing fences may be too low to shield you from view. Sometimes the problem can be solved by stepping the deck down in stages. Or plant shrubbery and trees that are the right height.

You may have to take direct action to achieve privacy. You don't have to build an unfriendly, solid wall to avoid the feeling you are being watched. If you feel overexposed, a well-placed trellis can give you some nice climbing

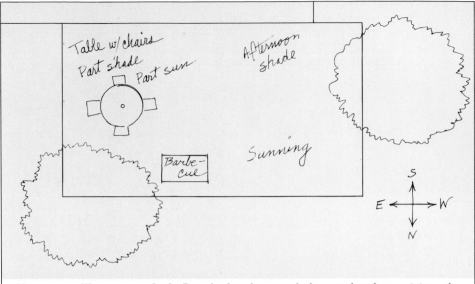

**How you will use your deck.** Rough sketches can help you develop a vision of how your deck will be used.

plants to look at as well as providing a pleasant enclosure.

Family members need some privacy among themselves as well. By building with different levels, including a conversation pit, or even just by let-

ting the deck ramble a bit, you can make for areas that are separate without being walled off.

**Balancing openness and enclosure.** Think about whether you want your deck to feel airy and open to the

*A deck with varying levels allows family members privacy without being walled off.*

world, or cozy and secluded. These effects can be achieved in many ways. A small deck will feel cozier than a large deck. Low benches and railings designed with large open spaces in them give an open feeling. A deck that hugs the house will have a more sequestered feel than one that juts out into the yard. Foliage plays an important role as well.

**Enjoying the view.** Plan your landscape along with your deck, to maximize your viewing pleasure. Orient the deck so that you will be looking at the best features of your yard.

**Planning for children's play.** The idea here is not to build a jungle gym into your deck, but to provide an inviting place where kids can play. Build your steps extra wide and deep or have a series of descending platforms, and children will spend hours playing with dolls and trucks and letting their imaginations run wild. Have a place on the deck where you can relax while keeping an unobstructed eye on the little ones in your yard.

**Including a pool or whirlpool.** As long as you use lumber that is very rot-resistant, wood makes an ideal surface next to a pool or whirlpool. It's softer than tile or concrete, and is slightly absorbent, making it a pleasant place to sit or lounge after you've gotten out of the water. An inexpensive above-ground pool gains a lot of class when you surround it with a deck. If you are putting in a whirlpool or hot tub, position it for privacy as well as an unobstructed view of the stars and supply comfortable sitting areas around it.

**Container gardening.** It is almost impossible to put too much foliage on or near a deck. And almost anything that can be grown in your yard can be grown in containers. Find planters that will go well with your deck and your house, or plan to build some from the same material as your decking. With small, moveable planters you can move flowers around. With enough sun, tomatoes, peppers, and all sorts of vegetables do well. An herb garden flourishes without a lot

*A railing of planters topped by a beam for hanging plants results in a wall of foliage that creates privacy without the need for a solid, unfriendly wall.*

*A whirlpool or hot tub is a natural for a secluded corner of a deck.*

of work and still looks great after a bit of harvesting. The avid gardener may consider putting cold frames or even a greenhouse on or next to the deck.

## Traffic Patterns

Make your deck easy to get to. The more entrances, the better. Wide doorways—sliders and French doors are good—will make it easy to flow from house to deck. Large windows that look onto your deck will entice people outside. If you plan to do a lot of eating on your deck, make sure it's close to the kitchen. If you can open a window and hand food out to the deck, so much the better.

Consider what the walkways to and from your deck will be like. Will people have to skirt around furniture to get there? Will the kids be tracking dirt on a living room carpet? Will there be a bottleneck during a party? Coming off the deck into your yard, will you want some sort of patio surface to ease wear and tear on the grass? Walk around your house and your future deck site while you discuss these questions.

## Weather Considerations

Consider what your future deck will be like during all the seasons when you are likely to use it. The three main variables affecting your use of the deck are sun, wind, and precipitation. In Chapter Two, "Developing and Drawing Your Plans", we will discuss construction techniques for building a deck that withstands the elements.

*Small containers made of the decking material blend into the deck and allow you to move your foliage around.*

**Sun.** Decide how much sun and how much shade you want, and take this into account when siting your deck. If you live in the northern hemisphere, a north-facing space will be in shade most of the day. This can be an advantage if you live in a very hot climate and a disadvantage for most everyone else. An eastern exposure gives the deck morning sun and afternoon shade; this is often the best choice in warm climates. In cold climates a southwest exposure provides full and late afternoon sun, making the deck usable as long as possible and keeping it warmer on many cool spring and fall days.

Also consider the position of the sun in the sky and the angle of the sun. The sun is highest in the summer and lowest in the winter. This means that in the winter a south-oriented deck will receive less direct sunlight than during the summer. A fence or tree that does not block out the high summer sun may block out sunlight during other times of the year, when the sun is lower.

Pay attention to the various areas of your deck. For instance, you may want continuous shade for a hammock, afternoon shade only for the eating area, and as much sun as possible for potted plants and a sunning area. To achieve your desired effect, you have several options: You may be able to position the deck for optimal use of light. Or you may need to change your foliage, adding or subtracting branches and trees. Perhaps an overhead structure may be your best bet.

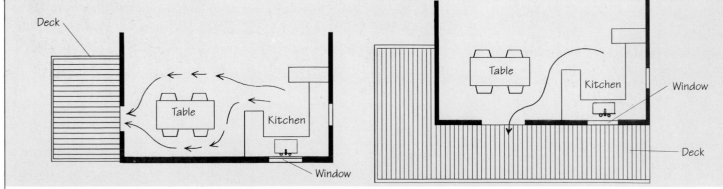

**Traffic patterns.** With the plan at left, traffic is routed around the dining room table, making it a chore to get food to the deck. Moving the deck and the door as shown at right makes deck access easier with less disruption of the dining room. Food can be handed through the kitchen window.

**Wind.** Take note of wind patterns on your property—the usual direction it comes from, whether it is pleasant or unpleasant. If heat is a problem and you want to maximize wind, or if you have too much wind, it may be possible to change your shrubs and trees to solve your problem—say, by pruning, or by planting new foliage. A raised deck will be windier than one closer to the ground.

For severe problems, you may need to construct a wind break of some sort. This need not be drastic; some sort of louvered or lattice arrangement with climbing plants is much more pleasant than a solid fence and in fact often does a better job of diffusing wind.

**Rain.** A deck is generally thought of as something you enjoy while the weather is nice; most people want to spend dreary days indoors. But you may live in an area where it rains much of the year, or perhaps you just like to watch the rain. If so, you might plan to extend the overhang of your roof so that part of your deck is sheltered. Or have the deck sit outside a large set of sliding glass doors, so you can enjoy the pattern of rain as it falls on your deck and potted plants.

# ENVISIONING THE CONTOURS OF YOUR DECK

You and your family can use some low-tech but effective methods to envision your deck. Set some lawn chairs out on your lawn, on spots where they might sit on your future deck. Take in the scenery, and open yourself to seeing your yard in new and unexpected ways. Imagine yourselves doing what you hope to do on your new deck. Where will the barbecue be? How about the tables and

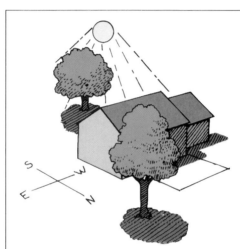

In the northern hemisphere, midday summer sun stands high in the sky; buildings and trees cast little shadow.

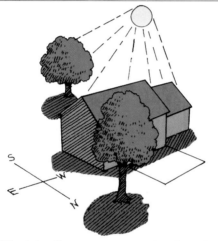

The late afternoon summer sun is as far to the north as it will go; there is a small amount of shade on the north and east of buildings.

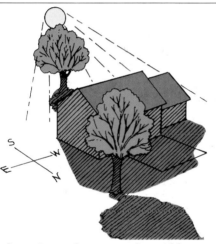

In spring and autumn, the midday sun is part way to its zenith; buildings and full-leafed trees cast considerable shadows.

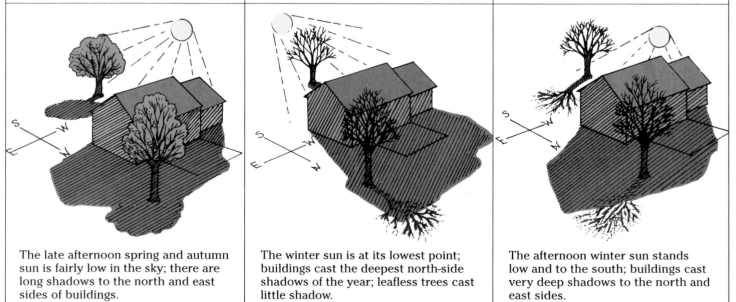

The late afternoon spring and autumn sun is fairly low in the sky; there are long shadows to the north and east sides of buildings.

The winter sun is at its lowest point; buildings cast the deepest north-side shadows of the year; leafless trees cast little shadow.

The afternoon winter sun stands low and to the south; buildings cast very deep shadows to the north and east sides.

**Weather considerations.** When deciding on a site for your deck it is important to consider the path of the sun at different times of the year.

**Envisioning the contours of your deck.** A length of garden hose or rope can help you envision the shape of your deck.

# ENHANCING HOUSE AND YARD WITH YOUR DECK

A deck usually does not stand alone; it is attached to your house and sits on top of your yard. So always consider not only how the deck itself will look, but also how it will fit in with its surroundings. This does not always mean striving to make the deck blend in; it is after all a different sort of structure than the house. But the contrasts should be pleasing rather than jarring.

Something to keep in mind: Although the decking will be the greatest amount of material you install, it will not be the most visible element from most perspectives. Railings, stairways, and fascia boards are often the things people will see first. If the deck is raised very high, the posts and understructure may become the most prominent visual elements.

chairs? Would a bench be good over there? Do you want to keep that grassy area as it is, or would it be better to have a deck over it? Have each family member choose his and her perfect spot for enjoying a relaxing summer's afternoon. In this way, you will come up with very general ideas about the shape and size of your deck.

If you have the space and the money, you may be tempted to build a very large deck. In most cases, this will be inappropriate; deck areas of more than 350 square feet can create a feeling of isolation unless you have an unusual amount of deck furniture. Plan deck areas that feel comfortable, that are scaled to human use.

Use a hose or rope to mark the possible outlines of your deck, and do some walk-throughs: Is there enough room for a planter here? Is this the right-sized space for a buffet area if we have a party of 15? If we put a table and chairs here, will it be easy for people

to seat themselves? Will the hammock fit over there? Would an L- or T-shape help give the right feel? What if we put some hanging planters or large potted plants over there, to give a sense of separate spaces?

*A new deck can look stuck on, particularly on an old house with plenty of architectural detail. This deck solves the problem by taking its color and architectural detail from the house. Where maximum privacy is desired the rail is covered with clapboards. Elsewhere, the railing uses simple balusters that mirror the window mullions.*

## Basic Elements

Though you probably do not want your deck to completely blend in with your house, you do not want it to be jarringly different, either. Elements to consider when seeking to match your deck with your house and yard are mass, shape, color and texture.

**Mass.** The size of a deck should suit the house. The more common problem is a deck that is too massive-looking. A large deck will overpower a small house, making it appear even smaller than it is. Decide which vantage points are the most important: How will your deck appear from where people are most likely to stand and look at it?

A deck's visual mass is not just a function of its actual size. Building low to the ground or designing railings that are low or light-looking will help the deck recede and thus appear smaller. Large visible beams, railings that are densely packed with boards, and wide fascia boards all will make a deck seem more massive. If your deck must

### Lower Your Deck for a Better View

A great many decks are built with a fundamental design flaw: they block the view. Railings usually stick up about 36 inches above the deck surface and can really get in the way when you look out your window. (This becomes increasingly true the wider your deck is.) If you want to gaze at your yard instead of your rails, consider stepping the main body of your deck down. Two steps can make a dramatic difference.

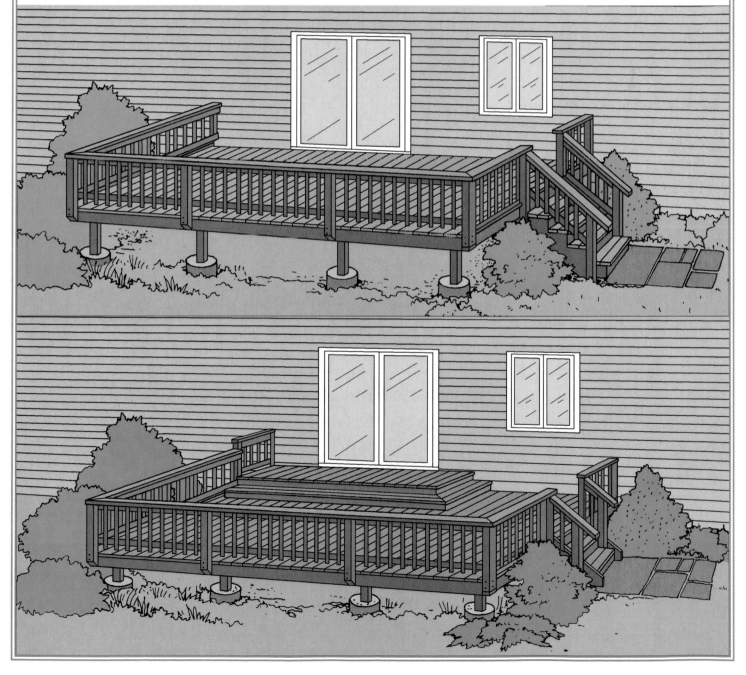

be raised 10 feet or more above the ground, you will have to use thick 6x6 posts (actually, the higher you go with these, the less thick they appear). You may be able to cover these with landings or deck sections that are more airy.

**Shape.** The shape you choose for your deck should harmonize with the lines of your house. First, consider the *general orientation*. The alignment of a deck should in most cases be much more horizontal than vertical. This will give it the light, breezy feeling that you want from an informal space. However, if you are building a raised deck, there will necessarily be up-and-down lines. If your house is tall and narrow, some of this vertical sense will be welcome, and you may want to repeat these lines. In many cases you will want to soften the vertical with a series of horizontal lines, using decking and railings.

*Lots of windows, lots of corners, and a natural brown color combine to give this house a cozy feeling. The light railings and natural wood of the deck harmonize with the house.*

*A massive house calls for a massive deck. The steep prominent roof and brick facade of this house bespeak substance. The wide fascia and hefty railings and benches of the deck hold their own.*

Second, think in terms of *overall shape*. If your house has a pleasing L-shape, for example, you can repeat that with a deck. A house with a confusing shape can be softened with a deck that is simple; a plain-looking house can be jazzed up with a deck that has a bold shape.

Most people choose to have a deck that is attached to the back of the house and leads to the backyard. However, you may want to consider other options such as the Japanese-style *engawa*, which wraps around the house, or a deck that incorporates a tree, an island deck or a peninsula deck.

*The bold shape of this deck adds visual interest to the simple facade at the back of this house.*

*Not all decks are attached to the back of a house. This peninsula deck creates an oasis in one corner of the yard.*

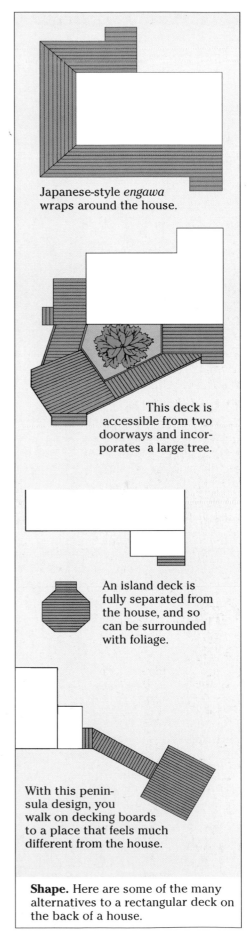

Japanese-style *engawa* wraps around the house.

This deck is accessible from two doorways and incorporates a large tree.

An island deck is fully separated from the house, and so can be surrounded with foliage.

With this peninsula design, you walk on decking boards to a place that feels much different from the house.

**Shape.** Here are some of the many alternatives to a rectangular deck on the back of a house.

*This deck could have just continued along in a boring straight line. Instead, it jogs to create an opportunity for a garden fountain.*

**Texture.** Natural wood has a fairly rough texture: Knots, minor cracks, and rough spots are usually considered part of the charm of a deck. Such casualness goes well with almost all landscaping, but may be unsuitable beside your house. If you need to clean up the lines a bit, buy more expensive wood with fewer or no knots. Composite materials—also referred to as "plastic decking"—have an embossed surface that imitates rough texture. Painting will smooth over some rough wood surfaces. Other options include metal railings, glassed (or Plexiglassed) windscreens, and latticework (which can be rough or smooth, depending on the material).

## Special Ways to Bridge House and Yard

Your deck will be a destination for outdoor living, but it will also be a visual transition point, a bridge linking your house and your yard. In fact, a well-designed deck will *feel* something like a bridge, not only because it is suspended over the ground, but also because it evenly balances the amenities of the indoors with the stimulation of the outdoors. In addition to the basic elements of mass, shape, texture and color, here are some specific ways

Third, imagine *individual lines*. Look at your house and your yard for existing lines: rectangles, curves, projections, even triangles. Use these as starting points, and think of your deck as providing variations on those themes. If your existing lines are a bit boring, you will want to liven things up a bit with some new angles—octagonal shapes and curved lines are good choices. But if you already have a good variety of lines, adding complex shapes with your deck will only make for a muddled general impression. Usually, simplicity is best: two or three sorts of lines artfully repeated are more pleasing than a jumble of shapes.

You most probably cannot change the shape of your house to suit your deck, but it is often possible to landscape in conjunction with building a deck. Garden edgings or patio surfaces can be designed to complement the lines of your deck.

**Color.** In most cases, people choose either to stain a deck to a redwood or cedar color or to let the wood turn grey over several years. These are good choices for the deck itself, because they project a relaxed, casual mood. And when many people think

of a deck, they automatically think of exposed natural wood. But if your deck will abut a formal portion of your house, or if the usual decking colors simply will not go with your house, do not hesitate to consider painting. Often a combination of natural wood and paint works— one good option is to paint the entire deck except for the cap piece that sits on top of the railing.

*A series of levels stepping down to a pond is much more attractive than any stair could be. Notice how the visual interest is heightened by changing the direction of the decking at each level.*

to ensure that your deck conducts a graceful passage:

**Stepping down.** Where possible, avoid long sections of stairway. Use a series of landings or multiple levels to bring the deck down in a way that feels more natural and graceful. Often the design problem here is to make sure that each level is a usable and visually pleasing space. This can be solved by making the levels cascade, that is, to have them fall off each other at different points or even at different angles, rather than just progressing downward in a straight line like huge steps.

And even if you go with a normal stairway, consider making it wider and/or longer than the usual size. A 36-inch-wide stairway, especially if it is more than six steps long, might look skimpy and stick-like next to your deck and/or your house. An accurately scaled drawing can help you visualize and make a decision.

**Configuring planters.** In the natural world any color combination looks great—Mother Nature does not have to agonize over paint chips. So it's hard to go wrong with foliage, as long as you can keep it healthy. And with some planning, you can do better than not going wrong. If, for instance, you make a planter of the same material as the deck, and place plants in it that are similar to those in your yard, you will have a very nice tie-in between deck and yard. And if you can build a planter that harmonizes with the house exterior, then you can tie in all three.

**Incorporating trees.** If you have a tree that looks great next to your house, avoid cutting it down for the sake of a deck. Build your deck around it instead, and you will not only have shade, but a harmonious juxtaposition of yard, deck, and house. Trees that are near the deck work well too, forming a sort of arch from yard to house,

*These planters create a beautiful transition between deck levels.*

with the deck in the middle. (See "Building Around Trees," page 107.)

Your deck need not lead down to a lawn. Consider a pathway at the bottom of your steps, made of materials

*Trees growing right through the deck provide natural shade and make the deck blend with the outdoors.*

*By repeating the angles of the deck, this patio becomes a harmonious extension of the deck.*

that in some way echo your house and also work well in a garden—bricks, concrete pavers, or crushed stone, which comes in a variety of colors. Patio materials can be rustic or formal, ranging from rough landscaping timbers to mortar-set tiles. Natural stone and brick, which are midway between formal and rustic, are often good choices. Pay attention to the direction of the lines in your patio—they are a continuation of the lines in your deck, which in turn should be tied to the lines of your house.

**Adding an outbuilding.** If a gazebo, shed, or play structure is in your future, include it in your plans now. There may be a simple way to tie it to the deck and the house—make the roof of the same material as your deck and paint the rest of the structure the same as your house, for instance. One exception: Garishly colored plastic playground equipment—red swings, yellow slides— usually seem okay because it is obviously for the kids. Or, you can build the play structures of the same materials as your deck.

# THEME AND VARIATION

As you look at other decks, you will encounter many design ideas that appeal to you. Consider them all, but in the end you must simplify. Strive for a sense of unity, rather than incorporating a bit of everything. The best decks take one or two ideas and then work out variations on those ideas.

The idea could be a gently curved line: you can put it at several places in your deck, and repeat it in smaller form in the benches. Or you may choose differently angled decking: have three or four sections that break off of each other at similar angles. If you have a large octagonal-shaped projection, you may be able to add a smaller version of it elsewhere on the deck or you can build a table or a bench with the same shape.

*Matching white railings and decking left natural do an elegant job of tying this gazebo to the deck.*

*Every deck should have a focal point. This deck zigzags its way to a unique fire pit.*

Remember that often the most visible elements of a deck are those that project vertically. Choose your railings or benches to harmonize with the overall structure. (To a certain extent, railings always match the structure, simply because they follow the deck.) Planters can take on shapes that mirror the deck structure.

A great deck will have a stunning focal point, something that immediately grabs the attention of everyone who enters. Perhaps you already have one—a beautiful tree, a lovely view, a nice pool. Or you can supply the eye-catcher yourself—a hot tub, a huge potted plant or a series of flower boxes, a well-kept greenhouse, a statue. Play to your strengths, and position the deck and furniture so as to accentuate your focal point.

## SOLVING PROBLEMS GRACEFULLY

At the same time as he or she is dreaming up visions of beauty, the successful deck designer must tackle nitty-gritty problems, both large and small. The idea is to make lemonade out of lemons, to turn knotty conundrums into pleasing points of interest. Specific solutions to these problems are given later in the book; but now is the best time to start thinking about them.

• Storage can be dealt with by providing access to the area under your deck, by building an attached shed, or by using interior space that has been freed up by the deck. List the things you need to store and make sure you have room for them, or they will clutter up your deck.

• Lighting can usually be dealt with after building your deck—low-voltage systems are often your best bet. But if you plan now, you can hide at least some of the wires by running them through parts of your deck.

• Drainage will usually only be a problem in the future if it is a problem

*Clever storage solutions can really enhance a deck. The bench under the bowl of fruit is hinged to swing up, taking the lattice beneath with it. If you look closely, you can see the hot tub cover stored under the bench.*

*By thinking carefully about deck lighting now, you can make your deck a pleasure to use at night.*

now. For minor problems, you may need to plan for a gravel-filled trench in the ground to collect runoff from your deck. If you have major problems, be sure to deal with them before you build.

A sloping site will make building more difficult, but also presents an opportunity for an interesting, multi-leveled deck.

• Trees on a deck site also present a chance to do something stunning.

Find out how quickly your tree will grow and plan to leave ample space.

• Pools and hot tubs require precise planning and cutting. Think carefully about how high and how wide you want the decking, for maximum sitting and sunning pleasure.

• Overhead protection, if you do not have the foliage to do the trick, can be achieved with some very nice louvered structures or with brightly colored awnings. For areas with heavy

rainfall, you can build an extension of your roof.

• Access to plumbing and electrical service must not be ignored; if you cover up something with a deck and it comes to need repair, you can be in big trouble. However, little trap doors that would look tacky inside are charming on a deck.

*An overhead lattice provides some protection from the sun without sacrificing the open feeling of a deck.*

# Chapter 2

# DEVELOPING AND DRAWING YOUR PLANS

Now that you've discussed what your deck should do for you, have made some general choices about its site and shape, and have scribbled some rough sketches, it's time to get serious about the drawings. In this chapter we show how to turn your dreams into definite plans that clearly lay out your deck design right down to the details.

When making plans, refer to other portions of this book to help make decisions. You will find information on materials in Chapter 5 and full explanations of framing configurations in Chapter 8, for instance. It's also a good idea to look ahead to gain a sense of what it will be like to actually do the work: You may be able to avoid planning something that is too difficult, or you may be able to find an easier way to do something.

## MAKING THE DRAWINGS

To plan properly, make four types of drawings. First, a *site plan* (also called a *base plan*) maps your house and yard. Second, a *plan drawing* gives an overhead view of the deck, showing where all the footings and lumber pieces go. Third, *elevations* depict your deck as it will appear from the sides and the front. And fourth, *detail drawings* show how you will deal with complicated portions of the deck, as well as how you will construct any deck enhancements, such as benches, storage boxes, and overhead structures.

Check with your building department to see what drawings are required and how detailed they need to be. As a general rule, however, it is a good idea to do more than the required amount of drawing. All these drawings may seem bothersome, but they will ensure that your deck is designed well, and they will save time and money when you build.

Formal drawings will help you think through all the aspects of your deck. As with the rough sketches, be prepared to redraw and redraw again, and don't be surprised if you find that, by solving one problem, you have uncovered another. The design process rarely proceeds in an orderly fashion, and you may find yourself skipping back and forth between elevations, plans, and details. However, the order in which we present things here is a useful way to begin.

## Tools and Techniques for Drawing

Your finished drawings must be to scale. The most common choice for overall deck plans is to have ¼ inch equal 1 foot, but you may have to change your scale so that the whole drawing fits on your sheet of paper. Detail drawings tend to be to a larger scale—for example ½ inch to the foot. For the site plan, though, you may need a smaller scale.

All you really need are large sheets of paper (12x16 inches is common), pencil, drafting square, ruler and eraser. But other tools will turn tedious work into something that is actually fun.

**Architectural scale ruler.** This handy tool will keep you from a lot of mental computations: it enables you to instantly convert to your scale: one side will give you numbers based on a ⅛-inch scale, another on a ¼-inch scale, and another on a ½-inch scale; these are the only scales you are likely to need.

**Drafting tools.** If you have access to them, a drafting board and a T-square will make drawing a series of parallel lines enjoyable rather than boring. Graph paper is a more low-tech solution, but can be quite effective. Tracing paper, either plain or with a grid printed on it like graph paper, can be purchased in large rolls from art and drafting supply stores. A drafting triangle will help you make perpendicular lines and establish angles. Compasses and templates with various sizes of squares and circles are useful only if you are designing a curved deck.

Tape the paper to your working surface, so it won't slide around while

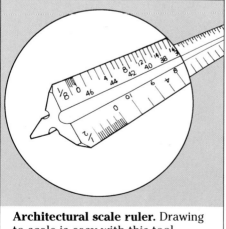

**Architectural scale ruler.** Drawing to scale is easy with this tool.

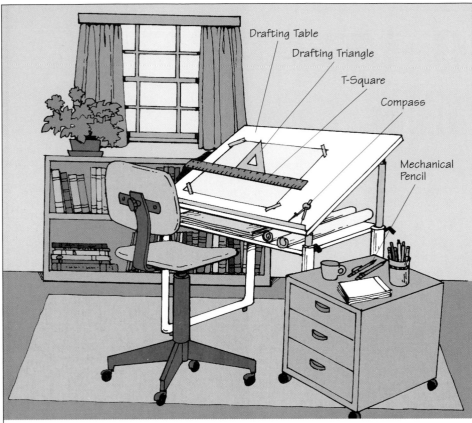

**Drafting tools.** Whether you have fancy drafting tools or are just using graph paper, pick a pleasant spot for drawing.

you use your tools. You may find it helpful to use overlays—set the tracing paper on top of a basic drawing and experiment with different ideas. If the idea works, you can incorporate it into the final drawing; if not, just throw it away. This helps you avoid a good deal of repetitive redrawing and messy erasing.

## Drawing a Site Plan

In most cases, you will be able to get some sort of scaled plan of your site. It may have come with your title when you bought the house. Or you may be able to get one from the outfit that built the house, or from the local building department. Check this drawing for accuracy, and use it as a starting point. You will probably have to re-scale it and add or subtract foliage, for example. Also, unless you are still casting about for the basic location of your deck, you do not have to draw your entire site—only where your deck will be.

### Computer Deck Programs

Your building supply house may have computer programs to assist in designing decks. These are of course always changing, but what we have found so far is this: Some programs simply give a readout of materials you will need, based on the size of your deck. These are generally accurate and are a good way to double-check your figures. Other programs go further and print out pictures of the deck. These are not as accurate: Sometimes they give designs that are not up to code, and sometimes they incorrectly place lumber pieces and footings. Also, they tend to be rather inflexible, allowing for only a few types of rail designs, for instance. And be aware that some lumberyards will give you the printouts only if you buy their lumber, which may be higher in price than elsewhere.

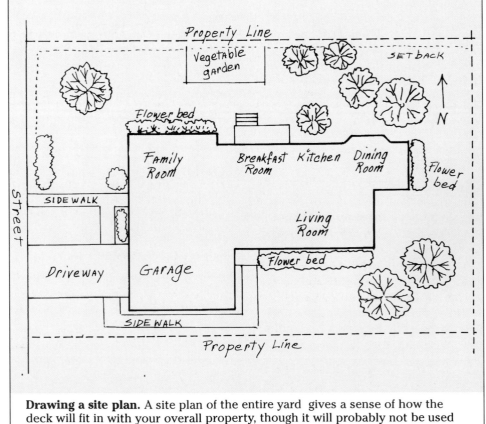

**Drawing a site plan.** A site plan of the entire yard gives a sense of how the deck will fit in with your overall property, though it will probably not be used when it comes time to draw the deck.

Include in your site plan everything pertinent to building your deck: the location of doors and windows looking out on the deck site; trees that provide shade for the deck; slopes; where the sunniest spots are. It is important to locate not only your property lines, but also the setbacks required by your local building regulations.

When you draw the trees, you want to keep in mind they will grow and the shade they produce on the deck will occupy a slightly larger area than their actual size. So draw them a bit large.

Indicate the exact locations of any pipes or wires that are buried on your site, so you can be sure to avoid hitting them when you dig your footings. Contact the customer service departments of the phone, electric, and/or water companies if you are not certain that you have reliable information. In most cases, they will come out and mark locations for free.

**Making photocopies or overlays.** Once your site plan is made, make several photocopies so you can scribble ideas on them, or use tracing paper for overlays. Keeping in mind the considerations discussed in Chapter One, indicate where you will locate the flower pots, benches, a hot tub, etc.

**Making a site elevation.** If you have a seriously sloping site, draw a site elevation. This will give you a more accurate idea of how far you have to step down with stairs or with different levels. With a helper or two, find out how far your yard slopes down by using a line level and measuring tape. Hook one end of the string to a reference point on the house. One person holds the other end of the string up in the air—he may need a step ladder. Another person checks the line level to see that the line is level, and a third person makes measurements from the ground up to the line.

Now that you have a site plan and a definite notion of the location and shape of your deck, it is time to start designing the deck itself.

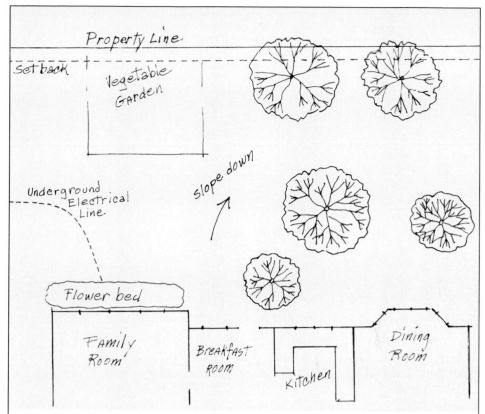

**Drawing a site plan.** This site drawing shows only the portion of the property on which the deck will stand. The existing back porch is not shown, so as to make planning easier.

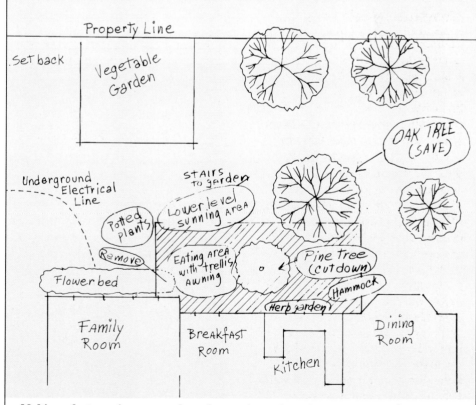

**Making photocopies or overlays.** Lay a piece of tracing paper over the site drawing to designate use areas and to make plans for the foliage. Draw the outline of the deck.

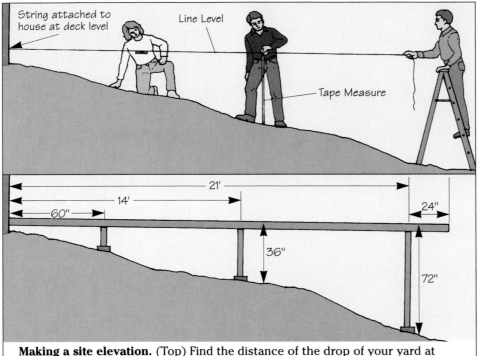

**Making a site elevation.** (Top) Find the distance of the drop of your yard at various points on the deck site. (Bottom) Use the measurements to draw a site elevation.

# DESIGNS THAT ARE "FORGIVING"

Even the most experienced contractors make mistakes; there's no reason you should expect to do a perfect job. So whenever possible, choose design options that either de-emphasize imperfections or allow for easy correction of mistakes. Here are some examples:

**Hiding the footings and the beam.** The most difficult thing to get right is the footings. You measure for them with string lines while there is no structure in place, and variations in the yard can throw you off a bit. When you dig the holes, it's easy to slide one way or the other. And once the footings are poured, there's no moving them. Of course, we will show you the best way to accurately align footings, and they can't be *too* far out of line, or the posts will not be entirely resting on them. But it is not unusual for footings to be off by an inch or two, meaning that some posts will sit off-center on top of the concrete. So it is best to place the footings well under the deck—so that the deck cantilevers out 24 inches or more—where people won't notice the imperfections. (However, if you want

to add a skirt under your deck, this design could make it difficult. See "Installing Skirts," page 117).

In addition, mistakes can occur in the overall layout for the posts and beam. Placing the footings well under the deck will mean that the beam is also hidden, so that if the deck is not perfectly aligned with the post, it will not show. There's another reason for doing this: The large timbers used for the beam—usually pressure-treated two-bys or four-bys—tend to be ugly and will clash with your deck if you choose cedar or redwood decking.

In a low deck especially, cantilevering past the beams can be very attractive

because it makes the deck seem to float over the yard.

**Let the lumber "run wild".** Of course, there are many elements of a deck that have to end up cut flush. Whenever possible, wait for a later stage of the building process to cut them off, rather than trying to get them to fit exactly at the beginning. Posts, beams and decking can in most cases be left too long when you first install them; you'll cut them off to size later. This is called letting the lumber run wild. It's an important technique for building decks that have a professional look, and our step-by-step instructions will point out every instance when you can apply it.

**Attaching built-up beams to the post.** In one type of construction, beams are set on top of posts. When that is done, the posts all have to be cut exactly to the right height before installing the beam, which can be tricky. An easier method, one that allows for correcting mistakes, is to let the posts run wild upward (that is, don't cut them to height yet) and build a beam composed of two two-by lumber pieces attached to the side of the post. This way, you can check and re-check the beam for level, and correct any mistakes as you work. The posts are cut to height only after the beams are in place.

**Using overhangs and underhangs.** It's easy to make mistakes in cutting lumber. And even if something is cut perfectly, there is a chance that it will shrink over time, leaving an unsightly gap. So as often as possible, avoid

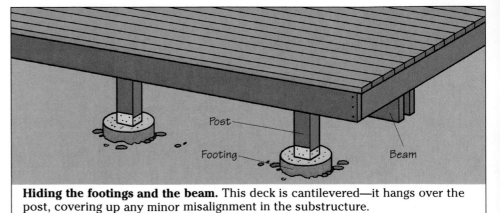

**Hiding the footings and the beam.** This deck is cantilevered—it hangs over the post, covering up any minor misalignment in the substructure.

having to cut something to fit precisely. This can often be done by planning to overhang members. In many cases, an overhang or underhang looks better than a flush cut anyway. Where possible, it is usually best to overhang decking; railing pieces often are best overhung as well. In addition, overhanging is often a good way to prevent water from collecting in joints. Less commonly, it is sometimes best to underhang members—as in the case of beam pieces if they are attractive.

**Use screws and bolts.** Nails are easy and convenient, but if you make a mistake and have to remove them,

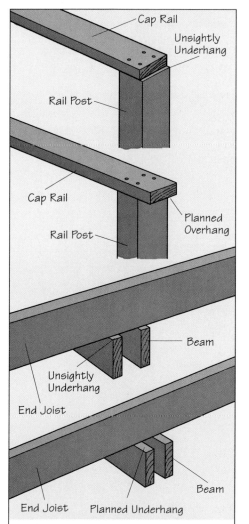

**Using overhangs and underhangs.**
A slight miscut or shrinkage of the rail post at top looks awful and exposes post end grain. A planned overhang solves the problem. If you end beams flush, bowed joists may leave you with a slight underhang. A larger, planned underhang looks better.

you will probably ruin the appearance of the lumber. If you use screws and bolts, it is much more likely that you will be able to re-use a piece of lumber that has been wrongly cut or placed.

**Install added-on railings.** As you will see later in this chapter when we discuss railing design, you can design a deck so that the posts supporting the deck come through the decking and continue upward to become part of the railing. However, that is a most *un*forgiving design; if the posts are not exactly aligned, or if they are not all perfectly plumb, then your railing will look bad. A much more forgiving arrangement is one that allows you to first build the deck, then add the rails. Such an arrangement can be quite strong and secure.

**Build the stairway after the deck.** Stairway design can be complicated; it takes some figuring to find out just where the stairway will end, for instance. So wait until the basic deck is finished before you figure the position of the stairway posts and the slab at the bottom of the stairs. The recommended design is first to install the stairs, then dig postholes in which to set the stair posts. (These posts will be the only ones sunk in the ground, which is a good idea since they are the ones most in need of lateral strength.)

## PRELIMINARY PLANNING CONSIDERATIONS

Before you get serious about drawing your plans, there are some site considerations you need to check out. These will not be a problem in most cases, but it's best to be on the safe side.

**Planning for drainage and stable footings.** If you are unfortunate enough to have any of the following problems, consult Chapter 7, "Installing Footings," for solutions.

If you have a site that is sometimes soggy, do not expect that a deck will solve the problem. In fact, in some cases, it can make things even worse. If your deck is not built with drainage in mind, you can end up with the same amount of water on the ground but less evaporation, since the site will now be in shade.

Footings must not be placed in unstable or mushy soil. If erosion is a potential problem—usually the case only if you have a very hilly site—take care of it before it undermines your footings.

**Planning for electrical and plumbing lines.** Check not only for buried pipes and lines, but also consider

**Planning for electrical and plumbing lines.** An access hatch in a deck can be built so that it is hardly noticeable.

moving any overhead lines that may impinge on your deck. If you hope to install any new water service—a handy faucet might be a good idea—it might be best to run some pipes ahead of time. The same goes for electrical lines: If you want to install new lighting with standard electrical wires, plan to bury as many lines as possible under the deck. (Check into low-voltage systems before you go to all this trouble—they can be cheap and require no burying of wires, since the voltage is so low as not to be dangerous.) Be especially careful about any access points to utilities—hatches for getting at the plumbing, septic covers, electrical boxes, and so on. If the deck is going to cover any of these, plan to provide a way to get at these things without tearing up the deck.

**Find out building and zoning codes.** Your building department will probably want to get involved with your deck; a large outdoor structure will be difficult to ignore. Take a trip to the office before you start planning to ask for a list of basic requirements—and to establish a reputation for yourself as a person who wants to do things right. There are requirements regarding footings; lumber sizes for various spans; how high your railings need to be; how far apart railing members can be; how close to your property line you can build and so on.

In this book, we will give span charts and other information as to generally accepted standards for lumber and concrete. Your local requirements may be more stringent, so always check them before making your plans.

# BASIC TERMS

The illustration on this page shows the essential parts of a typical deck. Starting from the ground and working upwards, here are some terms you should know.

A *footing* is a solid piece of concrete on which a post sits; the post is usually attached to the concrete with a *post anchor*, a metal fastener designed to keep the post from wandering and to inhibit rot by holding the post a bit above the concrete. *Posts*, usually of 4x4 or 6x6 lumber, are vertical members supporting either the deck or the railing. A *beam* is a massive horizontal piece of lumber—either four-by material or doubled-up two-bys—that supports the entire deck. *Joists*, made of two-by lumber and spaced evenly to

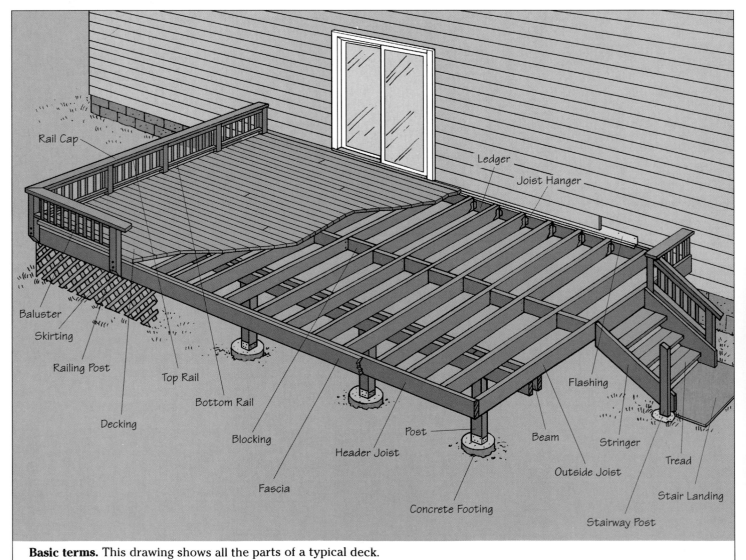

**Basic terms.** This drawing shows all the parts of a typical deck.

support the decking, usually rest on the beam on one end. Sometimes pieces of *blocking* (or solid bridging), made of the same material as the joists, are wedged between the joists to keep them from warping. On the other end they are supported by a *ledger*, a piece of lumber that is directly attached to the house. *Outside joists* and the *header joist* form the outside frame of the joist structure and are sometimes covered with a *fascia* board for the sake of appearance. *Decking*, the boards you walk on, is attached to the joists with nails or screws and is commonly made of 2x4, 2x6, or 5/4x6 material.

A typical railing setup includes posts for support and *balusters* (sometimes referred to as *pickets*), usually 2x2 or 1x4 vertical pieces evenly spaced between the posts. Balusters are attached to a *top rail* and sometimes a *bottom rail*, which run horizontally from post to post. A rail cap tops the whole thing off.

Stairways are composed of *stringers*, the angled-downward 2x12s on the sides which are the main support; *treads*, the boards you walk on; and sometimes *risers*, usually pieces of 1x8 that cover the vertical spaces between the treads.

## CHOOSING THE LUMBER

The type of lumber you choose will affect your plans. For instance, if you use 5/4x6 cedar decking, then your joists will have to be closer together than if you use 2x6 pressure-treated decking. It's usually best to choose the lumber first, based on your budget and taste, and then plan accordingly. Chapter 5 "Materials" presents a full discussion of the strengths and drawbacks of various materials.

Although there are many different types of wood available, chances are the best lumber choices for you will be pressure-treated lumber for the deck posts, beam, and joists and either cedar, redwood or pressure-treated for the decking, fascia, and rails.

## PLANS FOR THE SUBSTRUCTURE

In this section we will explain the basics of framing, to give you an idea of how to draw plans. For more detailed information, and for special situations—stepping down in level, turning corners, non-rectangular shapes, and so on—refer to Chapter 8, "Framing the Deck".

The substructure, the decking, the railings, and the stairway all need to work together; the way you do one will sometimes affect how you can do the others. In particular, make sure that your railing will work with your framing plan and that the joists are arranged to handle your decking pattern.

### Two Basic Framing Configurations

**Joists on beams.** The most common setup uses a beam (or more than one beam, if the deck is large enough) which supports joists. This arrangement allows for building large platforms and

**Joists on beams.** Joists are supported on one end by a beam and are attached to a ledger board with joist hangers on the other end. This beam is built of two 2x10s bolted to the 4x4 posts. Use this same arrangement when building an octagonal or curved deck.

Joist Hanger

Double Header Joist

Post

**Joists attached to posts.** Here, joists are joined directly to posts. If you set the posts in concrete rather than placing them on top of footings, you will need to be extremely careful to get them perfectly aligned—especially if you have the posts carry through upward to become part of the rail system.

gives you the option of hiding the beam and footings under the deck.

**Joists attached to posts.** Another arrangement doesn't use beams, but instead attaches joists directly to the posts. It can be employed where the deck is not too long in the direction of the joists. Often, because the header joist is acting as a beam, you will be required to double it.

There are three advantages to this configuration. First, it is simpler; you avoid building a beam. Second, the posts here can continue upward to become part of the railing system. (As we have noted, however, this is only a slight advantage—add-on railings can be built with great strength.) Third, this way allows you to build closer to the ground, since there is no beam. The disadvantages: the footings will be visible; and this design is not "forgiving," because all the posts have to be exactly correct for it to work. We suggest you use this arrangement when you need to build close to the ground or when the deck is quite narrow.

## Posts and Footings

If your deck is 72 inches or less above the ground, you can build with 4x4 posts. Anything higher than 8 feet requires 6x6s, which are a great deal more difficult to handle and are often unsightly. Between 6 and 8 feet is a grey area—check with your local codes.

The most common post-and-footing arrangement calls for a post that is set on top of a concrete footing that has been allowed to set. The post is usually attached to the concrete in some way. Posts can also be set into postholes which are then filled with concrete or gravel, but under most

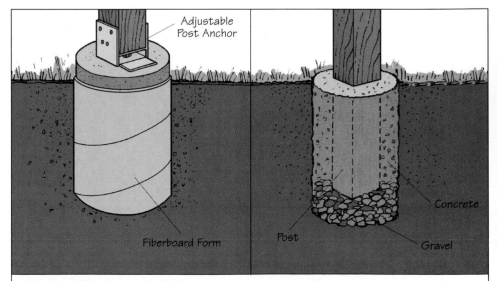

Adjustable Post Anchor

Fiberboard Form

Post

Concrete

Gravel

**Posts and footings.** (Left) Posts can be set on top of a concrete footing and attached to the footing with adjustable hardware. (Right) Or posts can be set in concrete or gravel below ground level.

circumstances we recommend this for the stair rails only.

You will probably need to dig and pour footings for each post. Include in your drawings the depth of the holes, the type of concrete forms you will be using, and the anchoring system. For your options here, see "Types of Footings," page 76.

## Beams

Beams can be made of single pieces of four-by lumber (4x8, 4x10, etc). This can save a good deal of time, since you won't have to construct your own beam. There are disadvantages, however. Lumber that is 4x6 and larger tends to be ugly and full of cracks; it's often difficult to find the sizes you want, and it's mighty heavy. You can run into difficulties when installing solid beams: The posts they sit on have to be cut perfectly to height and have to be held in place firmly before you can set the beam in place.

There are times you may want to use a solid beam, but usually it's easier to construct built-up beams with two-by lumber. You can sandwich strips of pressure-treated plywood between two two-bys, attach two-by pieces to either side of the posts, or laminate two pieces of two-by lumber together and attach them to the side of the posts with lag screws or bolts.

## Bracing for Elevated Decks

If your deck is raised 72 inches or more, you will probably need some sort of bracing—check to see what your building department recommends. Sometimes, certain pieces of specialized hardware will be enough to do the job, but often braces made with lumber will be required.

There are no hard-and-fast rules here, and fortunately you often can add bracing if the deck feels unstable after it is built. Bracing does not have to be an eyesore. Symmetrically placed pieces of lumber can add visual interest to an otherwise boxy shape. And in many cases, the

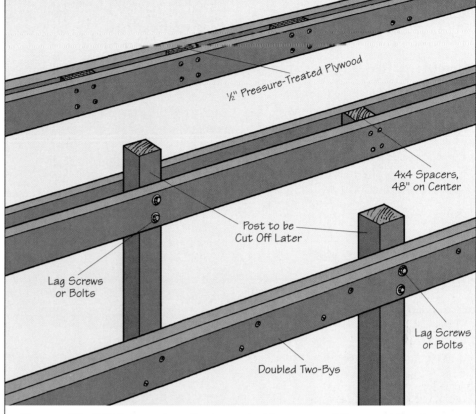

**Beams.** (Top) This beam is quite strong, but has some of the same disadvantages as does a solid beam, since it must be set on top of posts. Sandwiching the plywood makes it more susceptible to rot, as well. (Middle) This is a handyman-friendly beam: it's easy to handle the pieces, and you can let the posts run wild. (Bottom) Another forgiving method is to bolt doubled two-by beams to the posts.

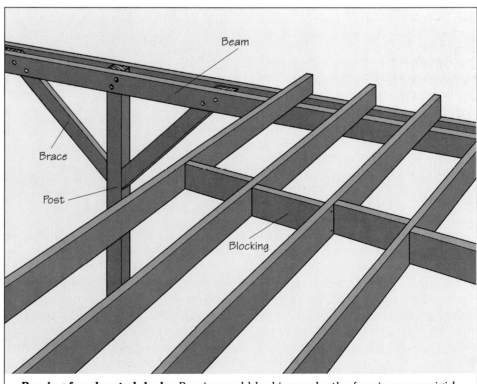

**Bracing for elevated decks.** Bracing and blocking make the framing more rigid.

bracing can be covered with skirting materials—sheets of latticework, for example.

## Blocking Between Joists

In some circumstances—especially when your joists span more than 10 feet—you may be required to install blocking, otherwise referred to as bridging or bracing. These are usually solid pieces of lumber, the same dimension as your joists, which are cut to fit snugly between the joists to prevent excessive warping. Blocking also adds strength and rigidity to the substructure if installed tightly.

## Choosing a Framing Configuration

When designing a deck, a choice you make regarding one aspect will often influence the design of other aspects. For instance, with 2x6 decking, you can space the joists 24 inches apart, whereas if you use 5/4x6 decking, the joists should be closer together, usually 16 inches. The length of the joists must be factored in when determining the size of the beam and how far apart the posts can be. And different species of wood vary in strength, making for even more variables.

As you delve into it, you will find that things are not as confusing as all this may sound. Once you have chosen your materials, use the charts in Chapter 8, "Framing a Deck", to figure the sizes and lengths of the beams and joists, as well as the positions of your footings and posts.

A major consideration as you design your substructure will be to get the most support from the least amount of lumber. To come up with the ideal arrangement, experiment with designs. For instance: Will larger joists mean that you can use fewer beams?

## CHOOSING DECKING SIZE AND PATTERN

In Chapter 9, Applying Decking and Fascia, you will find a variety of decking possibilities. If a complicated decking pattern catches your eye, do not think that it is beyond your capabilities: decking is actually one of the simpler aspects of deck construction, and with patience you can construct impressive-looking deck surfaces.

---

### Plan to Avoid Waste

Usually, when designing a deck you have a lot of leeway as to dimensions. It doesn't often matter, for instance, whether the deck is 16 and a half feet wide or 16 feet. You often are in a position to save some money by minimizing lumber waste.

Lumber is sold in 2-foot increments, so if you need a board that is 14 feet 1 inch, for example, you will have to pay for a 16-footer, and you'll have a possibly worthless 23-inch piece left over.

Planning in a manner as detailed as this may seem wearisome, but an hour or two of work could save you lots of work later, and plenty of money as well. And it's a good idea anyway to go over your plans in minute detail—you very well may find mistakes or ways to improve the design.

Design the decking to make the most of your joist boards. Plan the decking along with the joists. If your spans are too long for single decking pieces, plan where the butt joints will go, so as to use as much of decking boards as possible. (And for a sturdier deck, plan to double the joists under the butt joints, if possible—see

"Double Up for Decking Butt Joints," page 101.

Don't plan things too tightly, however. Sometimes you will need to cut off an inch or so to eliminate a split or unsquare end. (And though lumber is often sold with an extra ½ inch of length, that is not always the case, so don't count on it.) If, for example, you plan so that the decking will be 11 feet 10 inches (rather than 12 feet), you will be able to use 12-foot decking pieces with confidence.

It's easy to get confused and miss by an inch or three when figuring this, so here are some things to look out for.

• Include the overhang (if any) for decking boards.

• For decking boards cut at an angle, always figure the longest dimension.

• Be clear about which board overlaps which. For example, in many designs the outside joists will be either 1½ or 3 inches longer than the interior joists, because the outside joists overlap the header and ledger, while the interior joists butt against them.

---

**THE PROS KNOW**

### Do You Mind a Little Bounce?

Lumber requirements for decks are often less stringent than those for interior rooms in houses. This is because a certain amount of bounciness is considered okay in a deck. If you build your deck in a way that just barely meets the standards, it will be strong enough to last for many decades, but when you jump up and down on it, you will feel a definite flex that you would not feel inside your house. If you think this would bother you, then build on the heavy side, for instance, by using joists that are wider than what is required.

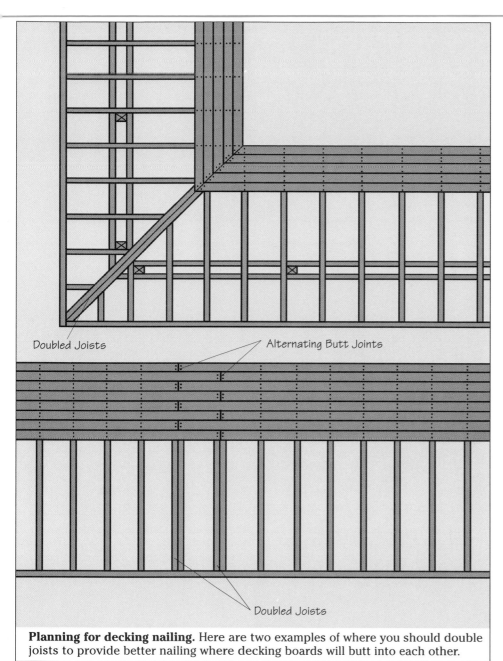

Doubled Joists

Alternating Butt Joints

Doubled Joists

**Planning for decking nailing.** Here are two examples of where you should double joists to provide better nailing where decking boards will butt into each other.

However, unusual decking patterns almost always mean that more lumber will be wasted, increasing your costs. And installing decking at an angle, for instance, will take you twice as long as installing boards parallel or perpendicular to the house.

One way to jazz up the surface of your deck without adding materials expense and without much extra work is to use different widths of decking in a pattern. You can alternate between 2x6 and 2x4, for instance.

**Planning for decking nailing.** Sometimes an unusual decking choice will require extra joist work. Think through the deck design, and make sure that every decking board will be well-supported at each end. If you know where the butt joints of your decking are going to be, it is a good idea to double up the joists at those points. This is particularly true for places where the decking makes a turn and you have miter-cut decking butting together. If the deck is too long for single decking pieces, plan on at least two doubled-up joists, so that you can stagger the butt joints.

# DESIGNING STAIRS

For normal-sized stairways, you will probably not be required to make a detailed drawing. But for your own purposes, you will want to find out

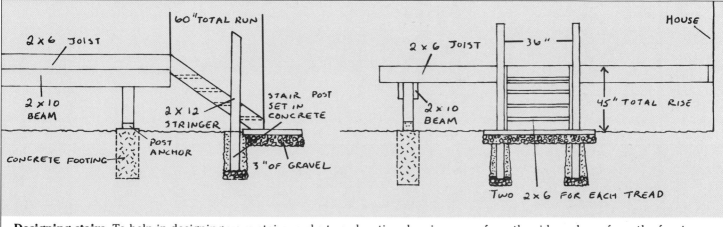

**Designing stairs.** To help in designing your stairs, make two elevation drawings, one from the side and one from the front. Note that these are not complete elevation drawings; they include only the elements that are pertinent to the stair design.

what size 2x12s you should buy for the stringers, how many treads there will be, and approximately where the concrete, masonry or gravel pad at the bottom will be. So figure as closely as possible how high your deck will be at the point where the stairs are and draw an elevation. (If you find this difficult to figure at this point, you may want to wait until you have built your deck, and then figure your stairs— as long as there is no danger that the stairs will end up where you don't want them.)

Laying out a stairway requires some fairly complicated figuring, so that all the steps will be the same height and so that you end up where you want to. In Chapter 10, "Building Stairs," we will guide you through this.

You can build a ramp either instead of or in addition to a stairway. Ramps are not only for wheelchair accessibility: If your kids will be bringing their bikes up and down regularly, for instance, a ramp can make things a lot easier.

# DESIGNING RAILINGS AND BENCHES

In Chapter 11, Adding Railings and benches, you will find many railing and bench options. There are three basic methods, requiring three different framing configurations. The first method is to attach decking posts to the outside joists (or to the fascia that covers them). This is the easiest to frame for, since you simply build the deck first and then attach the rail to it. In the second method, the deck posts continue upwards through the deck to become part of the rail system.The third method is used to accommodate a built-in bench. Here, joists cantilever out and provide support for the rear framing piece of the bench.

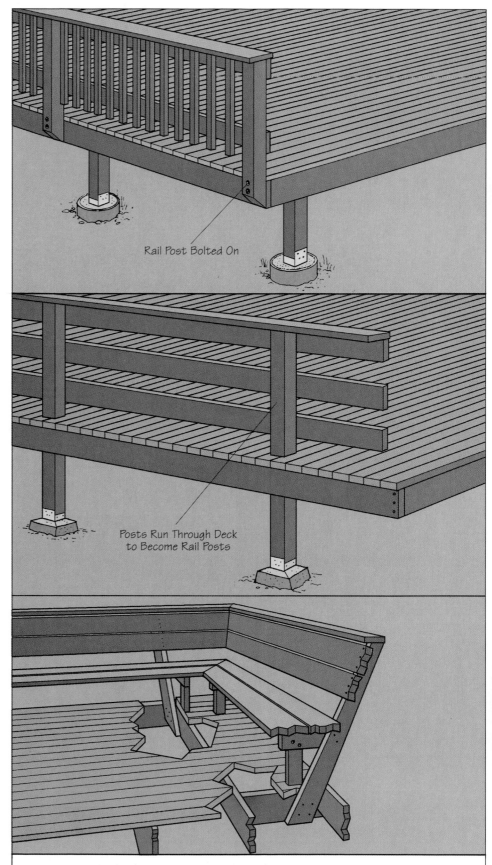

Rail Post Bolted On

Posts Run Through Deck to Become Rail Posts

**Designing railings and benches.** At top rail posts are attached with bolts driven through the fascia board into the outside joist. In the middle, deck posts continue upwards to become rail posts. At bottom, a bench, attached to joists, takes the place of a railing.

# DRAWING FINAL PLANS AND ELEVATIONS

Once you have made all your decisions regarding site, substructure, decking, stairs, and railings, you are ready to finalize your plans. The finished drawings should be clear: Do not rely on scribbled-over and often-erased sheets, but take the time to draw a clean set of plans.

There are a number of ways to provide the needed information on drawings. Your building department may want you to do things a bit differently, but here is an example of a set of simple plans and elevations, along with check lists. For examples of more complicated plans, see the "Deck Designs" section at the end of the book.

## Plan Drawings

Plan drawings show the deck framing as if it were viewed from directly above. For these drawings, it is usual to leave out the railings and decking. Be sure to include:

• Correct dimensional drawing of the perimeter.

• All joists, beams, posts and footings.

• Dimensions for all lumber.

• The distance spanned by beams and joists.

• Indication of size and direction of decking (it's not usually necessary to draw this).

• Hardware, such as joist hangers, angle brackets and bolts.

• Exact locations of doors and windows.

• Any electrical and plumbing fixtures and lines.

## Elevation Drawings

An elevation drawing shows the deck as if it were viewed directly from the side. Draw at least one elevation, including:

• A detailed drawing of the rail system, including all dimensions that pertain to local codes.

• Views of the footings, with dimensions showing how deep and wide they will be.

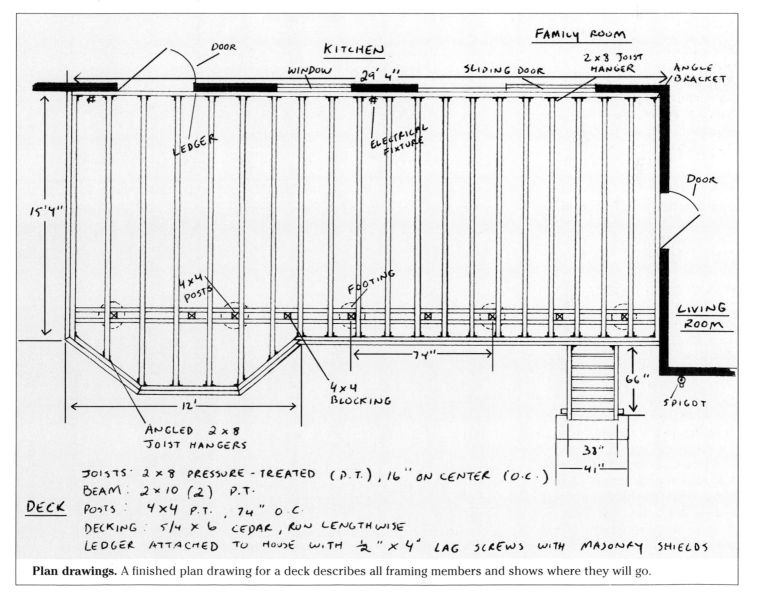

**Plan drawings.** A finished plan drawing for a deck describes all framing members and shows where they will go.

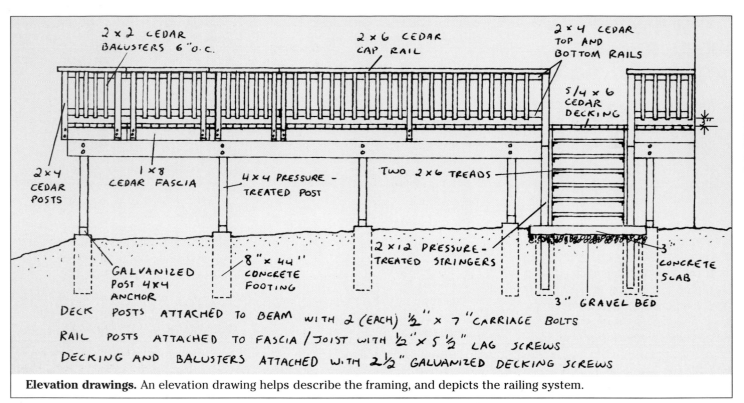

**Elevation drawings.** An elevation drawing helps describe the framing, and depicts the railing system.

- Hardware: post anchors, tread cleats, bolts.
- Height of the tallest post.
- A rough approximation of the site's slope.

## Detail Drawings

If you are going to build enhancements such as benches, planters, and overhead structures, make up some detailed drawings showing where these things will go on your deck.

It is also a good idea to draw close-up views of complicated spots on your deck. Sometimes you will need to make a detail drawing to satisfy the building department. At other times, you may need it for yourself, in order to figure things out.

Some common problem areas: where the stair railing meets the deck railing; hatchways for access to electrical and plumbing; framing around trees or hot tubs; changes in level, where special framing is needed. ledgers or other areas that need flashing or other special treatments to avoid moisture buildup. You will find examples of these sorts of drawings throughout this book.

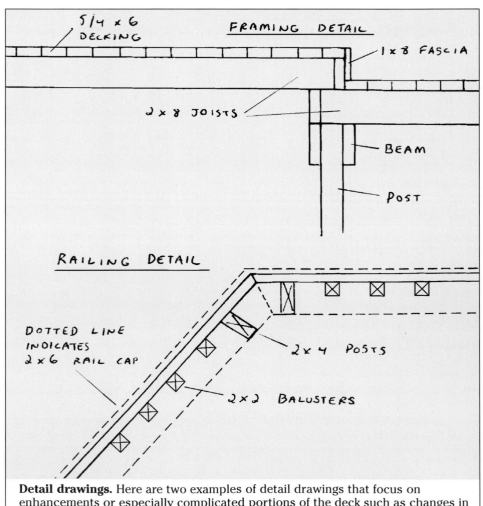

**Detail drawings.** Here are two examples of detail drawings that focus on enhancements or especially complicated portions of the deck such as changes in level or unusual rail configurations.

# CREATING A CONSTRUCTION STRATEGY

In addition to deciding what your finished deck will be like, it is important to plan how it will get constructed. Building a deck is not like remodeling an interior—your household won't be entirely disrupted. But nobody likes to see a yard full of unsightly holes and piles of lumber sitting for weeks. You want the job done well, and you want to get it done in a reasonable amount of time. With some prudent foresight and planning, you will be able to finish in good time and have some fun doing it as well.

## WHO WILL DO THE WORK?

First, take an honest look at the project before you and come up with the best way to use various types of labor: yourself, helpers, and professionals.

### Can You Handle the Project?

Read the following sentence carefully: If you are reasonably handy with tools, have been successful with another carpentry project or two, have a reliable helper or two at your disposal, and have the time and patience for a large project, you can succeed in building a deck that is not overly complicated and that is placed on an ordinary site.

Though a deck may look like an imposing project, taken step by step it is well within the reach of a moderately skilled non-professional. In fact, it's probably the most popular large-scale do-it-yourself project. Be honest about yourself, however: Can you cut a straight line with a circular saw? Do you tend to finish jobs, or are there lots of half-done projects around your house? Are you in a position to devote plenty of time to deck building, or are you woefully short on free time already? If these questions make you feel uneasy, consider hiring a professional, at least for part of the work.

### Designs that Require Professional Help

There are certain circumstances that require at least advice or assistance from a specialized contractor:

- A deck that is raised up high, say, 10 feet or more, can be dangerous to build without the right equipment and some experience.

- A deck cantilevered out from the house and supported by angled braces attached to the house (rather than to posts set on the ground) requires special engineering.

- A deck set in swampy or otherwise unstable soil will need the sort of foundations or pilings that a do-it-yourselfer cannot construct.

- A deck set on a site that is hilly can be a problem. If your yard is heavily sloped, think it through: Are you going to be able to set up and support every post, and set the beam as well? If you have doubts, call in someone who is used to situations like this.

- A deck that must support heavy loads, such as a spa or a hot tub, calls for professional assistance at least for the design.

- A roof-top deck may cause the roof under it to leak. Contact a roofing contractor before proceeding.

### Ways of Dividing the Work

The choice between doing it yourself and hiring someone else is not a strict either/or. Many contractors are reluctant to take on only portions of a project, but don't let a pushy carpenter talk you into giving the whole job to him if you want to do some or even most of it yourself. There are logical ways of dividing up a deck job. You can hire out for just the footings or for setting the posts and beam, for instance. And if there are design aspects you are not sure of, you can hire an architect or a deck builder to do the drawings for you.

Another option is to hire a carpenter for a day or two of labor. Some car-

> ### How Much Can You Save by Doing It Yourself?
>
> As a general rule, labor costs for a deck tend to be about the same as material costs. (Of course, in special situations, this can vary greatly.) You should be able to get about the same price for materials as a contractor— lumberyards tend to discount according to volume, and if you give them a total list of materials and make it clear that you are shopping around for a price, most of them will get competitive.

Swampy Site

Deck Elevated More Than 10'

Deck with Hot Tub

Severely Sloping Site

Deck Cantilevered and Supported by Braces

**Designs that require professional help.** These deck-building situations that probably will require the help of a professional builder.

If you decide to hire a professional to build your deck, it pays to spend some time finding the best one possible. Check first with friends and neighbors, who probably will not be reluctant to tell you their opinions of contractors they have employed. If possible, inspect a contractor's work. Ask his customers if he gave them the finished product they were hoping for, whether he finished on time, and if he responded quickly to any complaints. (And if your instincts about a contractor are good, don't be too rattled by one former customer's complaints. Check further. Customer expectations can be unreasonable.) If you cannot find a contractor by word of mouth, try contacting local trade associations. Get several references. The contractor should be insured for liability, property damage, and worker's compensation.

Interview and get bids from two or three contractors before hiring one. Don't just go for the cheapest deal: If he turns out to be incompetent or dishonest, you can end up losing a *lot* of money as well as time. Try to make sure he understands what you want and that he is agreeable with your goals and desires.

Have a lawyer take a quick look at your contract if you are at all unsure that everything has been covered. The contract should include the exact dimensions of the work to be performed (you should append the plans and elevations to the contract). All the materials to be used should be fully identified, including lumber grades and hardware types. You should specify some details about the lumber—#2 grade or better, no knotholes more than ½ inch in diameter, and no long cracks, for example. Include a timetable for the work to be performed.

penters will be reluctant to do this—they'd rather do a large chunk of work for a set price. But others will welcome the prospect of a day of labor without worrying about bidding. Good communication is the key to making this sort of arrangement work: The carpenter should have a clear idea of your deck design and should understand exactly what it is that you want done.

Some contractors you hire may be willing to lower their prices in exchange for your doing part of the grunt work, like digging holes and cleaning up. But be careful when setting up such a "sweat equity" arrangement. It's easy for misunderstandings to arise, and more often than not, both contractor and customer end up thinking they are doing more work than they were supposed to. Make sure your duties are clearly spelled out, and make sure you will be available to do your part of the work when the contractor needs you to do it.

If you decide to do it yourself, you will probably still need at least one helper. Building by yourself can be quite laborious and time-wasting. There are many moments when things go more than twice as fast with two people—for example, when one person holds the board and eyes the level while the other nails or screws the board in. Preferably your helper will be someone with carpentry skills, but you can probably make do with someone who is just there to help carry things and to hold things up while you do the skilled work. If possible, choose someone you enjoy being around.

## FROM PERMIT TO FINAL INSPECTION

Building codes and zoning ordinances generally apply to permanent structures, meaning anything that is anchored to the ground or attached to the house. So nearly every kind of deck requires permits and inspections from a local building department.

These departments are like feudal societies, and the inspectors you must deal with are lords of small domains. This is not necessarily a bad thing, since democracy obviously would not work well. Good inspectors tend to feel a lot of responsibility for their areas, since they are the last line of defense against shoddy work. They will get tough if necessary. In extreme cases, this could mean making someone tear down what they have built and start over again. So it's a good idea to build a solid relationship with these folks.

Whether you get a nice or a nasty inspector is largely due to things you have no control over: how big his (or her) caseload is, how many bad experiences he's had with do-it-yourselfers, the state of his love life, etc. There's no way of predicting what your guy will be like, but be prepared: you may get a stinker.

Inspectors have a natural distrust of handymen, and for good reason, since a lot of subpar work gets done by non-professionals. So show your inspector that you mean to do a good job. Check ahead of time about zoning requirements and property line setbacks. If you will be doing any plumbing or electrical work along with your deck, let your inspector know about it. Get a list of requirements ahead of time and find out what things are most important to the inspector. Present clean-looking plans that clearly address his concerns. Even if the inspector seems an annoying person, respect the fact that he is there to make your neighborhood a safer place to live in. If you do things well, you will probably find that even a hard-guy inspector will come to respect you.

You may think all this is not worth the hassle and the money and be tempted to skip the permit. But look on your building inspector as an asset. If he or she spots a design problem in your plans, it could save you a lot more money than the cost of the permit. And if you come to sell your home, it will be an advantage to have a document showing that your deck was inspected and certified to be safe and sound.

## Throwing a Deck-Raising Party

You'll probably be pleasantly surprised how many guys and gals will answer the call when asked to spend the better part of a Saturday helping build a deck. For many people who sit at a desk all week, the promise of building something solid can have a lot of appeal. And when it's someone else's project, and they don't have to worry about all the planning, that makes it seem more like a short adventure than a work project. You can sweeten the deal, of course, with the promise of free pizza and beer. (Avoid any food preparation that will take up your time and energy, and reserve the beer until the work is done.)

You want your party to be relaxed, but it will work only if you plan seriously. Choose a chunk of work that makes sense for your crew. Often the best plan is to do the footings and the ledger board yourself (since these involve some painstaking figuring, and you have to wait for the concrete to set for a day before proceeding) and invite the gang over for framing, a project that often requires numerous hands. Decking is also a good gang-work project.

Get all your ducks in a row before the group arrives; it would be a shame to have them all just standing around waiting while you make a trip to the hardware store, or while you take measurements that could have been taken the day before. Have all the lumber and hardware on site and inspected. Make sure you have plenty of tools, so everyone can feel like he or she is contributing.

If several people show up, don't be surprised if you spend most of your time supervising, rather than actually doing physical work. It is important that you carefully keep track of how everyone is doing, since a mistake could mean a whole lot of work re-doing things later. Remember, although they are your friends and want your deck to turn out well, they are not intimately familiar with your plan, as you are. And they may have lower workmanship standards than you. If you see someone making dents in the lumber, or spacing decking in a haphazard way, for instance, tactfully urge them to do better, or diplomatically give them a different job.

Your inspector will probably want to make two or even three inspections, for the footings, the framing, and the finished deck with rails and stairs. He will have his own ideas about when to schedule which inspection, but a good general rule is: Never cover up anything important that hasn't been inspected, and never force your inspector to crawl around to look at something. For example, if your deck will be raised, so that the substructure will be easily visible from below, you're probably O.K. putting on the decking before the framing gets inspected. But if your deck will be low to the ground, have him inspect the framing before you start decking.

## Neighborhood Regulations

You may also want to check with your neighbors or any local neighborhood committees. Some communities set their own architectural standards, either to preserve local traditions or to beautify the area. Not only will compliance with these standards help maintain good neighborly relations, but some communities actually codify these standards; if so, they carry the full weight of the law.

## Tax Effects

Like it or not, there's a good chance that your deck will affect your real estate tax bill. As soon as you apply for a building permit, your tax assessor will know that your house's value is about to increase. Once the deck is completed, there's a good chance that he or she will stop by to reassess your property. This is an annual cost, so it would be a good idea to visit the assessor's office to see what effects your project might have on your taxes.

## ADOPTING A REALISTIC SCHEDULE

Decks can go up quickly, but don't put yourself on a rush schedule. All sorts of things can slow you down: scheduling of inspections, trips to the hardware store for things you forgot to get rain or very hot weather correcting mistakes. Some days, you spend as much time dealing with unexpected little problems as you spend on the planned building.

How much you can get done in a day depends on many factors: your level of skill and that of your helpers; the site; the quality of the lumber; how far you have to cart things, to name a few. So there's no way we can tell you just how long it will take to build your deck. With all those caveats in mind, here are some projects that a skilled non-professional and a fairly skilled helper can expect to get done in one solid working day, if materials are on site and working conditions are good:

• Laying out and pouring up to seven footings, 8 inches in diameter and 42 inches deep.

• Building the substructure (Attaching a ledger board, setting and aligning posts, constructing and setting a built-up beam, and installing joists) for a deck that is modestly sized (200 square feet or less), not raised very high, and straightforward in design.

• Decking: 400 square feet if laid straight; 200 square feet if laid at an angle.

• Standard-design railings and stairway for a deck up to 400 square feet.

---

### Things to Ask Your Inspector

Inspectors come in a wide variety of dispositions: some are friendly, some are surly; some like to be asked for advice, some don't want to be bothered. But all will like you better if you appear organized and if you find a way to deal with problems ahead of time and quickly.

First, ask the office secretary for any literature that can answer your questions without bothering the inspector. Study it carefully; the inspector doesn't want to repeat what he has already written. Here is a list of common issues that may arise during the building of a deck, questions that will receive different answers from different inspectors. If the inspector seems inclined, get these questions cleared up early.

• How close can your deck be to your property line?

• What are the span and lumber requirements for posts, beams, joists and decking? If the office does not have a list, use our charts for decking, beams, posts and joists on pages 87-88 to make your drawing, and then run them by the inspector.

• How deep must your footings be? In areas where the ground freezes, this will depend at least partly on what your frost line is.

• Are there special requirements for the concrete footings? For instance, does he want you to install reinforcing bar?

• Which method of ledger installation does he prefer? (See "Ledger Design Options," page 89, for five typical options.) If he wants flashing, which type and method of installation does he prefer? Does he want joists slipped under the flashing or smashed against it?

• If your deck will be raised above the ground, will bracing be required? (There are no reliable rules here, and requirements vary greatly from area to area.) If you will be installing skirting below the deck, that may in some cases take the place of bracing.

• What are the requirements for the pad at the bottom of the stairway? Can you, for instance, use bricks or concrete pavers laid in a bed of gravel and sand, rather than laying a concrete pad?

• What are the codes for railings? These include how high the railing must be, how the railing is fastened and how big any gaps in the railing can be. These requirements vary from area to area.

Be conservative in your planning: it's much better to be surprised at how much you got done than to be disappointed because you didn't meet your day's expectations. Take plenty of breaks to stop and admire your workmanship—and to make sure you haven't made mistakes.

## TAKING CARE OF YOUR BODY

If you've never had back problems, that does not mean you are immune. Most people in the trades have had lower back pain, as have a large percentage of nonprofessionals. You don't have to do this sort of work for years to get it, and it's not usually caused by lifting very heavy objects. Sometimes all it takes is one day of lifting lots of things in a way that your body is not used to. So take it easy, lift with your legs rather than your back, and have someone help you even with

those pieces that you could have muscled into position yourself.

## PLANNING THE WORK SPACE

If you plan your work space with care, the project will proceed more quickly, you will be less likely to strain your muscles, and everyone—onlookers as well as workers—will be safer.

Centralize the power tools and cords, so you always know where the tools are and you're not always tripping over cords. Have a cord for every tool, so you don't have to keep stopping work to unplug one tool and plug another in. Use a work bench or a set of saw horses, so that you can do most of your cutting from a comfortable standing position.

Plan the location of the materials so as to cut down on toting time. Take care to stack lumber neatly, with the

boards packed tightly together to minimize warping and twisting. Make sure there are clear walking paths for all aspects of the job.

### Corralling Tools

Tools have an annoying habit of walking away from a work site (even when you're working by yourself). One way to prevent your tools from sprouting legs is to mark off a spot where each item should be returned whenever it is not in use. (An old blanket or scrap sheet of plywood works fine.)

At the end of the day, make it a point to put away your tools on your own. That way, you'll know exactly where something is because you're the person who put it there. This is also a perfect time to give everything a quick inspection, to check for dull blades, dead batteries, or other damaged or missing parts.

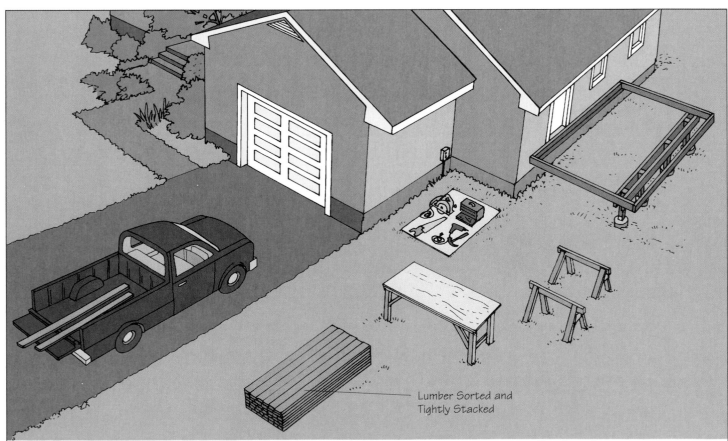

Lumber Sorted and Tightly Stacked

**Planning the work space.** In an efficient work site tools and materials are strategically placed to conserve steps while allowing you room to work.

# Chapter 4

# GATHERING TOOLS

You need only a modest set of tools to build most decks. More specialized tools will sometimes make the work go more quickly, but think before you buy: If you will use the tool only occasionally, is it really worth the price?

Your tools should be in good working order, or you can waste a lot of time and end up with a sloppy-looking job. But don't go overboard buying the best. You may feel pressure to buy fancy tools from the T.V. building expert who has all the right stuff or your neighbor who likes to show off his latest toys. But there's no reason to keep up with the Joneses—or with Norm and Bob, for that matter. If your budget forces you to choose between

a tool that will make things go a bit quicker and better-looking lumber, go for the lumber.

Purchase the least expensive tool that will do what you need it to do and then some. Often this means buying the mid-priced model, if the cheap version will not do a good job and the deluxe model is more than you need. A "bargain" tool will be no bargain if you are reminded of its limitations every time you pick it up, and an expensive tool will make you feel guilty the more dust it gathers in your garage.

Ask yourself the following questions before buying: Is it the right size and strength for the jobs I will be doing?

Will it work well on the sorts of material I will use it on? Does it perform to the tolerances I require? Will it withstand the abuse that my family and I will subject it to? How much garage space am I willing to dedicate to it? And, of course, does it make sense in the family budget?

## LAYOUT AND EXCAVATION TOOLS

**Reel tape measure.** For large decks, where you are laying out long distances, it's helpful to have a 50-foot or 100-foot reel tape measure. This tool is different from the handy 25- or

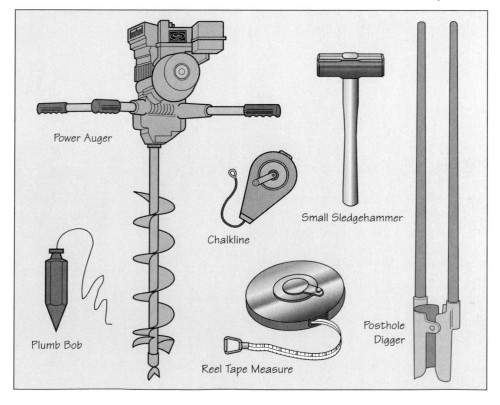

Power Auger

Plumb Bob

Chalkline

Small Sledgehammer

Reel Tape Measure

Posthole Digger

30-foot automatically retracting tape measure you'll carry in your tool belt for measuring lumber. Of course, you can use the shorter tape measure for layout if that is all you have available.

**Chalkline.** The tool that aligned the ancient pyramids, a chalkline will enable you to mark perfectly straight lines in just a few seconds. Use blue chalk, because other colors are so permanent that often they cannot be washed away. (Check the fine print on the chalk containers).

**Mason's string line.** Your string line will come in for some abuse and must be pulled tight, so get strong stuff—nylon is a good choice.

**Plumb bob.** To pinpoint the location of posts, you will need to drop a perfectly straight vertical line from a given spot. Use a plumb bob. Many chalklines are shaped to double as plumb bobs.

**Small sledgehammer.** For driving stakes, a standard 16- or 20-ounce hammer will usually do the job, but a small sledgehammer will make things go faster.

**Posthole digger.** In most areas of the country, you will need to dig deep, narrow holes for the footings. If you have only a few of these holes to dig, or if you have some cheap labor available, or if you can stretch the excavating job over several days, you can dig holes by hand with a posthole digger. This double-handled tool enables a single person to cut smooth, straight holes.

**Power auger.** For larger projects, consider using a power auger to dig postholes. These are powered by gasoline engines and work by drilling into the ground. They come in different sizes. Consult with your rental shop to get the right one for your job and your soil conditions.

In addition to the posthole digger of your choice, you may need a wrecking bar for breaking or prying rocks, as well as tools for cutting roots: a shovel, branch pruners, or even an axe.

## Safety Equipment

Common sense should tell you not to do carpentry without first having some basic safety equipment, such as eye and ear protection. Wear safety goggles or plastic glasses whenever you are working with power tools or chemicals... period. Make sure your eye protection conforms to American National Standards Institute (ANSI) Z87.1 or Canandian Standards Association (CSA) requirements (products that do will be marked with a stamp). Considering the cost of a visit to the emergency room, it doesn't hurt to purchase an extra pair for the times when a neighbor volunteers to lend a hand or when you misplace the first pair. The U.S. Occupational Safety and Health Administration (OSHA) recommends that hearing protection be worn when the noise level exceeds 85 decibels (db) for an 8-hour workday. However, considering that a circular saw emits 110 db, even shorter exposure times can contribute to hearing impairment or loss. Both insert and muff-type protectors are available; whichever you choose, be sure that it has a noise reduction rating (NRR) of a least 20 db. Your construction project will create a lot of sawdust. If you are sensitive to dust, and especially if you are working with pressure-treated wood, it's a good idea to wear a dust mask. Two types of respiratory protection are available: disposable dust masks and cartridge-type respirators. A dust mask is good for keeping dust and fine particles from being inhaled during a single procedure. Respirators have a replaceable filter. Both are available for protection against nontoxic and toxic dusts and mists. Whichever you purchase, be sure that it has been stamped by the National Institute for Occupational Safety and Health/Mine Safety and Health Administration (NIOSH/MSHA) and is approved for your specific operation. When you can taste or smell the contaminate or when the mask starts to interfere with normal breathing, it's time for a replacement. Work gloves are also nice for avoiding injury to the hands— catching a splinter off a board or developing a blister when digging post holes is not a good way to start a workday. Similarly, heavy-duty work boots will protect your feet. Steel toes will prevent injuries from dropped boards or tools. Flexible steel soles will protect you from puncture by a rogue nail.

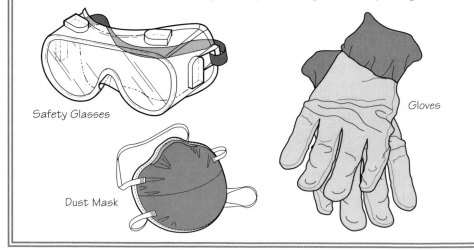

Safety Glasses

Gloves

Dust Mask

**Shovel, edging tool, hoe.** For excavating you may need some or all of these. A hoe is handy for mixing concrete; a special concrete mixing hoe which has two holes in the blade works even better.

**Wheelbarrow.** This makes a handy place to mix small amounts of concrete. It is also used to transport concrete and can come in handy if you have to carry heavy beams for a long distance.

# CARPENTRY HAND TOOLS

**Carpenter's level.** An accurate carpenter's level is one of the most important things to have when building a deck. A 48-inch level is a good choice; a 24-inch level will probably do, and an 8-footer is often awkward to use. A level made of wood and brass is more durable than the cheaper aluminum levels, but no more accurate. So, the aluminum model is an excellent choice for the occasional carpenter. Take care of your level; all it takes is one good drop or a hard hit to make it inaccurate. Test your level regularly: Set it on a smooth surface, and see where the bubbles are. Then flip it over. If the bubbles are in exactly the same place, your level is accurate; if not, either adjust it or get a new level.

T-Bevel

Sanding Block

Tape Measure

Chisel

Framing Square

Carpenter's Level

Angle Square

Combination Square

Block Plane

Water-Level

Pipe Clamp

Metal Snips

Line Level

Torpedo Level

Rachet Wrench with Socket

Flat Bar

Post Level

Cat's Paw

**Torpedo level.** You will find a torpedo level handy for small objects. It fits easily into your toolbox or your pouch.

**Line level and water level.** For some decks you will need to check for level over long spans. For this, use a line level or a water level. The water level is the more accurate of the two and more expensive. It is basically a long hose with two graduated vials attached to each end and works on the principle that water always seeks its own level. A line level consists of a single bubble vial that can be attached to a string line. When measuring, make sure the string is taut, and place the level near the center of the string line. Check the level by taking it off the string and reversing it. If the reading is the same both ways, then your level is accurate.

**Post level.** If you will be installing a lot of posts that need to be plumbed, consider getting a post level. This very specialized but inexpensive tool straps onto the post, so you don't have to keep holding a level up while you are moving things around. The post level indicates whether the post is plumb in both directions at once, saving you from having to first check one way and then the other.

**Framing square.** This large piece of flat metal measuring 16 inches in one direction and 24 inches the other is needed for laying out stair stringers and comes in handy for squaring up wide boards.

**Combination square.** This square has an adjustable blade which can slide up and down. It can indicate both 90- and 45-degree angles, and the adjustable blade is handy for transferring depth measurements and for running a line along the length of a board. Some types have level vials in them, but the vials generally are not of much use.

**Angle square.** Often called by the brand name Speed Square, this triangular piece of aluminum is tough enough to get banged around on the job and not lose its accuracy. Its trian-gular shape enables you to lay out a 45-degree angle as quickly as a 90-degree angle; it also enables you to find other angles quickly, though not with great precision. It can be held firmly in place, making it a serviceable cutting guide for a circular saw. You will probably find it the most useful of the squares.

**T-bevel.** If you need to duplicate angles other than 45 or 90 degrees, use a T-bevel (or bevel gauge). This has a flat metal blade that can be locked into any angle.

**Tape measure.** Get a good quality tape measure. A 25- or 30-foot tape is much handier than smaller measuring devices. And a 1-inch-wide blade is far superior to one that is ¾ inch wide, since it is more rigid and will not quickly fold when you extend it.

**Hammer.** Your hammer is always at your side and is used constantly, so get one that is comfortable. A 16-ounce hammer is a comfortable weight that will do the job, but you might like a 20-ouncer, which will drive 16d nails quickly into joists and beams. A straight-claw hammer is better for demolition work; a curved-claw hammer pulls nails a bit more easily.

**Nail set.** For places where the nails will show, you want to avoid the "smiles" and "frowns" caused by the hammer hitting the wood when you strike the nail with that last blow. Use a nail set, a small shaft of metal with one square end and one end tapered to a blunt point. With this, you can either drive nails perfectly flush with the wood, or countersink them into the wood.

**Utility knife.** No carpenter's apron should be without a utility knife. This inexpensive tool gets used for all sorts of things, including sharpening pencils, slicing away splinters from boards, shaving pieces of lumber, and opening bundles and packages. Get a better-quality, heavy-duty knife. Blades of cheap knives can slip out when you bear down hard. Replacement blades fit in the handle; replace blades as soon as they get dull. This will give you greater control and therefore greater safety. Either get a retractable knife or have a safe pocket in a leather pouch to insert a nonre-tractable knife.

**Tool belt or apron.** A tool belt or apron is a definite must; without it, you will spend untold hours looking for that tool you used a few minutes ago. You can get an elaborate leather belt or opt for less expensive canvas. Your belt should comfortably hold those objects you use most during a working day: your square, tape measure, hammer, chalkline, nail set, chisel, pencils, and utility knife; and it should have a pocket left over for a good-sized handful of nails. Be sure you can holster and unholster your hammer, pencil, and tape measure with ease.

**Pencils.** Have plenty of pencils on hand—they have a tendency to disappear. Flat carpenter's pencils are better than regular pencils, since they need to be sharpened far less often.

**Chisel.** This is useful for cleaning out dado cuts and finishing notch cuts. A 2-inch-wide chisel is most useful for this kind of work.

**Flat bar and wrecking bar.** The flat bar is more versatile, but the wrecking bar (sometimes called a crowbar) gives you more leverage. These are handy for demolition such as removing siding before installing a ledger board for you deck and for prying deck boards into position.

**Cat's paw.** This tool is used for pulling framing nails. By striking the back of its claw with a hammer, you can drive it under a nail head, even if the head is below the surface. Then you push or strike the top of the tool to pull the nail out. A cat's paw seriously mars the face of the board.

**Block plane** You may occasionally need a plane for trimming or smoothing wood and straightening irregular edges or bevels. Properly set, a block plane will trim one shaving off at a time, allowing you to achieve tight-fitting joints.

**Sanding block.** A more commonly used tool will be a sanding block. Use it for taking off rough edges, rounding sharp corners, and smoothing out splinters and rough spots. There are several types—choose the most comfortable—and they are all far superior to simply using a sheet of hand-held sandpaper. In most cases, a power vibrating sander will not do any better than a sanding block. Use a belt sander only if you are doing very heavy-duty rounding of edges.

**Wrenches, pliers, metal snips.** If you will be installing lag screws or carriage bolts, a ratchet wrench with the right socket will make things go much faster than a crescent wrench. Channeled pliers and locking pliers are useful for prying and pulling—especially when you need to pull out nails whose heads have broken off. You will need metal snips for cutting flashing.

**Clamps.** Pipe clamps are sometimes helpful for holding pieces of lumber in place temporarily. Large C-clamps or bar clamps can also come in handy for this purpose.

**Hand saw.** Though not used much any more, the hand saw can come in handy for finishing cuts that a circular cannot finish—as when you are cutting out stringers or cutting off posts in awkward places.

**Caulk gun.** Though it should be used sparingly on a deck, there are places that benefit from a good bead of caulk.

**Putty knife.** For filling holes in damaged wood or to fill holes left by countersunk nails or screws.

**Brushes, rollers, sprayers.** Depending on the product you choose, any of these can be used to finish your deck.

## CARPENTRY POWER TOOLS

**Circular saw.** The sound and feel of a good circular saw slicing through a piece of lumber and quickly shaping it to fit your design: this accounts for much of the satisfaction people feel

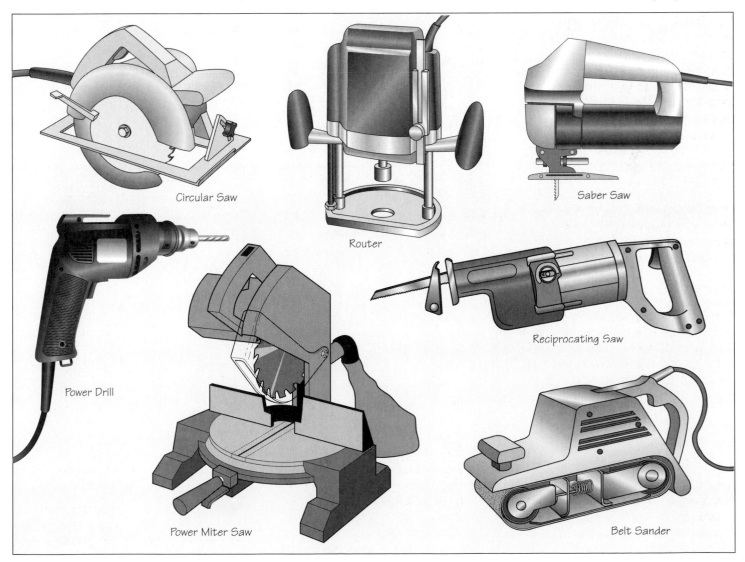

Circular Saw

Router

Saber Saw

Power Drill

Power Miter Saw

Reciprocating Saw

Belt Sander

while doing carpentry. A good circular saw will crosscut, angle cut, rip (cut lengthwise), and even bevel lumber easily and cleanly.

Most carpenters and do-it-yourselfers prefer circular saws that take 7¼-inch blades. This size will allow you to cut to a maximum depth of about 2½ inches at 90 degrees and to cut through a piece of two-by lumber even when the blade is beveled at 45 degrees.

Don't judge a saw's performance by its horsepower rating, but by the amount of amperage the motor draws and the type of bearings it uses. A low-cost saw will pull only 9 or 10 amps and will run its drive shafts and arbors on rollers or sleeve bearings. This will mean less power, a shorter life, a tendency to heat up during continual use, and sometimes less precise cuts because the blade will wobble a bit. Better saws are rated at 12 or 13 amps and are made with ball bearings. This combination of extra power and smoother operation makes for long life and more precise cutting. As is often the case, a mid-priced model may well be your best choice.

However, worm-drive saws—which are the most powerful saws and have the longest-lasting bearings—are heavy and take some getting used to; do-it-yourselfers should avoid them.

A plastic housing is no longer the sign of an inferior tool, since many plastics are highly impact resistant. Check out the base: if it is made of thin, stamped metal, it won't stay as flat as one with a thicker base that is either extruded or cast metal.

**Circular saw blades.** Use carbide-tipped blades in your circular saw. These cost a few dollars more, but last up to five times longer than

comparable blades made from high-speed steel. A 24-tooth blade is usually the best choice for deck construction and general use. (There is a trade-off between the number of teeth and cut rates and quality: A blade with fewer teeth will cut faster, but the cuts will tend to be ragged. More teeth will produce a finer cut, but your saw will have to work harder to move more teeth through the wood, and it will cut more slowly.) Have an extra blade on hand; wet wood and dense pressure-treated wood can dull your saw's blade quickly.

**Power miter saw.** If you need to make a large number of angle cuts, or if you don't feel able to make the precise angle cuts you need, it may be a good idea to buy or rent a power miter saw. These tools (also called chop saws or cutoff saws) are simply circular saws mounted on a pivot assembly so as to make precise angled cuts. Make sure you get a chop saw that will do the job: a standard 10-inch saw will *not* be able to completely cut a 2x6 at a 45-degree angle.

With a bit of extra work, you can put together a jig that will enable you to make accurate 45-degree cuts with a circular saw, although not as easily as with a chop saw. See "Cutting on an Angle," page 65, for information on how to make this jig.

**Saber saw.** This is a good choice if you need to make cutouts or if you want to cut on a curve. If you need to do a lot of this kind of cutting, buy or rent a heavy-duty saber saw. With a standard do-it-yourself model, you'll cut through two-by lumber *very* slowly, you'll break lots of those little blades, and the saw will have a tendency to wobble, making for a less-than-pleasing cut.

**Reciprocating saw.** For demolition and for cutting off posts, a reciprocating saw works well, but don't get one just for this job—a hand saw will do the job as well, though more slowly. Don't try to make precise cuts with a reciprocating saw.

**Power drill.** If you will be assembling much of the deck with screws, get a heavy duty drill; if you're using nails and need to drill only an occasional hole, a handyman drill will probably suffice. A good ⅜-inch, variable speed drill is what you want—no need for a big ½-incher. Screw guns or attachments designed to turn drills into screw guns automatically set the depth of the screw head, making the job a lot easier. However, if you are using a soft wood for the decking—cedar, for example—a tool like this may leave round indentations in the lumber. At the least, get a magnetic sleeve, and plenty of the small, cheap screwdriver bits that fit into it.

**Cordless drill.** If it's in the budget, a cordless drill is mighty nice to have. If you get a powerful enough one (say, 12 volts), it will do almost everything a regular drill can do—and without the bother of a cord. A good cordless drill will come with a quick recharger and an extra battery, so you never have to wait for your battery to charge.

**Belt sander.** Use this tool with care; it's easy to over-sand, especially if you are working with soft wood such as cedar or redwood. With practice, you can do a lot of rounding off in a hurry with one of these tools.

**Router.** Though by no means essential for deck-building a router equipped with a chamfering or round-over bit can be quite handy for adding detail to your deck.

# Chapter 5

# MATERIALS

You have lots of decisions to make about the materials to use for your deck. Take your time reaching these decisions, because the materials you choose have a lot to do with how your deck will look, how long it will last, and how much money you will spend. In this chapter we will discuss all the materials that go into a deck. The longest discussion will be on lumber because there are so many available options.

## CONCRETE

In building your deck, you'll most likely use concrete for footings to support the posts, and you may also pour a small pad for your deck stairs to land on. Concrete is composed of three elements: *portland cement* is a fine powder that becomes a cement paste when mixed with *water*. *Aggregate*, a mixture of sand and gravel, acts to bind the cement paste together. In addition, reinforcing metal in the form of a bar or wire mesh is often used to give the concrete tensile strength. For an extra cost, you can get concrete that is reinforced with fiberglass for extra strength.

It is important to get the right mixture. Too much water will weaken the concrete; too little will make it difficult to work with. So the general rule when mixing your own is to add just enough water to make it workable for your needs. It should be liquid enough to fill all the spaces in the form, but if it is soupy, it is too wet.

The compressive strength of concrete —the amount of weight you can place on it before it crumbles—is determined by the amount of cement in the mix. A standard mix of five bags of cement per cubic yard of concrete will yield concrete that is strong enough for most deck work. Occasionally you will get an inspector who requires some sort of proof that you are using concrete that is strong enough; if so, make sure you get straight exactly what he or she wants.

In Chapter 7, under "Calculating the Amount You Need," page 82 you'll learn how to figure the amount of concrete you will need and the different options for obtaining it: having it delivered by truck, using premixed bags, and mixing your own.

## LUMBER

All your work and craftsmanship will be wasted if you use poor lumber. Choose the best lumber you can afford, and make building your deck a pleasure.

This is an important decision, and it makes sense to invest some time in making it. There are many factors to be considered when choosing lumber. Among the most common deck woods—pressure-treated, redwood, and cedar—there are many varieties to choose from. It all may look complicated at first, but the time you spend reading this chapter and inspecting wood at your lumberyard will pay off in a deck that stays strong and keeps looking good for decades.

Deck wood must resist rot and insects. Most lumber that goes into a house gets covered in some way, but the lumber used on your deck will be exposed to the weather and to whatever little creatures lurk in your yard. Even if you treat or paint the deck after building it, there will be significant uncovered portions.

You also want wood that will not easily warp or crack. Once it's firmly attached with nails or screws, lumber cannot move much. But all wood expands when wet and shrinks while drying, so a certain amount of twisting, cupping and splitting can occur, and this should be kept to a minimum.

To get the wood you want, it's not enough to choose a certain species.

### THE PROS KNOW

#### Getting the Best Lumber

The easiest way to get your lumber is to just place an order and have it delivered. But lumberyards often deliver some very poor boards to homeowners who buy in this way. If you want to get the best wood possible for your money, go to the lumber yard and pick out the boards, one by one, yourself. If your lumberyard does not allow you to do this, either get solid assurances of quality and a promise that you will be permitted to return boards you do not like or go to another yard. You may have to carry the lumber yourself if you do the picking. This will seem like excessive drudgery at the time, but the results will be well worth the effort.

Other factors that influence a wood's performance include: moisture content, method of drying the wood, what portion of the tree the lumber was taken from, and the grade of the wood.

## Lumber Basics

**Size and surfacing.** The *nominal* size of a piece of lumber—for example, 2x4—refers to its size prior to drying and surfacing. So the 2x4 you buy will actually be 1½ inches by 3½ inches; a 2x6 is actually 1½ by 5½; a 1x8 is ¾x 7¼, and so on. (See the chart Nominal and Actual Sizes of Lumber.) In most cases, lumberyards carry pieces in 24-inch increments beginning at 8 feet: so you can buy 8-footers, 10-footers, and so on.

Most of the lumber you buy is surfaced—smoothed, with rounded edges—on all four sides. This is called S4S, meaning surfaced on four sides. If you want a rough-sawn look (for the fascia or for posts, perhaps), you should be able to find cedar or redwood that is either rough all over or is smooth on only one side. This lumber may be a bit thicker than S4S.

Many people choose to use ⁵⁄₄ decking, available in cedar and pressure-treated lumber, for the decking and sometimes for the top cap on the railing. This material is actually 1 inch thick and 5½ inches wide (though some are narrower). Its edges are rounded to minimize splintering. Often only one face will be useable, so choose your boards carefully. To satisfy most codes and to build a strong deck, you will have to space joists no more than 16 inches on center to use this material.

In addition to the ⁵⁄₄ decking with rounded edges, there is available a special crowned and grooved decking. The

### Nominal and Actual Sizes of Lumber

| Lumber Size (inches) | Nominal Size (inches) | Common Actual |
|---|---|---|
| **Boards** | 1x3 | ¾x 2½ |
| | 1x4 | ¾x 3½ |
| | 1x6 | ¾x 5½ |
| | 1x8 | ¾x 7¼ |
| | 1x10 | ¾x 9¼ |
| | 1x12 | ¾x11¼ |
| **Dimension lumber** | 2x2 | 1½x1½ |
| | 2x3 | 1½x2½ |
| | 2x4 | 1½x3½ |
| | 2x6 | 1½x5½ |
| | 2x8 | 1½x7¼ |
| | 2x10 | 1½x9¼ |
| | 2x12 | 1½x11¼ |
| **Posts** | 4x4 | 3½x3½ |
| | 4x6 | 3½x5½ |
| | 6x6 | 5½x5½ |

grooves provide some stability to the lumber, and the crown is designed so that water will run off each board easily. This material will allow you to build a deck that is perfectly level without worrying about puddles forming. However, it is not a big problem to build a deck with a slight slope, so unless you like their appearance, these boards may not be worth the extra expense.

Most people choose 2x6 or ⁵⁄₄x6 for decking, either because they like the wider appearance or because it is less work. But with smaller and smaller trees being cut down for lumber, the price of wider boards is growing, and 2x4 is becoming a more economical choice.

**Lumber density.** As a general rule, lumber of greater density—that is, lumber that is heavier when dry—will be stronger but also more prone

to splitting and warping. So the lighter (and weaker) the wood, the fewer splinters and twists you will get. This is because light wood can act like a sponge, sucking in moisture when the weather is wet and drying out when the sun comes out, whereas dense wood does not have this characteristic and so is adversely affected by weather. Pressure-treating lumber does not affect density but only adds weight in the form of moisture temporarily, until it dries out.

So dense wood—fir or southern yellow pine, for instance—works well for the substructure, where strength is important and splinters and warping do not matter much. For the decking and rails, which will be walked on and handled, lighter wood is a better choice.

**Heartwood and sapwood.** The wood near the center of the tree, which is inactive because it has not been growing for some time, is called *heartwood*. Lumber milled from this portion of the tree is more resistant to rot and insects and less porous than is *sapwood*, which is taken from the area of the tree near the bark. This is a serious difference: decking made of redwood or cedar heartwood will last far longer than will sapwood decking of the same species. Often

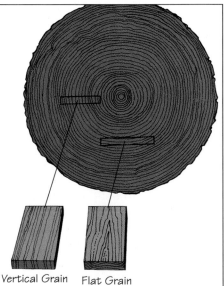

Vertical Grain    Flat Grain

**Vertical and flat grain.** A board will have vertical grain, flat grain or a combination of the two depending upon what part of the log it came from.

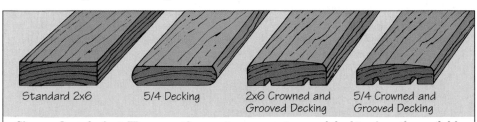

Standard 2x6    5/4 Decking    2x6 Crowned and Grooved Decking    5/4 Crowned and Grooved Decking

**Size and surfacing.** These are the most common types of decking boards available.

lumber containing a good deal of sapwood is given the more palatable name of "common" by lumberyards.

**Vertical and flat grain.** Lumber is cut from the log so as to have either vertical grain, in which narrow grain lines run along the board, or flat grain (also called plainsawn), with wider lines that often form sort of rippling V-shapes. Most boards are a combination of the two, and in any given load of lumber you will find boards that are both primarily flat-grained and primarily vertical-grained.

Vertical grain is superior. It is less likely to shrink and warp, is stronger, and looks better. You don't have to go to the extra expense of specifying vertical grain when you order; when you choose boards at the lumberyard, pick as many of the ones with narrow lines as possible.

**Lumber dryness.** Lumber companies cut trees while they are still alive, so they have a lot of moisture in them to begin with. And pressure-treated lumber gets saturated with liquid chemicals, making it even wetter. To what extent this lumber is dried after treatment varies quite a bit. Some lumber you buy may have a moisture content of as much as 30 or 40 percent.

Wood that is wet—whether from natural moisture or from chemicals—will shrink as it dries out. Wood shrinks more in width than in length, but the lengthwise shrinkage can become significant. Wood shrinks proportionally, so that the longer the board, the more it will shrink. Often shrinkage is not a problem, but in certain cases—especially when you are making butt joints—it can be disastrous. If you have a lot of decking butt joints and the boards are subject to shrinkage, you can end up with a deck that has unsightly gaps all over the place. Also, wet wood can warp, which makes it difficult to work with and can cause cracks after the lumber has been installed.

**Grading stamp.** This means it is best either to buy fairly dry wood or to dry it yourself. You don't have to go to

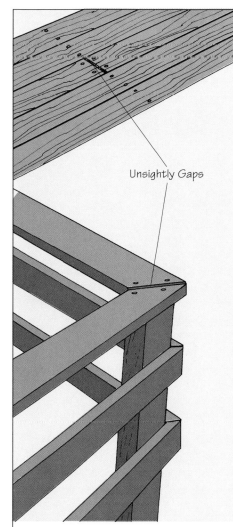

Unsightly Gaps

**Lumber dryness.** Unsightly gaps can occur if wood shrinks.

the extra expense of buying kiln-dried lumber (wood that has been dried in special procedures at the mill); if your lumber has a moisture content (MC) of less than 20 percent, shrinkage and warping will be minimal. Moisture content of lumber is indicated on the grading stamp.

Unfortunately, you cannot rely completely on the moisture content that is

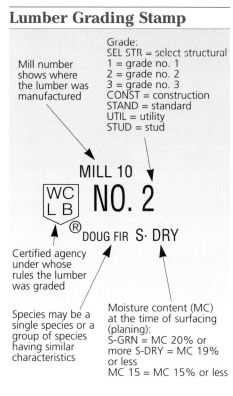

## Lumber Grading Stamp

Mill number shows where the lumber was manufactured

Grade:
SEL STR = select structural
1 = grade no. 1
2 = grade no. 2
3 = grade no. 3
CONST = construction
STAND = standard
UTIL = utility
STUD = stud

MILL 10
WC L B ® NO. 2
DOUG FIR  S· DRY

Certified agency under whose rules the lumber was graded

Species may be a single species or a group of species having similar characteristics

Moisture content (MC) at the time of surfacing (planing):
S-GRN = MC 20% or more S-DRY = MC 19% or less
MC 15 = MC 15% or less

**Grading stamp.** Knowing how to read the lumber grading stamp will provide lots of useful information about the piece of wood.

stamped on the board, since wood can pick up moisture through rainwater or humidity while sitting in the lumberyard. Your local lumberyard may be able and willing to give some sample boards a quick check with a moisture meter. Or you can check yourself in less technical but effective ways: Cut through a board crosswise, and feel for moisture or drive a nail into the board and see if any wetness appears.

**Stickering.** If your wood needs to be dried, *sticker* it by stacking it carefully with small pieces of wood in between each layer, which will allow air to get at all sides of the boards.

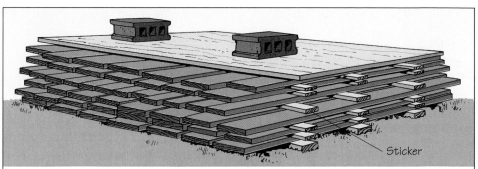

Sticker

**Stickering.** "Sticker" your lumber to enable it to dry out without warping.

**Lumber grades.** Lumber is sorted and graded on the basis of number and size of knots, milling defects, and drying technique.

*Lumber Grades*

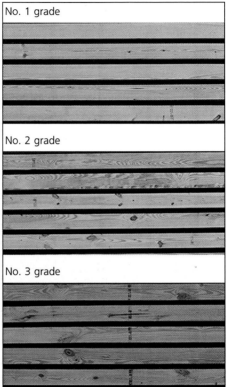

No. 1 grade

No. 2 grade

No. 3 grade

The highest-quality—and most expensive — lumber is called *select*. This lumber is clear—free from knots and other imperfections. If you sort through lumber yourself, you will often be able to find an occasional piece of select lumber.

Most often, you will be dealing with *common* lumber, which comes in grades, often listed as no. 1, 2, and 3. Sometimes lumber is graded Const (construction), Stand (standard), Util (utility) and Stud (stud-grade). No. 2 is the most common grade and will be fine for most applications. Chances are, your building codes will require "no. 2 or better." No. 3 will be very rough and should usually be avoided. For the railings and other areas that are highly visible and that get handled, you may want to spend the extra money to get no.1 or even select. This is a decision best made while you are at the lumberyard looking at pieces of lumber.

# LUMBER SPECIES

The species of lumber refers to the tree it is cut from—cedar or yellow pine, for example. Softwood lumber comes from evergreen trees, such as fir and cedar, while hardwood comes from leafed, deciduous trees, such as maple and oak. Nearly all decks are built entirely of softwood.

## Redwood

The redwood trees of California and the Pacific Northwest are legendary for their size and the quality of the lumber they provide. Redwood's beautiful straight grain, natural glowing color, and weather resistance have traditionally marked it as the Cadillac of outdoor building materials. It is a pleasure to work with, easy to cut and sweet-smelling. Unfortunately, overlumbering has made redwood expensive and in some areas hard to obtain.

In most cases you will want to use redwood only for the visible portions of your deck, because it is expensive. But redwood is strong enough to be used for structural support as well, though you may have to use larger members than would be the case if you were using pressure-treated lumber.

You can usually tell sapwood from heartwood by color: the sapwood is lighter and hardly makes one think of *red* wood. Redwood heartwood is extremely weather- and insect-resistant, but the sapwood may start to rot in two or three years if it has contact with the ground or if it will remain wet for long periods of time. Treat sapwood before applying it, and use it only where it will be dry for most of the year.

You can let redwood "go gray" by not treating it with anything; it will reach a light gray color and a slight sheen that many people find attractive. Or you can treat it with stains and a U.V. blocker to keep it close to its original color (see "Sealers, Preservatives, and Stains," page 150).

In some parts of the country, treated and stained redwood is available. The idea here is to make the sapwood both decay-resistant and similar in color to the heartwood. This is an expensive item, but if it comes with a lifetime warranty it will be worth it. Inspect a good number of pieces to make sure you like the color. The reddish-brown will fade after five years or so, at which time it will go a uniform grey unless you re-stain it.

Redwood grades are established by the Redwood Inspection Service of the California Redwood Association. The service has established two grading categories: *Architectural grades* are the best-looking most expensive grades of redwood. *Garden Grades* are more economical and have more knots. Both categories of redwood are available kiln-dried or unseasoned and are usually surfaced on four sides.

Architectural grades include:

**Clear all heart.** All-heartwood and free from knots, this wood is recommended for highly visible applications.

**Clear.** Similar in quality to Clear All Heart, except that Clear contains sapwood. Clear is ideal for highly visible applications where the wood won't be subjected to rot.

**B heart.** Containing limited knots, but no sapwood, B-Heart is a less costly alternative to Clear All Heart.

**B grade.** Similar characteristics to B Heart but contains sapwood; same uses as Clear.

Garden grades of redwood are suitable for most deck-building applications. They include:

**Construction heart/deck heart.** This is an all heartwood grade containing knots. It is recommended for work on or near the ground such as posts, beams, joists and decking. Deck Heart has a similar appearance and uses as Construction Heart but is also graded for strength. Deck Heart is available in 2x4 and 2x6 only.

**Construction common/deck common.** Containing knots and a combi-

nation of heartwood and sapwood, these grades are recommended for above-ground applications such as railings, benches and decking. Deck common has similar appearance and uses as Construction Common but is also graded for strength. Deck common is available in 2x4 and 2x6 only.

**Merchantable Heart.** This is the most economical all-heartwood grade. It allows larger knots and some knotholes. Used for garden walls or utility structures on or near the ground.

**Merchantable.** Having the same characteristics as Merchantable Heart but containing sapwood, this grade is suitable only for fence boards, trellises and above-ground garden and utility applications.

# Cedar

Cedar has many of the benefits of redwood and usually costs less. Like redwood, it is stable, easy to work with, and rarely splinters or checks. And like redwood, it is the heartwood of the cedar tree that is resistant to rot. Sapwood will rot quickly. You can often recognize cedar heartwood by its dark color and the hamster-cage smell you get when you cut it.

Cedar is fragrant and beautiful, though it tends to have a more informal feel than redwood, with its light brown color. Left untreated, cedar will turn grey.

Cedar is not quite as strong as redwood and is rarely used for structural support. You may want to use it in places where the structure will be visible, for example, for stair stringers. In other places, for instance the outside and header joists, it is usual to use pressure-treated lumber for the joists and then wrap them with one-by cedar fascia board for appearance sake.

However, unlike redwood and pressure-treated lumber, cedar is available in most any size, even up to 12x12 monster posts. So you might use it for unusually sized post-and-beam constructions.

Cedar is widely available and comes in a number of varieties. The most commonly used varieties are Western red cedar and Inland red cedar. You can purchase Clear All Heart, but this is quite expensive. Chances are, you will want to use no.1 varieties: Select Tight Knot, taken from new growth and containing some sapwood, works well for decking that will not remain wet for long periods. Appearance

Grade comes from old growth and should be used in places susceptible to rot. Stepping down from these grades you will find Tight Knot and no. 2. These will contain more knots, but probably have the same amount of rot-resistance. And you may like the look of the knots.

One of the most common and pleasing deck building materials is ¾ cedar decking. This has rounded edges so you will

### Redwood Grades

| | Construction Heart/Deck Heart | Construction Common/Deck Common | Merchantable Heart | Merchantable | Clear All Heart | Clear | B Heart | B Grade |
|---|---|---|---|---|---|---|---|---|
| Architectural | — | — | — | — | ● | ● | ● | ● |
| Garden | ● | ● | ● | ● | — | — | — | — |
| Knots | — | ● | ● | ● | — | — | ● | ● |
| Sapwood | — | ● | — | ● | — | ● | — | ● |
| Posts | ●○ | — | — | — | ● | — | ● | — |
| Beams | ●○ | — | — | — | ● | — | ● | — |
| Joists | ●○ | — | — | — | ● | — | ● | — |
| Decking | ● | ●○ | — | — | ● | ● | ● | ● |
| Rails | ● | ●○ | — | — | ● | ● | ● | ● |

● Suitable grade for use.

○ Most economical grade for use.

end up with virtually no splinters. But inspect this lumber for the qualities we have discussed. Just because some company has labeled it "decking" does not mean it will suit your needs.

Cedar with one smooth and one rough face (called S3S, meaning surfaced on three sides) is often used for fascia and other surfaces that will not be handled or walked on. With the rough side turned outwards, it has a pleasing rustic appearance. However, water often gets trapped between a fascia board and the lumber it is covering up; so treat these pieces well.

Sometimes cedar will develop black, slimy spots. While this could be mold (*any* surface can develop mold if it stays damp long enough), chances are it is natural extractives that have been dissolved by water and are leaching out. It can be easily washed away with water and a mild soap.

## Cypress

Bald cypress is the South's answer to redwood. Native to the swamps and lowland areas throughout the southeast, bald cypress is similar to redwood in hardiness and strength, although it is not as stable. In the southern United States, local sawmills can be a very economical source for decking lumber. Cypress is not usually stocked outside of its native region, but it can be ordered in the north.

## Pressure-Treated Lumber

Pressure-treated lumber is almost always the best choice for posts, beams, and joists. There is much to recommend it: Its cost is low—not much more than untreated wood, a good deal less expensive than redwood or cedar—and if you choose the right kind of lumber, it will last a lot longer than cedar or redwood. For these reasons, many people choose to build their entire decks with it, decking and railings included.

But consider this choice carefully because there are some drawbacks: Pressure-treated lumber will often

crack and splinter over time as the preservative in it dries out. Green pressure-treated lumber has a color that is distasteful to most people. Left unfinished, pressure-treated lumber will turn gray, but a dirty-looking gray, not the same pleasing color and sheen that you will get with redwood or cedar. Pressure-treated lumber sometimes has a series of incisions left over from the injecting process, and these will not go away over time, but can become little collectors of dirt. And then there is the worry over the chemicals used in treating the wood; the material is indeed basically safe, since the agents bond securely to the wood, but it is best not to have it come into contact with food or be in a place where babies may be tempted to chew on it.

On the other hand, if you use lumber without incisions, if you carefully choose dry pieces that are not starting to crack or warp, and if you stain it correctly or purchase it stained brown, you can come up with decking and railings that are similar to cedar or redwood in appearance and that will be highly resistant to rot and insects.

All pressure-treated lumber is not the same. There are a variety of species, all with their own strengths and drawbacks; and there are several ways of treating the lumber. So it makes sense to check several sources before choosing. Don't just go with the cheapest price.

Beware: some smaller outfits treat the wood insufficiently, so that the treat-

ing agent does not penetrate deeply enough to give you the protection you need. Good pressure-treated lumber will have a warranty from a company that will be around for years to come. Some companies carry two product lines, a fully guaranteed product, and a less expensive product that is treated lightly and is appropriate for use only in areas that are not subject to a lot of moisture.

In most parts of the country, you will find chromated copper arsenate (CCA) used for the treatment; less common are ammonical copper arsenate (ACA) and acid copper chromate (ACC). These chemicals are forced into the

### THE PROS KNOW
### Retreating Pressure-Treated Wood

Even after pressure treating, the chemical preservatives do not penetrate throughout the entire depth of a board. The Western Wood Products Association (WWPA) does not recommend ripping for width or resawing for thickness, because these operations can expose large untreated sections of wood on the treated board. Of course, some cutting is inevitable. The WWPA suggests brushing or dipping on additional preservative on all freshly cut surfaces until the wood is saturated. Most professional builders do not take this extra step, considering it not worth the effort. (It often involves stopping after each cut and performing a separate task, something that can greatly slow progress.) You may want to do it for places where water is likely to sit and soak into the end of a board.

lumber by means of special methods that a homeowner cannot duplicate.

CCA is still the best product. Though the treating solution is indeed toxic, it's not as bad as it may sound—arsenate is not the same as arsenic. More importantly, it has been shown in many tests that CCA bonds tightly and does not leach out of the wood. So once it has dried, it is quite safe to the touch. ACA is a water-based agent that is somewhat less toxic, but it does not bond to the wood as well as CCA, so it ends up actually being a greater environmental hazard because it can leach out of the wood for some time after installation.

After the treating process, the wood is very wet with chemicals. Sometimes it is kiln-dried after the treatment (and marked KDAT), which will make it more expensive. Or it may be air-dried to varying degrees. If you find your lumber is very heavy, chances are that it is still full of the stuff. As is the case with all lumber, the wetter the wood, the greater the chances of warping and shrinking. So for places like the railings, get dry wood, even if it means the extra expense of KDAT lumber.

In some areas you can buy KDAT lumber with a water-repellent. This is among the most expensive of pressure-treated woods, but is worth it under the right circumstances.

**Brown pressure-treated wood.**
Brown pressure-treated lumber is CCA-treated lumber with brown pigment added, so it has the same resistance to rot and insects as the green stuff, but with a different color. The brown color typically will last two to three years in areas with traffic and/or sun exposure, and five to seven years in less-exposed areas. When the color fades, you can restain or let it go grey (keeping in mind that, like the green stuff, brown treated wood will not turn the same sort of gray as you will get with redwood or cedar).

**The right wood for each job.**
Southern yellow pine is often the best pressure-treated product available, especially for decking and railing:

it is strong and hard, and receives the treatment well, so there are usually none of the ugly incisions used on other woods. However, southern yellow pine has drawbacks: it has a tendency to warp and splinter. You can control the warpage by stacking the wood carefully and by attaching it securely at all points; the splintering can be greatly reduced if you seal it soon after installation.

Pressure-treated Douglas fir is often used for structural members. It is a bit less expensive that Southern yellow pine and just as strong. And in fact, "Doug fir" is the best lumber among those that get treated: it resists splitting, warping and checking well. But because it doesn't soak up the treatment easily, it usually gets incised with a series of unsightly cuts to increase the penetration. Because it is not prone to warping, it is a good choice for pieces that will not be firmly attached at all points—for instance, joists and beams. Larch performs similarly to Douglas fir, but is not commonly available.

A new way of treating Douglas fir has been developed which makes it a good choice for decking. A high-density incisor is used on the bottom only—that's where rot is most likely—leaving the visible surface free from the marks. This product is available with a lifetime warranty. If your lumberyard has it, consider it over yellow pine even if it costs more, since it is more likely to stay free of warps and cracks, a very important consideration.

Pressure-treated woods of lesser quality include Ponderosa pine ("Pond pine") and hem-fir (not an actual tree, but a classification that includes various types of hemlock and fir). These will be cheaper and for good reason: They are weaker (see "Sizing and Spacing the Framing Members," page 87) and prone to warpage. In addition, they are sometimes insufficiently treated, since lesser-known companies are often the ones that use them. Check for assurances of long life. You may have to treat them annually to avoid checking and splitting.

However, keep in mind that "hem-fir" comprises a good number of trees that have grown at various elevations and so possess different qualities. So in certain areas of the country you can find wood in this classification that performs well. Check not only with your lumberyard, but also with deck owners in your area.

## Pressure-Treated Plywood

Plywood comes in 4x8 sheets and in various thicknesses. On a deck, you may use pieces of pressure-treated plywood as spacers for beams or the ledger. Because it will not be visible, a rough grade ("CD" is the most common) is fine.

This stuff may not look impressive, and if you've worked with regular plywood you know that it doesn't hold up to the weather at all well. But because it

Decking

Joists

**The right wood for each job.** The decking here will be nailed securely at all points, preventing warpage, whereas the joists will hang free at the bottom. Use lumber that is appropriate to each situation: The joists must be very warp-resistant, but the decking need not be.

is thin—¾ inch is the thickest—the treating liquid can fully saturate the sheets, and it holds up well. And plywood, because it has wood grain running in both directions, is quite strong. But it is never a good idea to allow water to sit on end grain, and plywood always has exposed end grain. So cut and install it in such a way that water will run off.

## Plastic-and-Wood Composites

For extra money you can purchase a decking and railing material that is nearly maintenance-free, free of splinters, and completely immune to rot and insects, and you will be doing something ecologically responsible to boot. Composite material typically contains more than 90 percent recycled plastic, with a bit of wood thrown in to make for a permanently skid-resistant surface. It cannot be used for posts, beams, or joists.

Composite is easy to work with. It cuts smoothly with a circular saw—however, you'll want to use a drop cloth to collect all the shavings. Deck screws sink into the material until their heads are nearly buried and invisible.

However, most people are put off by the plastic appearance. Though the material is basically indestructible, be aware that certain colors will fade in time, and there will be no way to stain or paint the surface to bring it back to its original color.

## Ironwood

If you have a big budget and a taste for the exotic, you may want to look into South American hardwoods (sometimes called ironwoods), such as ipé and pau lope. These are extremely strong and durable; they are used increasingly by park services and owners of golf courses, which find that they can use boards of half the dimensions of pressure-treated lumber and have the same strength, along with a nearly unlimited life span. Much of the wood comes from plantations rather than rain forests, so the environmental

impact does not seem to be any worse than building with other woods.

As you may expect, these woods are quite expensive; using ironwood for only the decking and railings could well triple the materials cost for your whole deck. (As they become more popular, the price will probably come down.) Ironwoods are also slow to install—cutting is arduous, and you may have to predrill for every screw or nail.

# LUMBER DEFECTS

You will rarely find a perfect piece of lumber, but you can avoid wood that has problems which will adversely affect your deck. Here is a list of lumber defects, with descriptions that will tell you whether you can live with them or not.

*Bow* is a bend in the wood along the wide face, from end to end. It has no effect on strength and can be used as long as you can straighten it as you fasten it in place.

*Cup* is a bend in the width of a board. If it's not severe, it can be straightened out with nails or screws (for decking) or blocking (for joists).

*Crook* is a bend in the wood that you can see as you sight along the narrow face from end to end. Most long boards have some crook—the high portion is called the "crown," and joists are always installed crown side up—but excessive crooking makes wood unsuitable for framing. Deck boards with moderate crooking can be pried straight and fastened into place.

*Twist,* if severe enough to be noticeable at first glance, renders lumber unsuitable for decking or framing.

*Lumber Defects*

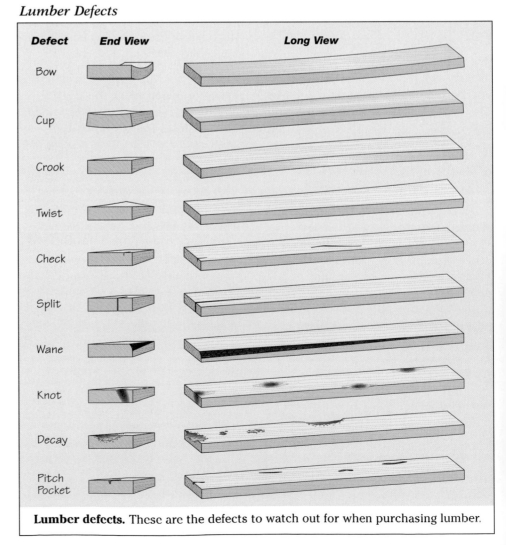

**Lumber defects.** These are the defects to watch out for when purchasing lumber.

*Check* is a rift in the surface caused when the surface dries more rapidly than the interior. It produces patches that look a bit like alligator skin. These are usually only cosmetic and do not affect the structural strength. Kiln-dried wood almost never checks.

*Split* is a crack that passes completely through the wood. It constitutes a serious structural weakness. Lumber with splits should not be used on any part of your deck.

*Wane* is the presence of bark or the lack of wood along an edge where bark once was. Wane has little effect on strength. Any bark should be removed from lumber, since it will promote rot.

*Knots* are the high-density roots of limbs. The knots themselves are strong, but they are not connected to the surrounding wood. Avoid large knots in decking, which may come loose over time. Large knots (over 1 inch) in the bottom third of a joist (that is, the side opposite the crown) will weaken it.

*Decay* is the destruction of the wood structure by fungi or insects. Decayed wood should not be used on any portion of your deck.

*Pitch Pockets* are accumulations of natural resins. They have little effect on strength, but will cause discoloration if you paint or stain the board.

# FASTENERS

Be sure that your fasteners will last as long as your lumber. (It does sometimes happen that nails actually rust away while they are embedded in wood that is not rotten.) Also, choose fasteners and fastening techniques that will not harm your wood.

In deciding what length fastener to use, the general rule is: The fastener's penetration into the bottom piece should be equal to or greater than the thickness of the top piece. So unless the fastener will be countersunk into the top board, it should be at least

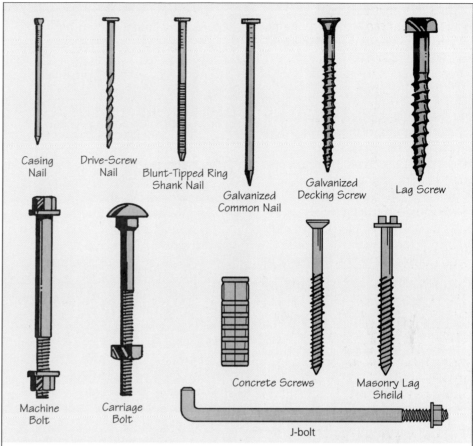

**Fasteners.** There's a huge variety of fasteners to choose from. The right choices will ease your work and result in a strong, long-lasting deck.

twice as long as the top board is thick. For example, when installing 1½-inch boards, you should use 3- or 3½-inch fasteners.

## Nails

The most common, and usually quickest, way of fastening wood together is to use nails. If you choose the right nails and install them properly, the joint will last for many decades.

Nails are denominated by the term *penny*, which is abbreviated *d* (which stands for denarius, an ancient Roman coin—we're talking some very old terminology here). The number originally referred to the cost of 100 nails of that size, but today it indicates the nail's length. For fastening two-by lumber together, use 16d nails (unless you are toenailing; then use 8d or 10d). For ¾ decking, 10d works best.

Unless you are working in a place where the nails will not be exposed to

### Avoid Galvanic Corrosion

Whenever you are attaching metal such as flashing or joist hangers make sure your nails are of the same material as the metal, or you can get galvanic corrosion, a chemical reaction that will produce stains.

weather (something that rarely happens when you are building a deck), it is usually best to use hot-dipped galvanized nails. These have little chunks of stuff stuck to them, which makes it difficult for them to work loose, and they resist corrosion well. However, they are not perfect and sometimes the galvanizing comes off the heads, so hit them with sealer after the deck is finished.

Stainless steel and aluminum nails resist rust more effectively, but have slightly less grabbing power than galvanized. Stainless steel is very expensive, but may be worth the price in very wet situations. Aluminum is soft and bends easily.

There are a number of "deformed" nails designed to have greater fastening power. Drive-screw nails actually rotate as you drive them in and hold much like a screw. Some specialized deck nails have blunted tips to minimize splitting and are ring-shanked to hold well. Be advised that a ring-shanked nail, though it holds well if it stays completely in place, loses much of its holding power if it becomes pried outward even the slightest bit.

Galvanized casing nails are basically thick, galvanized finish nails. They get their name because they originally were designed for fastening window and door casing. Casing nails do not have the holding power of nails with heads, though they grab a bit better than finish nails because they are thicker. (The thicker the nail, the more wood surface it touches and the more wood it displaces, and so the better it holds.) Because most parts of a deck are subject to weather and so need to be held firmly in place, casing nails are not usually appropriate, even though they look nicer when first installed. You might, however, use them for attaching fascia or other finishing touches such as nosings.

## Screws

There are a number of good reasons for choosing screws over nails. Screws offer more holding power than nails and can pull boards together more easily than nails. Screws can be installed without the "smiles" and "frowns" that hammering often

### Be Prepared

Even if you are going to be fastening with nails, have on hand a pound each of 1⅝-inch, 2½-inch, and 3-inch deck screws, for those places that are too tight to swing a hammer in, or for situations where you need extra strength.

produces in the wood. They can be removed without marring the wood, so that you may not have to throw away a board after making a mistake. (If using screws saves even one board, this could make up for the extra expense.) Once you get the technique down, screwing down decking with a good drill can be just as fast as nailing.

**Deck screws.** These screws are bugle-headed, which allow them to easily be driven flush to the surface of the wood (or even buried in the wood, though this is not usually recommended since it can split boards). Two kinds of screw heads are available, Phillips and square-holed. Phillips-head screws are easier to load onto your bit, but the bit has a tendency to slip out. It may take a second more to insert a square-headed bit, but it will stay in place more securely (this is especially important if you are screwing into hard wood). The bits are cheap, so you may want to experiment to find which works best for you. Do not use screws designed to accept both types of bit; by trying to do both, they end up doing neither well.

Phillips — Square Drive — Combination Phillips and Square Drive

**Deck screws.** Deck screws come in three head configurations. The combination Phillips Head and Square Drive is not recommended.

**Lag screws.** Also called lag bolts, these are thick screws with coarse threads and heads that will accept a wrench. Always use a washer or the head will sink into the lumber and will not hold as firmly. Use them for attaching the ledger board to the house, and for other places where you need extra strength but can only reach one side of the connection.

For attaching ledger boards to concrete or brick, use lag screws with masonry shields. The shields expand as you tighten the board in place, making for a firm connection. You

will need a masonry drill bit to make the hole for the shield.

For places where you need to attach lumber to masonry but do not need a lot of strength, concrete screws provide a quicker method. You can drill the pilot hole even while the board is in place, and then drive the screw directly into the masonry.

## Bolts

Bolts are used where connections must be extremely strong. The most common uses on a deck are tying together built-up beams and fastening a post to a beam.

Bolts with nuts and washers pass all the way through the members they join (or are "through-bolted") and are secured with washers and nuts. Hexagonal-headed (or "machine") bolts are easy to install, since you can put a wrench on the bolt head; make sure you use washers under both the head and the nut, or they will sink into the lumber. Carriage bolts have a rounded head that requires no washer; use them in places where you want a finished look.

# HARDWARE

Besides screws and nails, there is a variety of other metal fasteners that are used in the construction of a deck.

## Deck Fasteners

You can purchase deck hardware that will make your deck free of visible nail heads. You have two options here: deck clips and continuous deck fasteners. Both are expensive—continuous fasteners more so than clips. And they will probably take more time to install than screws or nails. But it may well be worth the extra time and expense to have a clean, nail-free surface, especially if your decking boards are beautiful cedar or redwood.

However, do not use deck clips if your decking is subject to shrinkage. They will lose holding power as the wood

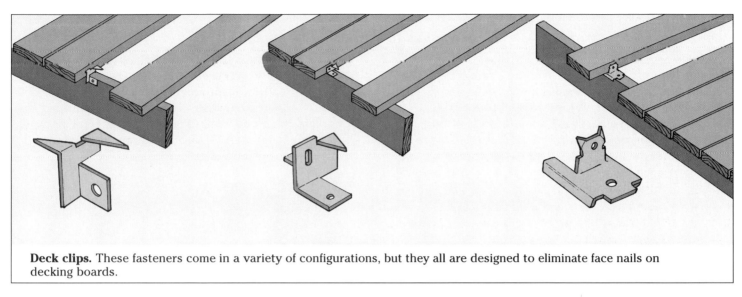

**Deck clips.** These fasteners come in a variety of configurations, but they all are designed to eliminate face nails on decking boards.

shrinks. Also, avoid using deck clips near the end of decking pieces or at butt joints because splitting can occur.

**Continuous fasteners.** Continuous deck fasteners use screws driven up through the bottom of decking boards. As a result, they hold better than clips. Continuous fasteners make for good butt joints and avoid splitting problems.

## Framing Hardware

Several companies have lines of framing hardware, designed to hold specified framing members securely in

**Continuous fasteners.** Continuous fastening systems allow you to fasten decking with screws driven from underneath.

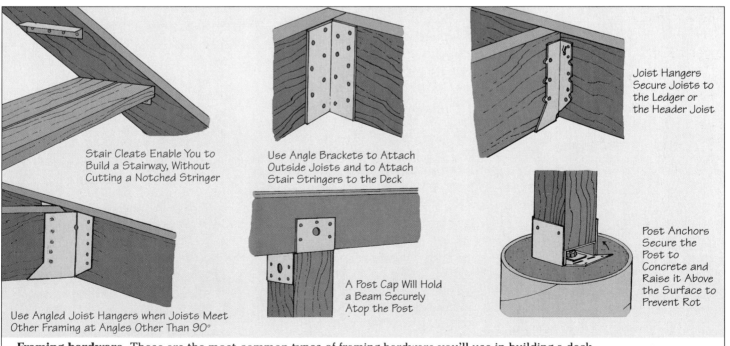

Stair Cleats Enable You to Build a Stairway, Without Cutting a Notched Stringer

Use Angle Brackets to Attach Outside Joists and to Attach Stair Stringers to the Deck

Joist Hangers Secure Joists to the Ledger or the Header Joist

Use Angled Joist Hangers when Joists Meet Other Framing at Angles Other Than 90°

A Post Cap Will Hold a Beam Securely Atop the Post

Post Anchors Secure the Post to Concrete and Raise it Above the Surface to Prevent Rot

**Framing hardware.** These are the most common types of framing hardware you'll use in building a deck.

## Alternatives to Framing Hardware

Framing hardware is not built for beauty and so you may want to eliminate it in some circumstances. Often, this will be possible, since decks and porches were built for many years without these metal pieces. Framing hardware sometimes is stronger than nailing or screwing, but often it is no more than a convenient alternative to traditional joinery.

Consult your inspector to see if he will let you do things another way. Three examples: If your joist work will be visible, you might choose to back-nail or back-screw, rather than using ugly joist hangers. Wood cleats can be used to support stair treads. And a side nailer can replace a post cap to hold a beam in place on top of a post.

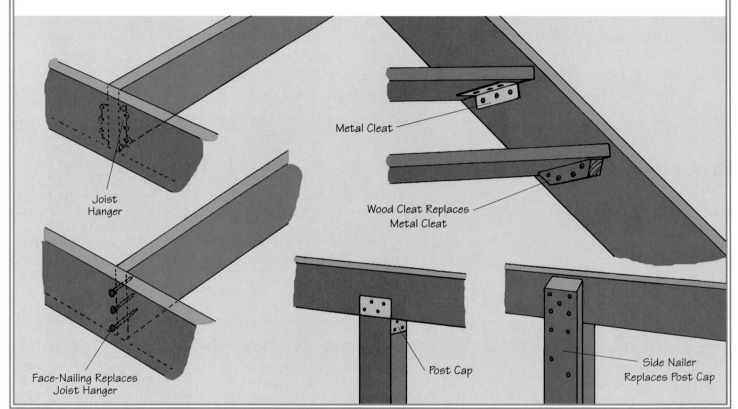

Joist Hanger

Metal Cleat

Wood Cleat Replaces Metal Cleat

Face-Nailing Replaces Joist Hanger

Post Cap

Side Nailer Replaces Post Cap

place. Your local building department may have specific requirements for joist hangers, post anchors, and so on, so check with them before buying.

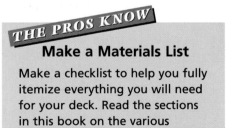

### Make a Materials List

Make a checklist to help you fully itemize everything you will need for your deck. Read the sections in this book on the various aspects of deck construction. It is easy to overlook things, so pore over your drawings several times, walk through the site again, and consult with your supply sources. To get the best price and quality, you may end up going to several different sources.

## Flashing

Flashing can usually be installed quickly and easily as long as you get the correct material. Find out what the inspector wants you to use, and describe your needs very specifically when you buy it. When possible, buy preformed pieces that are in the exact shape you need. In certain circumstances, you may have to buy a roll of flat sheet metal (sold as roll stock) and form it yourself.

Aluminum flashing will last practically forever, but it has a tendency to expand and contract with changes in weather, causing nails to come loose and leading to leaks. (Make sure you use aluminum nails with aluminum flashing, or corrosion will occur.)

Galvanized flashing might develop rust spots after some years, but it is thicker and stronger, and does not react to temperature changes as much as aluminum does.

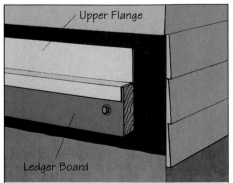

Upper Flange

Ledger Board

**Flashing.** This is the most common type of flashing used on a deck. The upper flange slips under the siding, while the lower portion protects the ledger board.

# Chapter 6

# CUTTING, JOINING AND FASTENING TECHNIQUES

Here we will cover basic carpentry techniques. Specific methods, such as figuring stairs or erecting framing structures, will be covered in future chapters. Readers with a lot of carpentry experience may just want to skim this chapter.

## MEASURING AND MARKING

Good carpentry begins with accurate measuring and marking. Get in the habit of using the same techniques every time, and your work will be much more pleasurable.

## Using a Tape Measure

Most of your measuring will be done with a tape measure. This is much faster than the old folding wooden rules and just as accurate. You will notice that the shiny metal hook at the end of the tape measure is a bit loose. It is made that way on purpose: it moves back and forth ⅛ inch, which is also exactly how thick it is. This means that you will get the same measurement when you hook the end of your tape measure to the end of a piece of wood as you will get when you butt it up against something.

Sometimes there's nothing convenient to hook your tape on and it helps to

have a helper hold one end. But more often than not, you can hook the tape and reel it out a good long way yourself. If there is nothing to hook to you can tack a nail and use that.

Some things to watch out for: Take care to see that your tape is straight when you measure. If it curves in any way, you will get a reading that is too long. If a helper is calling out measurements for you to cut, make sure that his tape measure agrees with yours—sometimes the hook gets bent which can throw your cut off by ⅛ inch or so.

## Measuring in Place

When possible, the easiest and most accurate way to measure is *not* to use a measuring device, but rather to hold a piece of lumber in place and mark it. This usually involves butting one end exactly to the spot where the board will rest and marking the other end.

Sometimes it's best not to measure at all, but instead let the piece run wild,

### Check for Square Ends

Often, the lumber you buy will have one or two ends that are not square. If necessary, square-cut the end you will hook your tape measure to before making a measurement. It's a good idea to go through a pile of lumber checking for square ahead of time, since it is easy to forget when you are in the midst of measuring and cutting.

---

**THE PROS KNOW**

### Subtract an Inch

If you need to hold the end of your measuring tape at a starting point instead of hooking it or butting it into something, you'll get a more accurate reading if you align the tape's 1-inch mark to the starting point instead of trying to align the hook to the point. Don't forget to subtract an inch from the measurement at the other end!

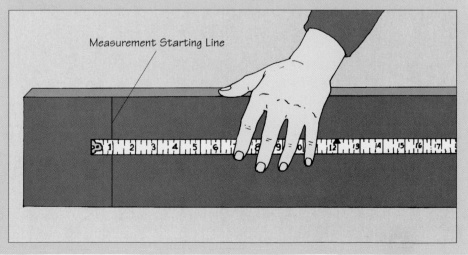

Measurement Starting Line

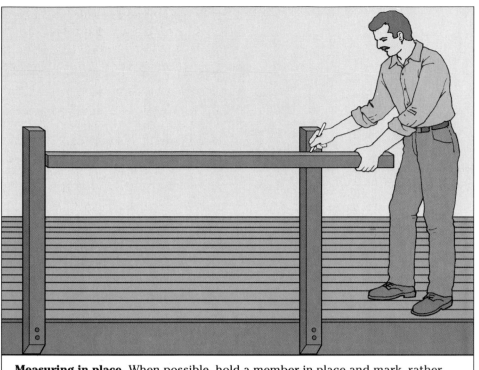

**Measuring in place.** When possible, hold a member in place and mark, rather than measuring.

that is, attach it in place with one end long, and cut it later. For example, to make post tops level with each other cut them to final length after they are set. Another common practice in deck-building is to let the decking boards run wild, then snap a chalk line and cut them all off in place.

## Marking for Cuts

When you make that little pencil mark in the wood indicating the exact length to cut, make sure you know which end of the mark is the right one. Most carpenters make a "v," with the bottom point indicating the precise spot. Using your square, draw a line through it, and make a large

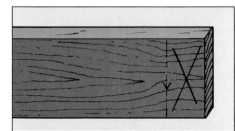

**Marking for cuts.** Here's how to mark a piece of lumber for cutting to length. The "X" indicates waste; the thickness of the saw blade will cut to the right of the line.

"X" on the side of the board that will be waste. (Your saw blade is ⅛ inch thick, and you don't want to cut on the wrong side of the line.)

To make long lines, snap a chalk line. Either have a helper hold one end, or tack a nail and hook the clip onto it. Pull the line very taut, make sure it's in position on both ends, then pick the line straight up several inches and let go. For long lines, or a wavy surface, you may need to first snap your end and then have your helper snap his.

## CUTTING WITH A CIRCULAR SAW

You'll use your circular saw so much in the course of building a deck that you'll soon become comfortable with the tool. That's good in that practice increases accuracy and speed. But it can also be bad because comfort breeds complacency. And when it come to power tools, complacency can be very dangerous. With a circular saw, you are holding in your hands a tool that can do you great harm in a fraction of a second if you are careless.

So take basic safety precautions: Know where your power cord is at all times. Make sure your safety guard works properly. Avoid kickbacks by correctly positioning the board you are cutting. And use a sharp blade that won't bind.

Since your circular saw will be your constant building companion, it's more than worth your time to perform some simple maintenance procedures that will ensure that it works as safely and as well as possible.

## Squaring the Blade

No matter what circular saw you have, you can't expect the angle markings stamped on the saw to be accurate. To ensure square cuts, use a square to set the blade.

Unplug the saw, turn it upside-down, and loosen the angle adjustment. Set a square on the base and hold it against the blade. Make sure you hold the square against the body of the blade and not the teeth; the teeth are offset from the body and will throw off your adjustment. Tighten the angle adjustment when the blade and base bear evenly on the square.

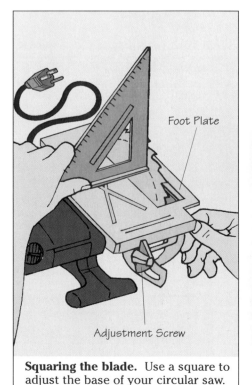

Foot Plate

Adjustment Screw

**Squaring the blade.** Use a square to adjust the base of your circular saw.

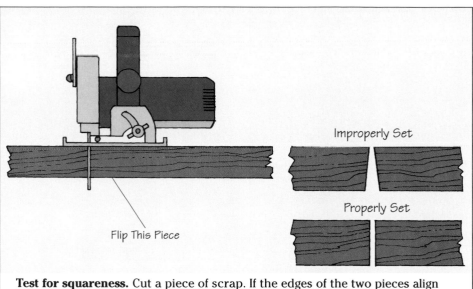

Improperly Set

Properly Set

Flip This Piece

**Test for squareness.** Cut a piece of scrap. If the edges of the two pieces align when you flip one, the blade is square.

**Test for squareness.** Crosscut a scrap piece of 2x4. Flip one of the cut pieces and hold it up to the other so that the two cut edges are aligned. If your blade is not square to the base, you'll see a gap at the bottom or the top equal to twice the amount your blade is out of square. If you see a gap, unplug the saw and try squaring it again, until it tests out as square. Check the stamped markings on your saw. You might want to make your own square mark with a sharp piece of metal or a small file.

## Making Accurate Square Cuts

1 **Position the workpiece.** Before making the cut, your workpiece must be well supported on a stable surface that won't move during the cut. To avoid dangerous kickback, make sure that the piece you are cutting off can fall away without binding. For instance, when using sawhorses, *always* cut to the outside of one of the horses and *never* between them.

If the piece of lumber you are cutting off will be long, you don't want to just let it fall. If you do, the weight of the unsupported offcut will cause the board to break, leaving a jagged piece sticking out at the end of the cut. If the offcut isn't too long, and the piece you are cutting is heavy enough not to move during the cut, you can support it with your left hand (or right hand if you are sawing left-handed). Or, you can provide something for the cutoff piece to fall onto that is only an inch or two below it. One way of doing this is to make your cut on top of a stack of wood, as long as the stack is neat and stable.

2 **Align the blade to the line.** The area occupied by the material a saw blade turns to sawdust—in others words, the slit made by your saw—is called the *kerf*. Most saw blades cut a ⅛-inch-wide kerf. This is a significant amount when you are attempting to fit pieces together precisely. So make sure you cut to the waste side of the line, so that you will not be ⅛ inch short.

As we mentioned, the teeth on a circular saw blade are offset. One tooth veers to the left, the next to the right, and so on in an alternating pattern. Take this into account when you cut:

Offcut

Offcut

**1** Position the workpiece so you can support the offcut with your hand or so that it will fall only an inch or two.

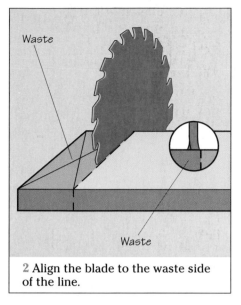

2 Align the blade to the waste side of the line.

3 Cut with a smooth, confident push of the circular saw.

Select a tooth that's offset toward the cut line and align the saw so that tooth just touches the line.

3 **Make the cut.** A beginner will find that it is helpful to use an angle square as a guide when mak-

ing crosscuts and may be tempted to use it all the time. But it is a bad habit to get into. A guide is useful for the occasional cut that must be very precise; however, if you want to make a lot of cuts with some speed, you should learn to cut freehand.

This actually takes only a bit of practice. Choose a time when you don't have to get any work done, and pick out some scrap pieces to work on. Get in the habit of keeping your eye on the leading edge of the blade, and become acquainted with the best way

## Kickback

As you cut with a circular saw, beware the dreaded kickback — when the saw suddenly and without warning jumps back at you while you are making a cut. This occurs because the teeth on the rear part of the blade catch the edge of the kerf (the slit made by your saw) and make it pull violently backwards. Despite the safety features of your saw, there is a chance that kickback could cause injury. So as soon as you feel the saw start to kick back, stop and correct the problem before continuing.

Leading causes of kickback:

• Binding board. Occasionally, stresses in the board itself—conflicts in the grain, you might say—will cause the kerf to close up as you cut. More often, however, binding occurs when the board is incorrectly positioned so that the cutoff cannot fall freely.

• Twisting blade. A circular saw is not a saber saw. If your cut is going off the line, do not try to correct your error while you are cutting. Stop the saw and wait for the blade to stop, back up, and start the cut over again.

• Backing up while the saw is running. Don't do it. Always release the trigger and wait for the blade to stop before backing up the saw.

• Dull blade. A dull blade will heat up and bind, which will make it prone to kickback. It pays to have a spare blade handy.

Though you can drastically reduce the chances of kickback by following correct procedures, unfortunately it can happen even to the most experienced carpenters. For this reason, it's important always to keep your hands well away from the blade or cut path and position yourself to one side of the cut— never directly behind it.

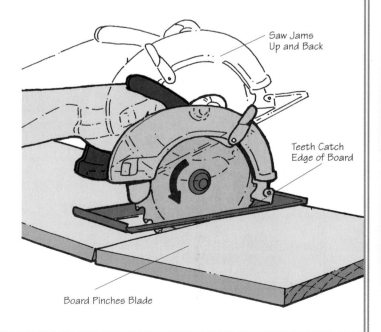

to align your saw. When you cut, push through smoothly, without micromanaging the cut by making little turns back and forth. Soon you will easily be making cuts that are accurate enough for framing.

For precise cuts, use a guide. An angle square works well. Make sure your foot plate butts up well against the guide and won't easily slide over on top of it. Hold the square in place against the edge of the board and set the base of your saw so that its edge bears firmly against the edge of the square. Slide the square and saw until the saw blade lines up with the cut line. The main trick now is to make sure the guide does not move as you are cutting, so brace the square securely against the board when you make the cut, using the square's edge as a guide. Saw with a light, steady pressure, allowing the blade to set the feed rate.

## Cutting on an Angle

Angle cuts can be hard to get exactly right. Sometimes the blade guard gets in the way a bit at the beginning of the cut, making it difficult to start straight. You are working at an unusual position, which takes some getting used to. And because angle cuts are longer, there is more of a tendency to try to correct yourself in midcut—always a bad thing to do. So if you have a lot of angle cutting to do, you may want to rent a power miter box. (If you do so, make sure it is large enough to make the cuts you need to make.)

Another option is to make a simple jig that will help you cut 45-degree angles with a circular saw. Use a straight piece of 2x2 that is about 36 inches long; a flat piece of ¾-inch plywood with one good factory edge, about 12x12 inches; and four 1¼-inch decking or drywall screws. Use a square to draw a line that is 45 degrees in relation to the factory edge, and fasten the 2x2 along that line, making sure that the front edge of the 2x2 sticks out extra long. Trim off the excess plywood. The first time you use the jig, continue cutting so that you cut off the front end of the 2x2; now the

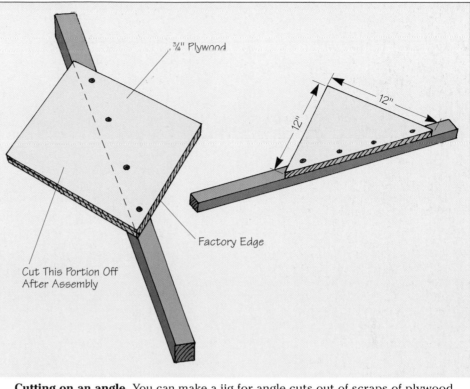

**Cutting on an angle.** You can make a jig for angle cuts out of scraps of plywood and 2x2.

front end of your jig will act as a guide for the length of your cuts. Of course, a jig like this can be made to cut angles other than 45 degrees.

**Cutting with the angle jig.** To cut with the angle jig, hold the jig tightly against the far side of the board. Butt the saw base tightly against the plywood of the jig, and align with your

cut line by sliding the jig and the saw in tandem forward or back. Hold the jig firmly in place, and keep the saw base butted to the jig as you saw.

## Ripping

When ripping lumber with a circular saw—that is, cutting it the long way—you will often need to secure

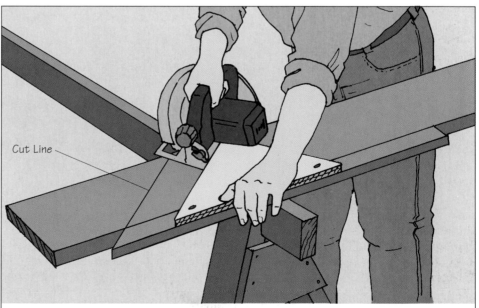

**Cutting with the angle jig.** Hold the jig tightly against the board, line up the cut with the front end of the jig, and make the cut.

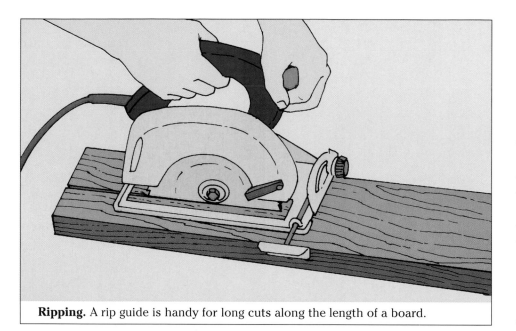

**Ripping.** A rip guide is handy for long cuts along the length of a board.

the board with a nail to keep it from creeping along as you cut. For accurate cuts, a rip guide comes in handy. This is a steel guide designed to fit your particular saw and usually attached to the base with a thumbscrew. The guide has a shoe that runs along the side of the board as you cut it along its length.

## Cutting Notches

The most common reason you'll need to cut notches in deck-building is to fit a decking board around a railing post. The first step is to mark for the notch.

**1 Mark the notch.** First, hold the piece to be notched against the

piece it needs to fit around. Mark the width of the notch. Now measure how deep the notch needs to be and lay out the notch with your square; as shown in the drawing the depth of the notch is equal to the amount the board to be notched overlaps the board below plus any gap you want to add between boards. If you keep the board nearly in position while you make your marks, so that you can visualize as you go, you will be less likely to make the common mistake of measuring on the wrong side of the board.

**2 Make first two cuts.** A notch at the end of a board will have a seat cut and one shoulder cut. A notch

that's not at the end has two shoulders and a seat. Start the shoulder cut or cuts by cutting in with a circular saw until the cut meets the seat cut layout line. If the notch is at the end of a board, start the seat cut the same way, cutting in from the end of the board.

When you move a circular saw along a cut line, wood is removed from the top of the board before it is removed from the bottom. This means that the cuts won't be completed. Finish the two shoulder cuts (or for a notch at the end of the board one shoulder and the seat) with a saber saw or reciprocating saw if you have one of these. Or use a hand saw, being careful to hold the saw perpendicular to the board.

**3 Finish the notch.** If the notch is not at the end of a board, you still have the seat cut to make. If the wood is straight grained with no knots in the way, you can make the seat cut with one sharp chisel chop. Place the chisel along the seat cut line with the flat part facing away from the waste. Make sure the chisel is perpendicular to the board and give it a sharp hammer blow. Otherwise make the seat cut with a saber saw or reciprocating saw. Another option is to nibble away the waste with repeated circular saw cuts into the seat cut as you did for the shoulder cuts. Then clean up with a chisel.

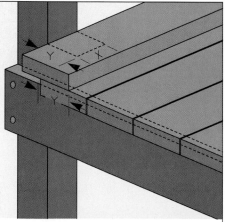

**1** To fit decking board around a post, hold the board in place and mark the width of the notch (X). The depth of the notch (Y) will equal the amount the board to be cut overlaps the board below plus any gap.

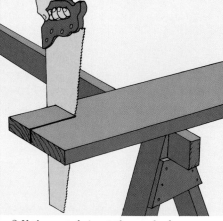

**2** If the notch is at the end of a board, use a circular saw to cut to the intersection of the seat and shoulder cuts, then complete the cuts with a hand saw, saber saw or reciprocating saw.

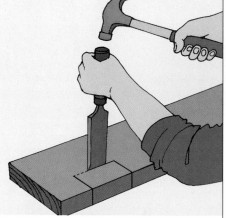

**3** If the notch has two shoulders, you can usually make the seat cut with one sharp chisel blow.

# Cutting Dadoes and Rabbets

Technically, a *dado* is a groove cut across the grain of a board. A *rabbet* is similar to a dado, except that a rabbet is on the end of a board. In deck building, you might cut dadoes into posts if you want rails to be flush to the post. You might rabbet the top of a post to receive a beam.

**1** To make a dado in thick stock, first cut the shoulders to the proper depth, then slice up the waste with multiple kerfs.

**1 Kerf the board.** To make a dado or rabbet, first set your circular saw blade to the exact depth of the cut; experiment on a piece of scrap wood to make sure you've got it right.

Mark the shoulders of the dado (or the rabbet's single shoulder) on the board. Cut the shoulders, then make a number of closely spaced kerfs through the waste area.

**2 Knock out the waste.** Holding your chisel with the flat side up, hit it with your hammer to knock out the bulk of the waste.

**3 Pare the seat.** Finally, use your chisel flat side down to clean up the seat of the dado or rabbet.

## Making a Plunge Cut

Occasionally you have to make a cut in the middle of a board, so that you cannot begin the cut from the outside of the board. You could use a saber saw (drill a ½ inch-hole first, for the saber saw blade to fit into). But for a straighter line, use your circular saw to make a plunge cut (sometimes called a pocket cut).

Make sure your power cord is out of the way, and grasp the saw with both hands. Position the saw and raise up the back, using the front of the foot

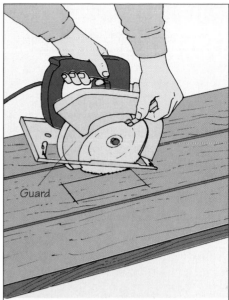

**Making a plunge cut.** Raise the guard, turn on the saw and slowly pivot the saw into the cut.

plate as a fulcrum. Now hold the blade guard so that the blade is exposed, and lower the saw until the blade is just above the right spot. When you are sure everything is safe and aligned, pull the power trigger and slowly lower the blade down to make the cut. If you do not twist as you go, you will be able to move forward with the saw after you have plunged through the board; make sure the foot plate is resting fully on the board before you do so.

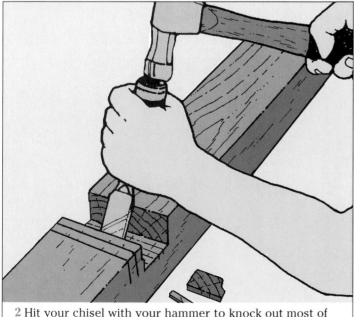

**2** Hit your chisel with your hammer to knock out most of the waste.

**3** Clean out the seat of the dado or rabbet with your chisel.

## Cutting off 4x4s

Your circular saw will not cut all the way through a 4x4 in one pass, so you need to cut from two sides. Using a square, draw a line all the way around the 4x4: If the last line meets up with the first, you know your layout lines are square. Then make cuts on two opposite sides. If your blade is square and you cut accurately, the entire cut will be fairly smooth, but don't expect perfection. (In nearly every case, the top of a 4x4 will be covered up by other pieces of wood later on.)

If you are cutting off a 4x4 that has a piece of lumber (such as a built-up-beam or outside joist) attached to it, first cut whatever you can get at with a circular saw, then finish with a hand saw or reciprocating saw.

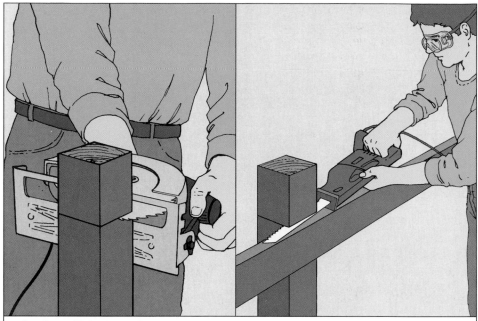

**Cutting off 4x4s.** Make two cuts with a circular saw, or use a hand saw or reciprocating saw to cut off 4x4s.

## LAYING OUT AND CUTTING CURVES

For short curved edges, mark with a compass—don't just eyeball it and expect it to come out right. For longer curves, make your own compass out of a pencil, a length of string, and a nail. Experiment with centers and compass openings until you find the curve that pleases you. Tack a nail at that point, and tie your string to it. Tie the other end to your pencil, and experiment to make sure you've got

it right. (It's easy to make mistakes, so do a "dry run" without making any marks first, or make very light marks.) Be sure to hold the pencil at the same angle at all times.

When cutting on the curve, be sure you have a heavy-duty saber saw, one that cuts with ease and does not wobble. Spend some time practicing on scrap pieces of lumber first—a mistake here might be difficult to correct. Clear the area of all obstructions. If you find yourself going a little off the line, correct it slowly rather than making a quick adjustment.

## NAILING

Good nailing technique, once learned, becomes second nature. But it is just as easy to develop bad nailing habits that will take the fun out of carpentry work and could, over time, result in serious damage to the tendons in your hand.

## Reducing Stresses and Misses

Many handymen and even some carpenters do not have good nailing technique. The most usual mistake is

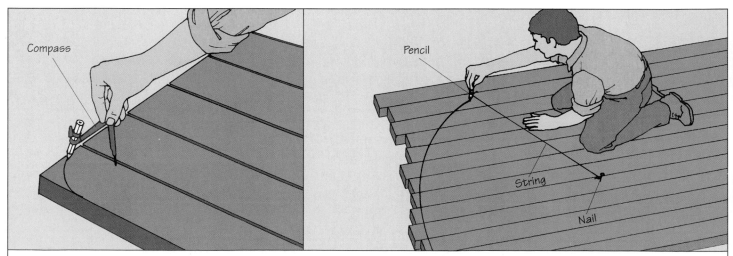

**Laying out and cutting curvers.** Use a compass to mark for accurate short curves. For larger curves, make a compass from pencil, string and nail.

to hold the hammer too stiffly, with the wrist locked in place. Instead, let your wrist flex a little, and finish each stroke with a snap of the wrist. Spend some time practicing; as you gain confidence, you will become more relaxed, and letting the wrist flex will come more naturally. One way you will know if you are hammering incorrectly is if your arm gets tired quickly.

Start with a hammer that feels comfortable when you swing it. Holding the nail in place, tap it gently once or twice until it can stand on its own. Then drive it home with several increasingly powerful strokes.

## Avoiding Splits

Whenever you are nailing near the end of a board (or near what will be the end of the board once it is cut off), take precautions to minimize splitting. Remember that any little split you see now will only get larger in time; and some spots that look O.K. now can develop splits later.

There are two techniques. First, you can predrill each hole. This may seem bothersome, but if you can do a whole row of nails at once, it really doesn't take much time. And the extra 15 minutes you spend now will mean a much better deck for years to come. Use a drill bit whose diameter is slightly less than the diameter of your nail shaft.

Another less effective but easier technique is to blunt the nail before

### Starting a Toenail

To prevent a nail from slipping when toenailing, place the nail upside-down on the spot where you want to start your toenail, and give it a few light taps. Not only will this method give you a flat spot to start driving, but it will also blunt the nail, reducing its chance of splitting the wood.

driving it. Rest the head of the nail on something firm—for example, the head of a nail that has already been driven into the wood—and tap the tip of the nail until it is no longer pointed. (When you drive this nail, it will tend to push some wood forward rather than to the side, thus reducing the outward strain that the nail puts on the board.)

## Skewing

Skewing means simply to drive two nails at opposing angles. This creates a sounder connection by "hooking" the boards together as well as by reducing the possibility of splitting.

## Toenailing

Most of the time, when two boards need to be joined at a right angle, you can backnail—drive a nail through the face of one board into the end of the other. But sometimes the face you would prefer to nail into is inaccessible, or the piece you have to nail through is too thick. In cases like this, toenail the pieces together. Toenailing means nailing at an angle through the end or toe of one board into the face of another. Position an 8d or 10d nail at least 1½ inches from the end of the toe. Start the nail at a 60- to 75-degree angle. Once it gets started, adjust it to a 30- to 40-degree angle. Move your hand and drive the nail home. If possible, drive two nails on each side of the board.

**Predrilling.** Because you are nailing so close to the end of the board, cracks often appear when you toenail—especially when you drive the head home. This not only looks bad, but also greatly weakens the joint. The

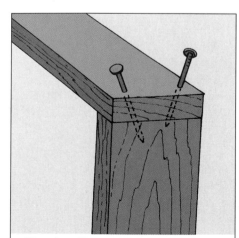

**Skewing.** For a stronger joint, "skew" the nails, by driving them in at opposing angles.

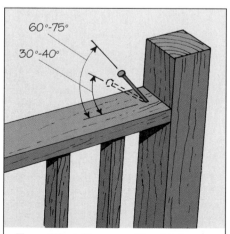

**Toenailing.** Decrease the driving angle after you start the toenail.

**Predrilling.** When pre-drilling for a toenail, press the chuck into the wood to make a depression.

best, though most time-consuming, way to avoid this is by predrilling. When you drill, allow the front end of the chuck to dig into the board a bit to accommodate the head of the nail.

# USING A POWER DRILL OR SCREW GUN

Though nailing has its advantages, there's a lot to be said for fastening with screws. Screws hold more firmly than nails and can be more easily removed or retightened, should problems with your deck arise years down the line. Their extra expense is a very small part of your materials cost. And once you get used to using them, they can actually be easier to use than nails.

## Driving Screws

It does take some practice before you can drive screws comfortably with a power drill or screw gun, without stripping the head or slipping and marring your wood. You also want to drive all your screws to a uniform depth, just barely below the surface of the lumber. (A sunken screw head is a place for water to collect, leading to rot.)

A screw gun or a special attachment for your drill can help: it sets the depth, and makes it difficult to slip

completely off the screw head. Some units have an automatic clutch, which disengages the drive when the resistance reaches a certain point. Test any of these first, however, especially if you are using soft cedar or redwood decking, to make sure they produce the correct depth and to ensure that you are not making unsightly dimples in your decking. With some practice, you should be able to drive screws accurately using only a magnetic sleeve with a screwdriver bit.

Choose either Phillips head or square head screws. (You may want to experiment with each, to see which you are most comfortable with.)

To drive screws, first position yourself in the best way possible: You should be stable, and the more body weight you can bring to bear, the better. If necessary, hold the screw in place—loosely and not touching the threads, so you won't cut your fingers. Start at a slow speed until the screw takes hold, and increase the speed until the screw is set. Maintain constant, steady pressure parallel to the screw, and do not stop until it is all the way in. Friction exerted on these fasteners can sometimes catch the screw, and you may snap it if you allow the wood fibers time to bind. Depending on your drill and the lumber, you may have to let up on the trigger just before the screw head is all the way in, and let it "coast" for the last fraction of a second. When the head is slightly countersunk into the wood, lift the drill as you take your finger off the trigger.

# AVOIDING ROT AND PLANNING FOR SHRINKAGE

In addition to choosing the best wood possible, certain construction methods will help reduce rot and minimize the effects of wood shrinkage.

## Protecting Open Grain

When you look at the end of a board, you are looking at the open grain. If you have ever painted a structure that had some areas of open grain, you will remember that this is where the paint got soaked up like a sponge. Open grain will soak up rainwater in the same way, making it the most vulnerable part of a piece of lumber.

For this reason, open grain should be covered whenever it is possible to do so effectively. This is especially important when the open grain is facing up, so that water can sit on it. Deck railings can usually be designed to eliminate horizontal open grain.

**Avoiding trapped water.** Of course, a certain amount of open grain is unavoidable—most commonly, the ends of decking boards are cut off and exposed to the weather. This usually isn't a problem as long as the boards can dry out quickly after they get wet. In fact, covering vertical open grain with wood or butting it against the house often increases the likelihood of rot. Unless the wood is attached

**Driving screws.** This is the best position for driving screws to fasten decking boards. Maintain constant pressure to prevent slipping.

**Avoiding rot and planning for shrinkage.** To prevent open grain from being exposed to weather you can cap posts or design railings to cover post tops.

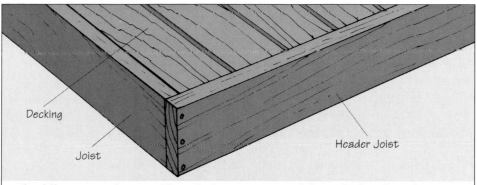

**Avoiding trapped water.** Though the open grain of these decking boards appears to be covered, this design actually offers greater possibilities for water to get trapped and not dry out—making it more apt to rot than a deck with uncovered open grain.

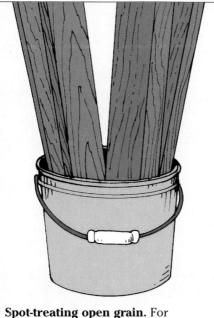

**Spot-treating open grain.** For lumber pieces at great risk of rot, soak the ends in a bucket of sealer/ preservative.

so that it remains tightly butted for years, there will be small gaps in which water can collect and sit.

## Tightening Butt Joints

If possible, plan your decking so as to minimize butt joints—places where you must join two decking boards together. This may mean spending extra money for longer boards, but you will end up with a deck that has fewer problem spots where water can seep in and damage your deck.

When you make butt joints, take steps to ensure they will remain tight for years. Choose dry lumber to minimize shrinkage. After you have firmly installed the first board, firmly tap the second towards the first before you install it. Drive your nails or screws at an angle so that they pull the decking boards tightly together.

## Spot-Treating Open Grain

If you are worried about open grain exposure, apply preservative/water repellent to all the places that are at risk (see "Sealers, Preservatives, and Stains," page 150 for products to choose from). For boards that will get a lot of contact with moisture, the most effective way is to set the end of the board in a container of

the preservative and let it soak for ten minutes or so. The wood will suck the stuff up. A more usual solution is to brush it on. Keep an eye on the open grain: if it becomes dry quickly, then apply another coat or two. Plan ahead: In some places you can brush preservative on after the deck is built, but in other places (for example, where the decking meets the house) you will not be able to do so.

## SMOOTHING AND ROUNDING

It's a good idea to spend some time smoothing rough spots and rounding off sharp edges. For a comparatively small amount of time and effort, your deck will take on a more finished, hand-crafted look. And your family and friends will be much less likely to encounter splinters.

Smoothing can usually be handled with a sanding block. You may have to start with a rough sandpaper and then go over it all again with a medium paper (80 grit is fine; a finer paper is rarely called for). Whenever possible, use long, smooth strokes rather

**Tightening butt joints.** For butt joints, tap the second piece in place, and angle your screws or nails towards the first piece.

## To Caulk or Not to Caulk?

Usually, a deck requires little caulk. That's because decks are made of rot-resistant lumber that is installed with few exposed joints. And most of the exposed surfaces of a deck get walked on or handled, making them unsuitable for caulking.

You may be tempted to cover up all the lines that don't look tight, but consider before you caulk:

• Will the caulking really keep moisture out or will it make a pocket for water? If you cannot completely caulk a spot so that no water can enter, you are better off not caulking it at all and allowing the lumber to dry out between rainfalls.

• Unless you are going to paint your deck, any caulk lines may appear as unsightly smears.

• Will your caulk get walked on or rubbed? If so, it may well come loose in time, leading to an incompletely caulked line that looks bad and promotes rot.

If you do apply caulk, choose a type that combines long life with good stickability. Plain latex caulk sticks well but will not last long; straight silicone caulk will last forever but could well peel off. A siliconized latex caulk is one good choice.

Some possible places for caulking are where decking is cut to go around a post, a ledger board that is pulled tight to the house, and where rail cap meets the house. Countersinking for a bolt exposes a bit of open grain and provides a place for moisture to sit, so these places should be filled with caulk. Simply installing the bolt and washer flush to the board avoids this problem.

Unless you are going to paint your deck, it is best not to finger-smear your caulk after you have applied it. That means you need to apply a good, clean bead of caulk the first time. This takes skill, so practice on scraps first if you are not experienced. Cut the tip of the caulk tube so that you will have a bead that spans the gap you are covering. Have a wet rag handy (it should be soaked with either water or mineral spirits, depending on your caulk) and wipe any mistakes away immediately. Take care to get in a position that will be comfortable for the entire caulk line, take a deep breath, and move the gun smoothly as you pull the trigger.

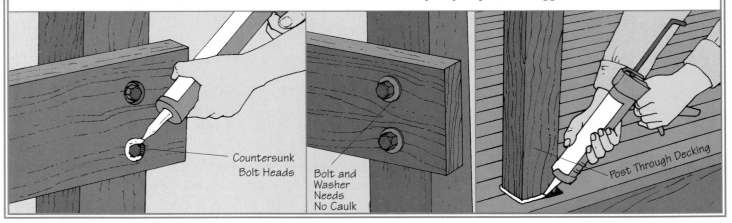

Countersunk Bolt Heads

Bolt and Washer Needs No Caulk

Post Through Decking

than short quick ones. And it doesn't pay to press down hard; a moderate amount of pressure usually lifts off just as much. Usually, the only areas on a deck that you should consider smoothing are those places that will be handled or rubbed against— rail caps, seats, tables, areas where children will play.

For rounding off, the trick is to decide how much you are going to round off, and then stick with the same pattern. If some parts are only slightly rounded while in other places a lot has been taken off, the deck will look sloppy and haphazardly built.

For softer woods, a sanding block will do a moderate amount of round-ing off. Though it may take some fairly heavy work, the advantage of a sanding block is that you can-not make a big mistake. For more extensive jobs or for hard woods, consider a belt sander, but beware that if you hold it too long in one place you can end up with an unsightly indentation that cannot be removed without deepening your roundoff. One other option: use a router with a roundover bit. If set properly, this is a nearly mistake-proof method of rounding. But be aware the router will probably not be able to reach every part of your deck that needs rounding, and you will have to finish some spots by hand.

### Protect Your Lungs

It is best to avoid sanding pressure treated wood. But if you must sand it, be sure to wear a dust mask. All those nasty chemicals in treated lumber are safe in most circum-stances because they are bonded to the wood. But when sanding, you are releasing tiny particles of that chemical-laced wood into the air all around you.

Some good places for rounding are the edges of decking; rail caps, built-in benches and exposed posts and beams.

# Chapter 7

# INSTALLING FOOTINGS

Take the time and trouble necessary to make your foundation accurate and strong, and the carpentry will go much quicker and more pleasantly. A house foundation is continuous, spreading the load to the entire periphery. Your deck's foundation, however, is made of individual footings. So even though they carry less weight than a house, your footings do need to be strong and stable. And if you don't place them correctly, you will spend many frustrating hours compensating for your mistakes.

## EXCAVATING, WEED CONTROL AND DRAINAGE

In most cases, little excavating needs to be done. If your deck is raised so that you can walk under it, you may have to change the foliage later on, because the area will be in shade. If the deck is low so that the area underneath will be covered up, knock down any high spots to make sure your joists will not rest on soil. The shade provided by your deck will usually discourage plant growth, but to be safe, lay down some plastic or landscaping fabric and cover it with some gravel, since it will be difficult to do so after the deck is built. Landscaping fabric is usually a better choice than plastic, because it does not trap moisture.

If you live in an area where vegetation is extremely lush and tenacious, consider removing it all—grass, plants, and roots—from the site by digging it away. Then apply landscaping fabric and gravel.

## Solving Special Site Problems

You may, however, be among the minority of people who need to take further steps to avoid landscaping problems. Look at the following list to make sure you are not one of them.

**A site that is already wet.** You can build over a soggy site, as long as it's not *too* prone to standing water. The deck *may* reduce the amount of water that falls on the ground beneath, if the deck is properly sloped and the decking is running downhill. Note that if you use crowned decking (see "Size and Surfacing," page 50), just about all the water will slip through the cracks. But a deck also puts the site in shade, so that sitting water will evaporate more slowly, especially if your deck is very near the ground. Any water

Footing

Landscaping Fabric

**Excavating, weed control, and drainage.** (Left) If you are concerned with weed growth under your deck, lay landscaping fabric on top of the grass, and cover it with 2-3 in. of gravel. It is usually easier to do this after the footings are in place. In some areas, you need to remove all grass, plants, roots and wood before laying the fabric and the gravel.

standing under a deck can breed mosquitos and smell none too good on hot summer days. And it will be very difficult indeed to provide drainage after the deck has been built. So deal with the problem before you build.

The simplest way is to grade the site —to make sure it is sloping uniformly away from the house, with no valleys or pits. In most cases this can be handled by shifting dirt around with a shovel or two. Another method is to slope your deck so that most of the water runs off. Of course, then you will need to provide drainage for the water that runs off. This can be done after the deck is built and you have a good idea of how big your problem is.

For more severe problems, consider digging a drainage ditch. This will collect water and carry it away from your site. Slope the section of yard where the deck will be located toward the ditch, and dig a trench about 12 inches deep at its highest point, sloping downward at least 1 inch per 10 feet of travel. Lay 1 inch of gravel in the bottom of the ditch, install a perforated drain pipe, cover with more gravel, and top off with soil. At the end of the ditch, have the water pour into a dry well—a large hole filled with stones.

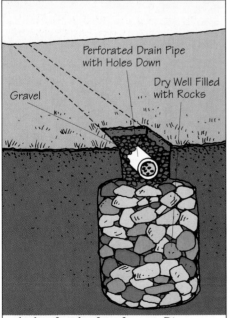

**A site that is already wet.** Dig a drainage ditch and a dry well and install perforated pipe, for severe drainage problems.

**Runoff from the deck.** It is often hard to predict how much water will run off your deck onto the ground surrounding it. You may end up with a little moat every time it rains. That's okay, though, because you can solve this drainage problem after the deck has been built. For minor puddling, try ringing your deck with plants in a wood chip bed. For larger problems, you may need a bed of gravel 6 inches deep, or you may even need to install a drainage ditch as described for a site that's already wet.

**Runoff from the roof.** If you have downspouts that dump water on your deck site, plan to change your gutter system so that it will empty out elsewhere.

**Erosion from water.** On a very hilly site, you might have erosion problems; little gullies left by rain are the usual tell-tale sign. This can be especially problematic if it threatens to undermine your footings. Be sure that none of your footings will be in danger of having some of the surrounding soil removed by rain.

Erosion can be limited by planting suitable foliage; check with a local nursery. Or you may need to provide drainage: Simple trenches might solve the problem, or you may need to dig a drainage ditch as described for a site that's already wet.

**Unstable soil.** Soil can be unstable if it is swampy, if it has been excavated recently, or if a significant amount of topsoil has been laid on it. If certain areas of your deck site are mushy or unstable, that's okay as long as you will not be putting your footings there. Any concrete or posts sitting in a posthole, however, must sit on undisturbed soil, which is almost always reached by the time you dig down 16 inches or so. If your conditions vary from this, or if you are unsure about your soil's stability, consult a local contractor to see how he has dealt with the problem. Or you can talk with your local building department, where they should know a good deal about local conditions and what sorts of foundations work best.

## DISTRIBUTING THE LOAD

To determine the locations of your footings, you need to have a total framing plan, giving the locations, lengths, and sizes of all your posts, beams, and joists. The charts in Chapter 8 ("Decking," "Beams," and "Joists," page 87) will give you the information you need to make such a plan. Here's some information that relates specifically to the foundation of your deck.

The total weight of a deck and all its permanent fixtures (railings, planters with soil, etc.) is called the *dead load*. Your footings must support not only the deck itself, but also the nonpermanent weight called *live load*— snow, people, wind resistance, and furniture, for example. Building departments usually mandate that a deck support 40 pounds per square foot of live load and 10 pounds per square foot of dead load. So your footings must be strong enough to handle 50 (or 60) pounds per square foot. If you anticipate higher-than-average live loads—heavily attended parties or hefty furniture, for instance—it is a good idea to exceed requirements.

This load gets distributed through the framing structure to various points on the ground. The ledger will easily shoulder its portion, since it relies on your house's foundation. Depending on their positions, different footings may have to carry different portions of the load. For instance, if your deck cantilevers out beyond a beam, the beam will carry more than the ledger. (Think of two people carrying a piece of lumber: the person who grabs the board at the very end will carry less weight than the one who picks it up two feet from the end.)

The illustration on the next page gives one example. It shows a deck that is 180 feet square, and so must be able to handle a load of 9,000 pounds. If the beam were at the very end of the deck, the ledger and the beam would be required to carry the same amount—4,500 pounds. But because

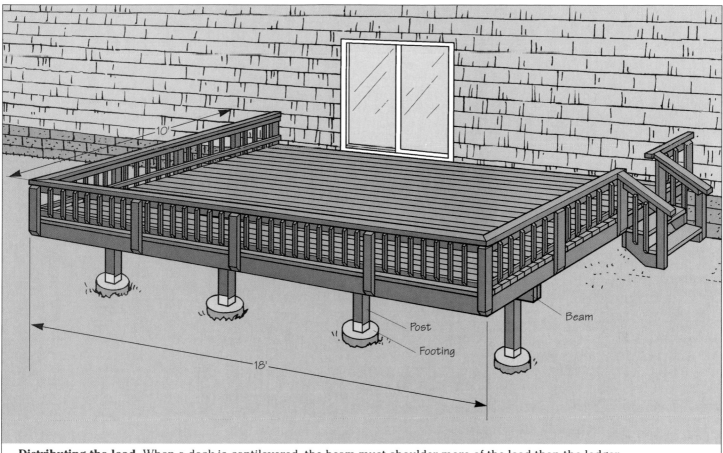

**Distributing the load.** When a deck is cantilevered, the beam must shoulder more of the load than the ledger.

the deck is cantilevered, the beam must handle more load than the ledger—5,500 pounds should more than suffice. If each of the four footings under the beam can handle 1,500 pounds, then there will be more than enough foundation strength (1,500 X 4 = 6000).

If you have soil that is loose, it may not be able to support much weight —perhaps as little as 500 pounds per square foot—which can mean that you will need more or wider footings than you would with firmer soil. By increasing the area of the footpad— the base of the footing, where it sits on the ground—you can compensate for loose soil: If your soil carries 800 pounds per square foot, a 12x12-inch footing can carry only 800 pounds, while a footing with a 24x24-inch pad can carry 1600 pounds. Some soils, especially those with a lot of clay, may be quite firm when dry but will lose strength when they get wet. If you think your soil is different from most of the yards in

your neighborhood, ask your building department to assess the situation.

## DO YOU NEED TO POUR CONCRETE?

In a minority of cases, newly poured concrete footings are not needed. For example, if your site currently has a concrete slab, it probably makes the most sense to set posts on the slab, rather than tearing it all up and pouring new concrete. In this situation, you will have a deck that "floats" if you are in an area subject to frost and the slab does not extend below the frost line. This means that your deck will rise and fall perhaps an inch or two as the ground freezes and thaws, meaning that boards may crack. In such a case, you should not attach the deck to the house with a ledger; make it a free-standing structure that happens to be next to the house.

Long-lasting decks have been built without any concrete support. This is usually done by setting extremely rot-resistant posts directly into postholes with 3 inches of gravel in the bottom, and then filling the holes with more gravel. If the deck gets rained on only occasionally, the gravel will allow the posts to dry out. If your building department approves this, and if there are other decks in your area that successfully use this method, you might want to give it a try. It could save you a good deal of work. (It is best to wait until the last possible moment before filling the holes with gravel; that way, you can adjust the posts as you construct the framing.)

**Precast piers.** If you have a very stable site (especially if the ground has a heavy clay content), you might get away with simply setting precast concrete piers directly on top of undisturbed soil. These come in a variety of sizes. Some have a small block of wood embedded in them on the top, so you can attach a post anchor with

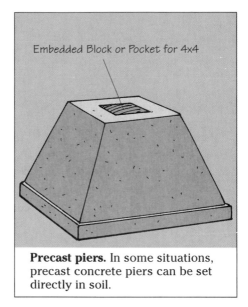

**Precast piers.** In some situations, precast concrete piers can be set directly in soil.

nails or screws; others are cast so that a 4x4 can fit snugly into a pocket on top. Remove any loose soil and provide a level spot where the piers can rest on level, undisturbed soil. Of course, such a foundation will float in areas with frost lines below the piers, which could damage the house as well as the deck.

## Types of Post Anchors

Choose your post anchors at the same time as you plan your footings because in most cases you must install at least part of the anchor while the concrete is wet. In some systems, the complete anchors are inserted into the concrete, while for others you insert a J-bolt or anchor strap while the concrete is wet, and add the rest of the anchor later.

There are two things to look for. First, we highly recommend that you choose an anchor that is laterally adjustable. Even the best carpenters do not expect to get their anchors in exactly the right location, so you should not be surprised if yours are off as well. Adjustable anchors will allow you to move your post an inch or two in either direction after the footing is set. Second, pick an anchor that holds the bottom of your post up above the concrete, so that the open grain can dry out. This goes a long way towards preventing post rot.

## TYPES OF FOOTINGS

Most likely you will need to pour concrete and make new footings. Choose your type of footing carefully to avoid unnecessary toil. Consult local codes and ask the following questions when choosing a footing:

• Will it be massive and stable enough to provide a solid resting place for the posts?

• If you want to avoid having a floating deck, will it be well below the frost line for your area?

• Will it be raised above the ground high enough to keep the post dry?

• Will local codes require you to add reinforcing bar to the concrete?

• Do you need to provide drainage beneath the footing? (You may be required to put some sand or gravel at the base of the footing.)

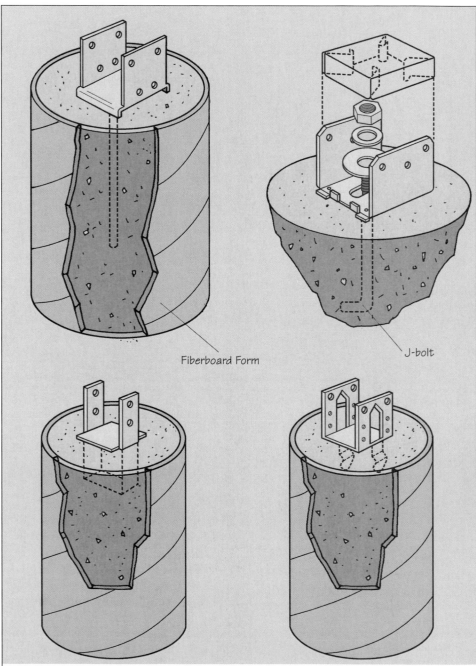

**Types of post anchors.** All the anchors shown, except the one at top right, are inserted directly into wet concrete, so they must be located perfectly. The anchor at top right allows you to adjust the post's location an inch or two in either direction after the concrete is set.

## Pouring Directly into a Hole

**No frost line.** In stable soil, you can simply dig a hole that will act as a concrete form. For areas with little frost, a hole that is, for instance, 12 inches in diameter and 8 inches deep will yield a substantial footing. Fill the hole completely with concrete, and taper it upward so that the center is an inch or two above grade. Insert an anchor or bolt directly into the concrete.

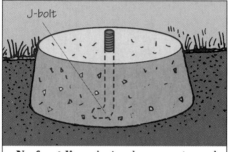

**No frost line.** A simple concrete pad will work for a footing in areas not subject to frost.

**Below the frost line.** Another option is to dig a cylindrical posthole that extends several inches below your area's frost line, and fill it with concrete. Flare the bottom of the hole a bit for stability. This method works best for footings with wide diameters, since it is difficult to dig a narrow posthole. A disadvantage: because post-

**Below the frost line.** In areas subject to frost you can dig a hole below the frost line and fill it directly with concrete.

holes cannot be dug with great precision, you will end up using more concrete than would be necessary with a precisely dimensioned concrete form.

## Additions to Hole-Dug Forms

The disadvantage of simply pouring into a hole is that the concrete is not raised much above the ground, which could subject your post to moisture. You can modify this technique by constructing a concrete form above the ground, using 1x6s or pieces of plywood.

**Precast pier on concrete.** Or you can purchase a precast concrete pier and set it into your bed of concrete. It is a good idea to paint the bottom of the pier with concrete bonding agent before setting it 1 to 2 inches into the concrete.

**Pouring into a tube form.** This is an easy and accurate way of pouring a footing. The tubes come in a variety of sizes, though 8 inches in diameter is the most common. The forms are made of fiberboard and are easily cut to length. A tube form has great advantages over just digging a posthole and filling it with concrete: It can be easily extended above grade to whatever height you desire; it makes inspectors happy because they know the exact dimensions of your footings;

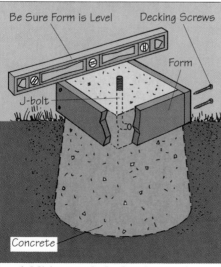

**Additions to hole-dug forms.** A form constructed above grade raises the footing above the ground.

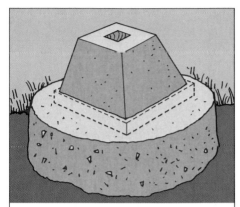

**Precast pier on concrete.** A precast pier can be set in a bed of fresh concrete.

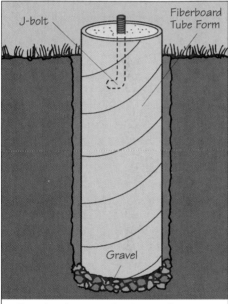

**Pouring into a tube form.** Concrete tube forms set in a hole save concrete and make the job easier.

and it makes your job easier because you don't have to mix extra concrete. The tubes are waxed, so you can easily strip away the part that shows above ground after the concrete has set.

## Continuous Posts

You can also set posts in post holes. It may seem that doing this adds a great amount of strength to a structure, but that is rarely so, especially in the case of a mostly horizontal structure such as a deck. Nearly all the lateral strength of your deck—what will keep it from swaying—comes from the way it all ties together. Every nail, screw, and bolt you install makes it a bit firmer. In addition, you will probably gain much stiffness by tying the deck to your house. So unless you are building a free-standing deck that is raised more than a couple of feet above the ground, concrete-set posts do not add significant strength.

And there are drawbacks to posts sunk in concrete or gravel: First, they are not "forgiving," especially if they're set in concrete, there's no correcting of mistakes. (However, if your design allows,

you can wait until the framing is finished before pouring the concrete, which will allow you to move the posts around a little during construction. Also, you do not have to worry about their height—you can run them wild and cut the tops off later.) Second, posts set into the ground are more likely to rot. And third, they are very difficult to replace in case they get damaged. So unless you have special reason to use them, we suggest them for the stair rails only.

However, continuous posts are required in some areas subject to earthquakes. They are also sometimes called for when the deck is raised high above the ground, to make sure the post bottoms won't move.

Continuous posts can be simply set into postholes that are then filled with concrete. Or they can be inserted into a large-diameter concrete tube form.

# LAYING OUT THE FOUNDATION

The footings will be the least visible element of your deck, so there is a temptation to treat them with nonchalance. But if they are not set accurately, the rest of the job will be a colossal pain. So take the time to check, cross-check, and recheck every step of the way.

It's best to have a helper for this, not only because you need someone to pull strings taut, hold one end of the tape measure, and to help make adjustments, but also because two heads are better than one.

**1 Locate the ledger.** The ledger board is usually the primary reference point for the whole deck. You may even want to install it first and then go on to the foundation. (See "Install the Ledger," page 89.)

In any case, to lay out the deck, you first need to mark the vertical edges of the ledger. In other words, you are marking its position from side to side, not its height at this time. In doing

### Watch Those Slopes!

When you measure horizontal distances, take care that your tape measure is held fairly level. If it angles downward, this will seriously alter your measurements. If your yard has a pronounced slope, you may have to work with ladders and levels to get precise measurements.

this, take into account the outside joists and the fascia board, if there will be any. If you will be applying one-by fascia, your ledger board will be 2¼ inches shorter than the finished deck on each end (1½ inches for the framing lumber plus ¾ inch for the fascia). If you plan to overhang the decking past the fascia board, be sure to take that into account as well.

If you are building a free-standing deck, you may want to use your house or another nearby building as a reference point, and establish a line that is parallel or at a right angle to it.

**2 Draw a reference line.** Once you have marked the ends of the ledger on your house, use a level or a plumb bob to bring the line down to a place on the house near the ground, so you can use it for laying out the deck. If your yard slopes appreciably downward from the house, place this mark near the ground. If the yard is fairly level, make the mark a foot or so off the ground. Attach a screw or nail to this spot, so that you can tie a string line to it. If your house is

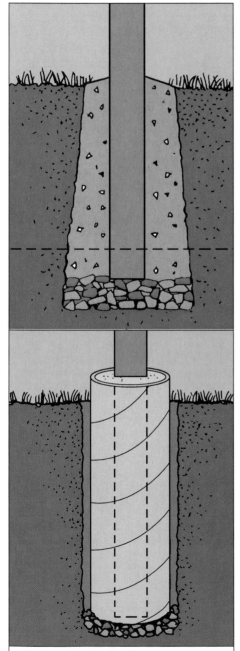

**Continuous posts.** (Top) A post can be set directly into a concrete-filled post hole or (bottom), the post can be set in a tube form, which is then filled with concrete.

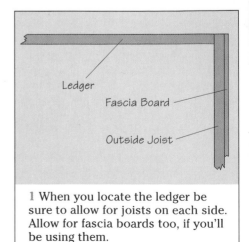

Ledger

Fascia Board

Outside Joist

**1** When you locate the ledger be sure to allow for joists on each side. Allow for fascia boards too, if you'll be using them.

2 Use a level and a straight board to reference the ledger to a point near the ground.

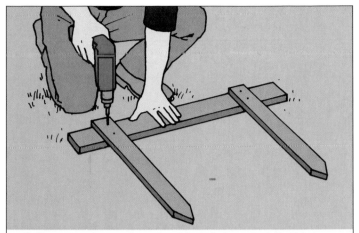

3 Construct batter boards of 2x4, 2x2, or 1x4. Build them strong enough to withstand accidental bumps.

masonry or concrete at this point, drive a stake firmly into the ground and attach a screw or nail to it.

**3 Assemble batter boards.** For each outside deck corner you will be locating, construct two batter boards. Make these by attaching a 36- or 48-inch-long crosspiece squarely across two stakes. You can buy pre-made stakes at the lumberyard, or simply saw pieces of 2x4 or1x4 to a point on one end. Although they are temporary and will be used only to hold string lines, the batter boards must be sturdy—there is a good chance they will get bumped around.

**4 Roughly lay out perimeter.** Measure from the ledger to determine where your posts will be, and roughly mark lines, using a string or long pieces of lumber. You want this line to run through the center of the posts, meaning that you have to take into account thicknesses of beams and outside joists: a two-by is 1½ inches thick, and the center of a 4x4 is 1¾ inches from either edge. The drawings show the most common situations. Pound a stake into the ground at the (again, rough) intersections of the lines.

**5 Establish the centers of the corner footings precisely.** Firmly pound two batter boards into the ground 16 inches or so beyond the stake in either direction. Run string lines from the ledger to the batter boards, and from batter board to batter board in the other direction. On the ledger,

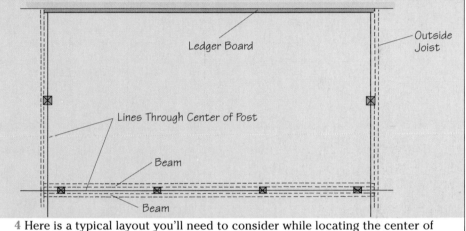

4 Here is a typical layout you'll need to consider while locating the center of your posts.

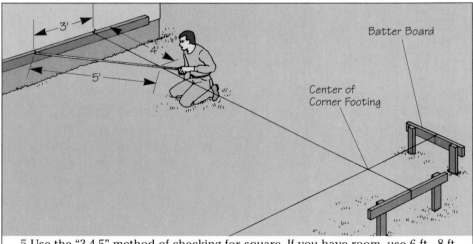

5 Use the "3-4-5" method of checking for square. If you have room, use 6 ft., 8 ft., and 10 ft., or 9 ft., 12 ft., and 15 ft. instead.

the string line will usually be run 1¾ inches in from the outside edge of the ledger. Pull the strings taut, and wrap them around the crosspieces several times so they will not move. Check the post line again, to make

sure it runs through where you want to locate the center of your posts. Pull up the stakes from the ground.

Now check for square using the "3-4-5" method: Measure along your house (or ledger board, if you've already

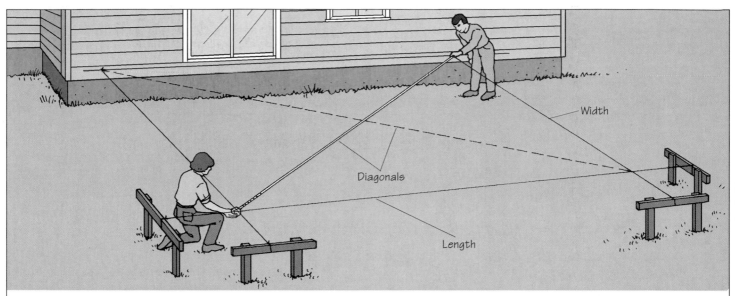

**6** As a final check, make sure that parallel sides of the layout are equal in length and that diagonals also are equal to each other in length.

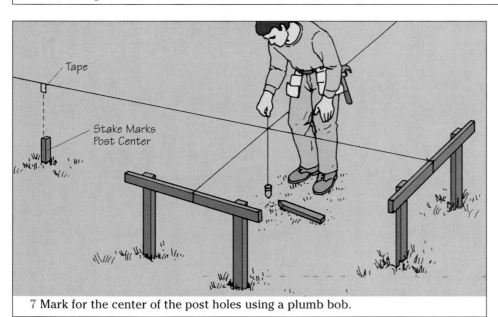

**7** Mark for the center of the post holes using a plumb bob.

ground that will be the center of each post—and therefore, the center of each posthole. For the corner posts, bring a plumb line down from the intersection of your lines. Hold the line until the bob (or chalkline body) stops swaying, and mark the spot with a small stake. For postholes not located at corners, measure along the string, taking care that you do not move the strings as you measure. Use pieces of tape to mark the string line.

# DIGGING POSTHOLES

This is usually the most physically demanding part of building a deck, so think about some options before you grab that posthole digger.

Digging postholes can be grueling work indeed, but you may be able to avoid the pain without spending a lot of money. Check the yellow pages and call up some fence companies. Many of them will have a small drilling rig that attaches to the back of their truck and powers out holes with ease. (The larger rig will probably be too expensive to hire.) Their hourly rate will be high, but they can do it so quickly that the expense may not be much more than renting a power

installed it) and mark a point 3 feet in from the nail holding the string. Now measure along the string and use a piece of tape to mark a spot 4 feet from the house (make sure you remember which edge of the tape is the right one). Finally, measure the distance between the two marks. If this is exactly 5 feet, then you have a square corner. If not, adjust the string line until it comes out right. Repeat this on the other corners. If you have the room, you can be more accurate by using multiples of 3, 4, and 5: 9, 12, and 15 feet, or even 12, 16, and 20 feet.

**6** **Check lengths and diagonals.** Double-check for square by taking

three pairs of measurements: the two lengths of your rectangle should be equal to each other, as should the two widths and the two diagonals. All this measuring may seem bothersome, but it is an effective way to double-check for something that is extremely important.

Once you have established that your lines are square, attach them securely to the batter boards, using a nail or screw to make sure they cannot slip sideways when someone bumps into the string.

**7** **Mark for postholes.** Use a plumb bob to mark the spot on the

auger. Be clear about the exact width and depth of the holes and how clean their holes will be. Chances are, you will scrape them smooth yourself with a posthole digger. And be on hand while they dig, to make sure they drill in exactly the right spots.

If the job is not too large, or if you have some strong-backed help (a local high school kid in need of a few bucks can often do the trick), you can do the work with a simple clamshell-style posthole digger.

For larger projects, you'll thank yourself for renting a power auger to speed up the job. These are powered by gasoline engines and work by drilling into the ground. They come in different sizes. Consult closely with your rental shop to get the right one for you. Some are designed to be handled by one person (though it certainly wouldn't hurt to have a helper), and the larger ones require two fairly brawny people. If you hit a rock or large root, the auger can suddenly bind, putting a sudden strain on your back muscles as you try to keep the handles from spinning. But all in all, augers are less work than digging by hand. You will still need a posthole digger to clean out the holes when you are finished with the auger.

**1 Dig the holes.** Once the marker stakes are all firmly established, it is usually a good idea to remove the string lines—but not the batter boards. You'll be putting the string lines back in place later, so leave clear marks on the batter boards showing exactly where they should be reattached.

As you dig, it's easy to lose track of where the center of the hole should be and often rocks or roots cause the hole to shift to one side. So carefully dig up the circumference of each hole before you start digging, so that it will always be clear exactly where the hole should be.

Whether you are using the auger or a posthole digger, if you run into a rock, you'll need a wrecking bar (also called a breaker bar or a crowbar) to break up stones or pry them loose. If you

run into roots, chop at them with your posthole digger or shovel, or use branch pruners. In extreme cases, you may have to go in there with an axe.

**2 Tamp the bottom and reattach string lines.** The bottom of your footing hole should be firm. Even if you have reached undisturbed soil, there will be an inch or two of dirt crumbs left over from the digging process, so tamp it down with a piece of 4x4.

Now is probably the best time to put your string lines back in place. It may sound wearisome at this point, but it really is a good idea to recheck them for square. Your batter boards may have been bumped.

**3 Install forms.** Once you have dug the holes, install the forms of your choice (see "Types of Footings," page 76), making sure they are secure. Remember that concrete will exert significant outward pressure. If you are

1 (Left) If you have only a few post holes and your soil is soft, a clamshell- style posthole digger may be all you need. (Right) A hand-operated power auger can be tough to handle but makes the work go quicker.

2 Tamp the bottom of the hole with a piece of 4x4.

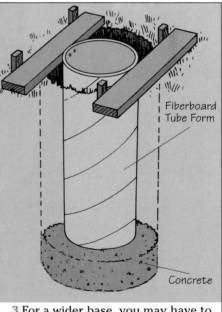

Fiberboard Tube Form

Concrete

3 For a wider base, you may have to hold up and support the tube form with stake-held 2x4s.

using a fiberboard tube form, you can usually just backfill it with dirt to keep it stable, but in some cases—as when you are required to have a wide base at the bottom of the footing and the form must be suspended—support it with stakes and two-by-fours.

Some designs call for leveling all the footings with each other. To do this, first backfill all the tubes so they are stable. Then mark all the tubes with a water level, and cut them off with a hand saw.

**4 Add gravel and reinforcing bar.**
Pour 2 to 3 inches of gravel into the bottom of the concrete form. (If you're using a tube form, this can be done before inserting it into the hole.) This provides drainage, which keeps ground moisture from compromising your footing.

If called for by the building inspector, add reinforcing bar. Usually, this means pounding a piece of "rebar" into the ground so that it runs through the center of the form. Do it carefully, so the rebar will be at or near the center of the concrete. Make sure it does not stick out of the form.

Gravel

Concrete

Reinforcing Bar

**4** Install gravel and reinforcing bar in the concrete form. Check to see that the top of the form is level.

# MIXING AND POURING CONCRETE

Now it's finally time to actually begin forming a part of your deck. This means more heavy physical work that doesn't produce anything of beauty; but once the concrete is poured, you will be ready to start the more pleasurable parts of the job.

## Calculating the Amount You Need

The math involved here may look daunting at first, but with a simple calculator it will probably take only minutes to figure. And you can always have your supplier check your figures. Chances are, you will be pouring a number of footings that are all the same size, so you can just figure one of them and multiply that amount by the number of footings.

First, a little basic math: A cubic yard is 3 feet by 3 feet by 3 feet, or 27 cubic feet. There are 1,728 cubic

inches in a cubic foot. Pi ($\pi$) is 3.14. The radius of a cylinder is half of the diameter. And the figure $r^2$ means that the radius should be squared or multiplied by itself.

For *box forms* multiply the inside length times the inside width times the depth in inches. Divide the result by 1,728 to convert into cubic feet, then divide by 27 to convert into cubic yards. Let's say, for example, you need to pour seven footings that are all 18 inches by 18 inches by 8 inches deep. Multiplying 18 times 18 times 8 gives you 2,592 cubic inches. Dividing 2,592 by 1,728 gives you 1.5 cubic feet. Divide again by 27 to find you need .055 cubic yards of concrete for each hole. Multiply .055 by the seven holes to find you need .39 yards of concrete.

To figure *cylinders*, the formula is: volume = $\pi r^2 h$. That means that you multiply pi (3.14) times the radius squared, times the height, to get the amount of cubic inches. Then you convert that into cubic feet, then cubic yards. For example, let's consider a case where you need to pour 9 cylindrical footings that are 8 inches in diameter and 42 inches deep. First figure the cubic inches for each footing: the radius is 4, and 4 squared is 16. So multiply pi, 3.14, x 16 to get 50.24; multiply that by the height, 42, to get 2110 cubic inches per footing (you can round off the tenths). Divide that by 1,728 and get 1.22 cubic feet per footing. You will have nine of these footings, so 1.22 x 9 = 10.99, or basically 11 cubic feet. Dividing this figure by 27 gives you the number of cubic yards: 0.4.

## Options for Obtaining Concrete

There are three basic ways to get concrete: you can add water to premixed bags, mix your own from raw materials, or order ready-mixed concrete delivered in a concrete truck. Which of the three you choose will depend primarily on how much concrete you need, what your site is like, and how much your labor is worth to you.

**Delivery by truck.** If you need ¾ of a cubic yard or more, you may be better off having it delivered in a truck, even if the concrete yard's minimum is 1 full yard. Concrete delivery varies greatly from region to region, so call several companies to see what is feasible and how much they will charge.

You need to be completely prepared before the truck arrives. These guys generally have little patience with small jobs and may expect to just dump the entire load as soon as they arrive. Arrange things ahead of time if you need the driver to wait while you distribute the concrete (you may have to pay an extra fee for this). Map out where the truck will park, and where the arm of the truck will reach to wheelbarrows. (If you're lucky, you may be able to pour directly into the forms.) Line up helpers. Have more than one wheelbarrow on hand if possible, and provide clear pathways so that they can quickly get to all the footings.

**Using premixed bags.** You can buy bags that have the cement, sand and gravel already mixed. These can be convenient: All you need do is mix with water and pour. However, the bags weigh 80 pounds, so this is not light

work—in fact, mixing from raw materials can sometimes actually involve less heavy lifting. A wheelbarrow makes a good container for mixing.

You do pay a price for convenience, since these bags usually cost more than it would cost to mix your own. Each bag yields about ⅔ of a cubic foot, so a typical 8 inch by 42 inch cylindrical footing will take two bags, and ½ of a cubic yard will require about 20 bags.

**Mixing your own.** For in-between amounts, or for sites where truck delivery would be difficult, consider mixing your own concrete. This can be done in a wheelbarrow or on a sheet of plywood using a hoe (preferably a mason's hoe with holes in it). Or, for larger amounts, you can rent an electric mixer. This last option is cost-effective only in areas where ready-mixed concrete is very expensive.

The key issue here may be delivery: If you can get the materials delivered on site inexpensively and in the spots where you want them, that is a big plus. The cement, sand, and gravel needed for ½ yard of concrete may be too heavy for a standard-duty pickup truck.

## Mixing and Pouring

The basic technique is the same here whether you are using premixed bags or combining your own dry ingredients. You can build a mixing trough, but the easiest method is simply to mix right in the same wheelbarrow you will use to transport the concrete.

**1 Mix dry ingredients.** If you're mixing your own dry ingredients, shovel them into the wheelbarrow, trying to keep the amount on the shovel equal in size: Usually, three shovels of gravel, two of sand, and one of cement. Thoroughly combine the ingredients with a concrete hoe (do this even if you are using premixed bags).

**2 Add water.** Hollow out a hole in the center of the dry ingredients, and pour in some water—not as much as you will end up using, but enough to get everything damp. (If you use a garden hose, set it for a trickle so you don't add too much water.) Mix thoroughly, then slowly add more water, testing the concrete as you go for the right consistency. Don't make it soupy. It should be just fluid enough so that it will pour into

1 Mix proper proportions of sand, gravel and cement in a wheelbarrow.

2 Make a depression in the dry ingredients and add enough water to make the ingredients damp. Mix thoroughly, slowly adding water until the concrete is pourable.

3 After filling the form with concrete, strike it off level.

4 Use a plumb bob and your string line to make sure the hardware is centered in the footing.

your form and fill all the spaces, and no more.

**3 Pour and strike off the concrete.** Pour the concrete directly from the wheelbarrow, or do it with the shovel. Clean up any excess as you go. Poke a 2x2 or a piece of rebar deep down into the concrete in several places to get out any air bubbles. Once you have filled the form, "strike it off" with a scrap piece of 2x4, to obtain a smooth, level top surface. (Or mound the concrete up a bit towards the center, if that is the design of your footing.)

**4 Install post anchor hardware.** Install your J-bolt or post anchor immediately. Wiggle it a bit as you place it, to get rid of air bubbles. Then line up the hardware with your string line and a plumb bob to make sure it will be in the center of the post. Be certain that it is sticking up the right distance out of the concrete, and use a torpedo level to make sure it's plumb.

Loosely cover the top of your footings with plastic, so they won't dry too quickly. You can start to build on the footings after 24 hours. But remem-

ber that concrete takes three weeks to fully cure, and it will be prone to chipping if you bang into it during the first few days.

## Installing Posts in Postholes

If you have chosen to sink your posts into the ground, take special care to get things right, because you won't be able to fix things later. It is a good idea to soak in preservative the parts of the posts that will be sunk; at the least, give the bottoms a good brushing.

**1 Dig flared holes.** For additional stability, flare your holes so that they are 3-4 inches wider at the bottom than at the top. Throw 2-3 inches of gravel in the bottom, for drainage. (One option here is to stick in a large-diameter concrete tube form, into which the post can be inserted before pouring the concrete. This makes more efficient use of concrete, and also makes it possible to bring the concrete several inches above grade, lessening the possibility of moisture sitting next to your post.)

**2 Check the posts for length.** You will let the posts run wild and cut them to their exact height later, after the concrete is set. For now, however, make sure that none of them is too short. Use a line level to check.

1 Dig a hole that flares slightly outward at the bottom, for extra stability. Place 2 to 3 in. of gravel.

2 Use a line level to make sure none of your posts are too short.

3 Adjust the posts until they are both plumb and aligned with the string, and temporarily brace them.

**3 Brace posts in position.** Reattach your string lines, but in a different position: You now want them to be on the outside edge of the posts rather than the center, so you will have to move them over 1¾ inches. Align the posts with the lines, being careful not to bend the string. At the same time, make your posts plumb in both directions. Once you have things roughly in place, attach two braces to each post, using only one nail so they can be adjusted, and pound a stake in the ground next to each brace. Have one person check for plumb and the other pound the nail into the stake. This is a painstaking operation involving many shiftings and reshiftings. The posts should just barely touch the strings, so that the posts don't move the strings out of alignment.

**4 Pour the concrete.** As you pour, poke a long pole or piece of reinforcing bar into the concrete on all four sides of the post, to release any air bubbles. (This is especially important in a situation such as this, where the concrete forms a long, narrow ring around the post.) Use a trowel to slope the top of the concrete upward, so that rain water will drain away from the wood.

4 As you pour, release air bubbles by poking a 2x2 or a piece of re-bar into the concrete.

# Chapter 8

# FRAMING THE DECK

Framing is the skeleton of your deck, the mostly unseen structure. This means that you usually don't have to be careful about how the framing looks, but you must build it correctly and build it to last.

A good deck frame will have its members placed so that the decking is supported everywhere it needs to be and so that any railings, stairways, and benches are amply undergirded. The lumber pieces will be correctly sized, so that the deck will not sag after a few years.

Most of this chapter will give step-by-step instructions for the most common types of deck frames. At the end of the chapter, you will find instructions for some special situations.

## FRAMING BASICS

In nearly every case, two-by or four-by pressure-treated lumber is the best choice for framing a deck, though in special situations redwood or even cedar can be used. Pressure-treated lumber generally costs only a little more

than standard fir or hemlock and will last much longer. For visible areas such as outside joists and header joists, use either good-looking lumber (brown treated may be a good choice), or cover the areas with fascia boards that match your decking and rails.

A deck frame is made of *posts, beams, joists,* and *ledgers*. Posts rest on your footings and are usually made of 4x4s; for a raised deck, 6x6s may be required. Beams are usually either

attached to the posts or sit on top of them. They can also rest directly on top of footings that are level with each other. They can be built up— made of a pair of two-bys—or they can be solid four-by timbers. Joists, the members to which decking will be attached, usually rest on top of the beam(s) on one end and are attached to the ledger board at the other end. Joists and ledgers are made of two-by lumber and are of the same width. The ledger is attached to the house.

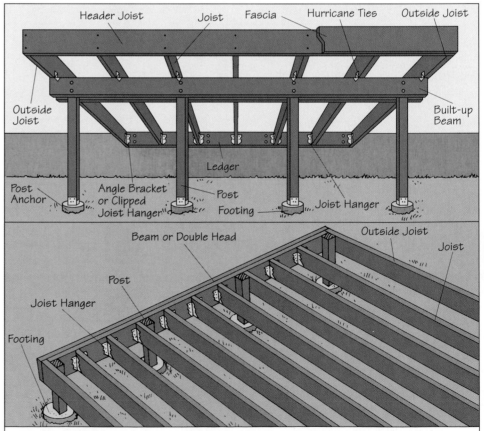

**Framing basics.** The deck at top has joists supported by beams below, probably the most common method of deck construction. The deck at bottom can be built close to the ground because its joists are supported in joist hangers attached to the sides of the beams.

### Plan Ahead for Rails, Benches, and Skirting

Though it is simple to add most rail- ings and benches after the deck is built, some designs require that you begin their construction during the framing. Choose your rail or bench while you plan the framing.

If you are going to cover up the underside of your deck with a skirt, plan now for the structural pieces the skirt will be attached to. If your deck is cantilevered and the posts are set back, this could be a prob- lem: How will you attach the bottom of the skirt?

## SIZING AND SPACING THE FRAMING MEMBERS

The *recommended span* for a piece of lumber is the distance it can safely traverse without being supported underneath. If you exceed a recom- mended span—for instance, if you use a 2x6 joists, spaced 16 inches apart, to span 10 feet—your deck will feel flimsy, and there is a good chance it will sag over time.

The span charts presented here are conservative, and if you follow them, you will end up with a firm, long-last- ing deck. However, local codes vary— it's not unusual for neighboring towns to have much different standards. For example, all the deck projects pre- sented in Part Two of this book were approved by the building inspector in the municipalities in which they were built. But some of those decks do not comply with the charts presented here. So check to see if your local building department has literature you can refer to.

Notice the charts specify species. This is important because stronger woods such as Douglas fir can span greater distances than weaker woods such as cedar.

These recommendations apply to nor- mal loads. If you plan to place heavy objects on your deck, such as soil-filled

planters, reduce the spans or beef up the lumber accordingly. Dimensions given in all the following charts are nominal, not actual. A 2x6 is actually 1½ inches by 5½ inches, and a 1x4 is ¾ inch by 3½ inches.

First, determine the decking span, that is, how far apart your joists will be. This will be determined by your deck-

ing material's size and lumber type and whether it will be laid perpendic- ular or at a diagonal to the joists.

## Joists

In planning joists, keep in mind the size and lumber type of the joists, as well as how far apart they will be spaced o.c. (on center).

### Recommended Decking Spans (maximum length of decking between joists)

| | |
|---|---|
| ¾x6 Southern pine or Douglas fir, perpendicular | 16" |
| ¾x6 Southern pine or Douglas fir, diagonal | 12" |
| ¾x6 redwood or cedar, perpendicular | 16" |
| ¾x6 redwood or cedar, diagonal | 12" |
| 2x4 or 2x6 Southern pine or Douglas fir, perpendicular | 24" |
| 2x4 Southern pine or Douglas fir, diagonal | 16" |
| 2x6 Southern pine or Douglas fir, diagonal | 24" |
| 2x4 redwood or cedar, perpendicular | 16" |
| 2x4 or 2x6 redwood or cedar, diagonal | 16" |
| 2x6 redwood or cedar, perpendicular | 24" |

### Recommended Joist Spans
(maximum length of joists between beams and/or ledger)

| | |
|---|---|
| 2x6 Southern pine or Douglas Fir, 12" o.c. | 10'4" |
| 2x6 Southern pine or Douglas fir, 16" o.c. | 9'5" |
| 2x6 Southern pine or Douglas fir, 24" o.c. | 7'10" |
| 2x6 Hem-fir, 12" o.c. | 9'2" |
| 2x6 Hem-fir, 16" o.c. | 8'4" |
| 2x6 Hem-fir, 24" o.c. | 7'3" |
| 2x6 redwood, 12" o.c. | 8'10" |
| 2x6 redwood, 16" o.c. | 8' |
| 2x6 redwood, 24" o.c. | 7' |
| 2x8 Southern pine or Douglas fir, 12" o.c. | 13'8" |
| 2x8 Southern pine or Douglas fir, 16" o.c. | 12'5" |
| 2x8 Southern pine or Douglas fir, 24" o.c. | 10'2" |
| 2x8 Hem-fir, 12" o.c. | 12'1" |
| 2x8 Hem-fir, 16" o.c. | 10'11" |
| 2x8 Hem-fir, 24" o.c. | 9'6" |
| 2x8 redwood, 12" o.c. | 11'8" |
| 2x8 redwood, 16" o.c. | 10'7" |
| 2x8 redwood, 24" o.c. | 8'10" |
| 2x10 Southern pine or Douglas fir, 12" o.c. | 17'5" |
| 2x10 Southern pine or Douglas fir, 16" o.c. | 15'5" |
| 2x10 Southern pine or Douglas fir, 24" o.c. | 12'7" |
| 2x10 Hem-fir, 12" o.c. | 15'4" |
| 2x10 Hem-fir, 16" o.c. | 14' |
| 2x10 Hem-fir, 24" o.c. | 11'7" |
| 2x10 redwood, western cedar 12" o.c. | 14'10" |
| 2x10 redwood, western cedar 16" o.c. | 13'3" |
| 2x10 redwood, western cedar 24" o.c. | 10'10" |

**Cantilevering.** If you plan to cantilever your joists over a beam—that is, let them stick out beyond the beam—the amount of the cantilever should be no more than one-fourth of the joists' span. Usually there is no good reason for a lengthy cantilever; a foot or so to help hide the beam and posts is often a good idea. When you cantilever your deck, you are placing more weight on the beam over which it juts out, so you may have to beef the beam up or add more posts.

## Beams

You can sometimes reduce your beam size by adding a post or two, thereby saving money in lumber—though it will require more work to install another footing. Allowable beam spans depend on the size and type of the beam lumber, as well as the span distance of the joists that rest on the beam.

If you are using a built-up beam, the figures may have to be adjusted, depending on your building department. The department may, for instance, consider a beam made of two 2x8s to be just as strong as a 4x8, or they may consider it weaker.

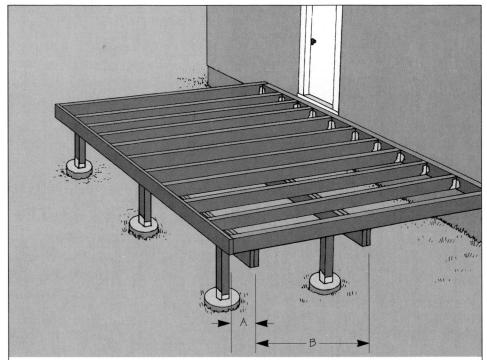

**Cantilevering.** The cantilever (distance "A") must be no more than one-quarter the distance spanned by the joists (distance "B").

This may also depend in part on how the built-up beam is constructed.

**Posts.** There is no need for a chart here. Unless your deck will carry an unusual amount of weight, 4x4s will work if your deck is 6 feet or less above the ground, and 6x6s are required for decks over 8 feet high. If you are in a gray area—between 6 and 8 feet tall—consult with your building department, or err on the safe side by using 6x6s.

## Recommended Beam Spans (length of beam between posts)

| Size of beam | With joists spanning up to | Beam can span up to | Size of Beam | With joists spanning up to | Beam can span up to | Size of Beam | With joists spanning up to | Beam can span up to |
|---|---|---|---|---|---|---|---|---|
| **Southern pine or Douglas fir** | | | 4x12 | 6' | 11' | 4x12 | 10' | 7' |
| 4x6 | 6' | 6' | 4x12 | 8' | 10' | 4x12 | 12' | 7' |
| 4x8 | 6' | 8' | 4x12 | 10' | 9' | 4x12 | 14' | 6' |
| 4x8 | 8' | 7' | 4x12 | 12' | 8' | | | |
| 4x8 | 10' | 6' | 4x12 | 14' | 7' | **Redwood, Ponderosa pine, Western Cedar** | | |
| 4x10 | 6' | 10' | 4x12 | 16' | 7' | 4x8 | 6' | 7' |
| 4x10 | 8' | 8' | | | | 4x8 | 8' | 6' |
| 4x10 | 10' | 7' | **Hem-Fir** | | | 4x10 | 6' | 8' |
| 4x10 | 12' | 7' | 4x6 | 6' | 6' | 4x10 | 8' | 7' |
| 4x10 | 14' | 6' | 4x8 | 6' | 7' | 4x10 | 10' | 6' |
| 4x10 | 16' | 6' | 4x8 | 8' | 6' | 4x10 | 12' | 6' |
| 4x12 | 6' | 11' | 4x10 | 6' | 9' | 4x12 | 6' | 10' |
| 4x12 | 8' | 10' | 4x10 | 8' | 7' | 4x12 | 8' | 8' |
| 4x12 | 10' | 9' | 4x10 | 10' | 6' | 4x12 | 10' | 7' |
| 4x12 | 12' | 8' | 4x10 | 12' | 6' | 4x12 | 12' | 6' |
| 4x12 | 14' | 7' | 4x12 | 6' | 10' | 4x12 | 14' | 6' |
| | | | 4x12 | 8' | 9' | | | |

# INSTALLING THE LEDGER

The ledger usually makes a helpful starting place for laying out the whole deck, so you may want to install it before you dig your footing holes. It is a major supporting member, so it must be firmly attached to the house. Make your ledger of the same two-by material as your joists. Pick a straight board that is not cupped, so the joist ends can fit snugly against it.

## Ledger Design Options

The ledger is a common trouble spot because rain and snow can collect between it and the house and damage both. In particular, if you have beveled horizontal siding (including wood, aluminum and vinyl) or shingles, simply attaching the ledger onto the siding is an invitation to big trouble: Water will collect in the V-shaped channel between the siding and the ledger.

There are five common methods for attaching a ledger:

**A** If you will be attaching to a flat surface (either siding or masonry), simply attach the ledger very tightly against the house, so that water cannot seep behind it. This is the simplest solution, and it works well if you can really squeeze the ledger tight to the house. However, there is a good chance that your inspector will want you to put in more work.

**B** For joining to a wall with siding (either flat or beveled horizontal), cut out a section of siding and fit the ledger into it, providing flashing that forces water to run down the face of the ledger.

**C** If you are attaching to a surface with beveled horizontal siding, take a piece or two of cedar siding of the same shape as the house siding, and install it upside down, thereby producing a plumb house surface. Install the ledger against this plumb surface, and either flash it or just let it be.

**D** Against a flat surface, install several washers or specially shaped pieces of lumber behind the ledger at each lag screw, thereby providing a space between the ledger and the house, so that water runs easily between them and can dry out between rains.

**E** For stucco or masonry surfaces, cut a channel above the ledger, into which flashing can be inserted.

All these methods have proved successful in various parts of the country. Opinions vary on which solution is best, and your inspector may favor one or the other. If he orders you to do it a certain way, it's a good idea to just do what he says. The point is to avoid having moisture trapped against the ledger or the house framing for long periods.

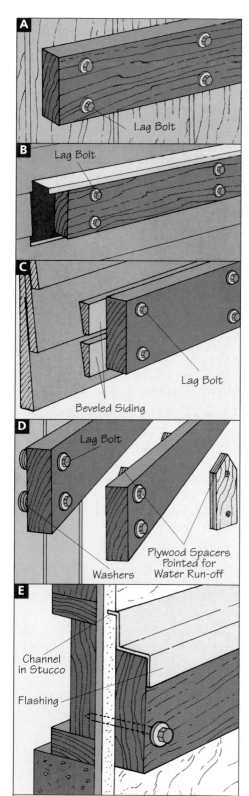

**Ledger design options.** There are five common ways to attach a ledger to your house. (A) Simply attach the ledger snuggly to the house. (B) Cut out the siding and install flashing. (C) Cut a piece of beveled siding to create a flat surface. (D) Hold the ledger off the wall, using washers or plywood for spacers. (E) Insert flashing into masonry or stucco.

# Preparing for the Ledger

If any of the following steps do not apply to your method, just skip to the next step.

1 **Locate the ledger.** It may sound like a good idea to have your deck surface level with your interior flooring, but if you do so you will be inviting rain and snow to seep under your threshold and into your house. So plan to have a small step down: ¾ to about 1 inch will go a long way towards keeping your home drier in most regions. If you think you need a greater step down, make it the distance of a normal stairway step (6 to 7½ inches); anything between 1-6 inches will feel awkward.

To locate your ledger, measure down from the level of your house's floor the thickness of your decking (1 inch for ¾ decking, 1½ inches for two-by decking), plus the amount you want to step down. Mark this spot, and then extend the mark the length of the ledger. You want this line to be perfectly level. (For purposes of drainage, you usually want the deck to slope away from the house rather than alongside it.)

To make marks that will ensure your ledger is level throughout its length, either use a water level, or set your carpenter's level atop a straight board. (Because few boards are perfect, it is best to place the level near the center of the board.) Tack a nail to the side of the house for one end of the board to rest on. Once you have made several marks, snap chalklines between them, and double-check those lines for level.

2 **Mark for outer joists, fascia and decking.** It helps to visualize all the dimensions of your finished deck, so mark for every lumber piece that will go up against your house. This means adding 1½ inches for the outside joist, plus ¾ inches for fascia (if any), plus the distance you plan to overhang your decking (if any).

3 **Cut out the siding.** If the ledger installation requires removing

1 You can use a long straight board and a level to locate the ledger. Or, when marking for a long ledger or one that makes a turn, use a water level to ensure accuracy.

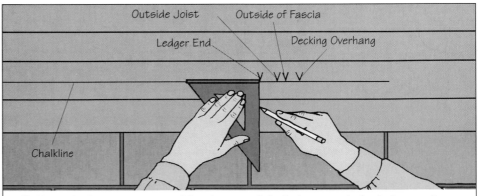

2 Along the line you snapped for the top of the ledger, mark the ledger ends and the positions of end joists as well as fascia boards (if any) and deck board overhangs, if any.

some of your siding, mark an outline for the cutout, taking into account everything that will fit into it: the ledger, the end of the outside joists, an extra ⅛ inch in width for the flash-ing (if any), and possibly the end of the fascia—but not the decking. Marking will be easier if you tack a piece of ledger-width material in place and draw a pencil line around it.

## Go for Level or for Good Looks?

Houses settle over the years and not always evenly. So it's not unusual for a house to be out of level. If your house has horizontal lines—if it is covered with brick or horizontal siding, for instance—then a perfectly level deck may look very awkward up against it. So you may want to align the deck to the house rather than to the earth. If you do so, however, make the header joist out of level in a way that is parallel to the ledger.

**3** Use a circular saw to cut out the siding for the ledger. Screw a piece of 1x4 to provide a flat surface for the saw when making vertical cuts in in beveled siding.

Cut it out with a circular saw. If you have aluminum or vinyl siding, follow manufacturer's directions; often it works best to reverse your circular saw blade when cutting these materials. Set the blade so that it cuts just through the siding and not much more. You will need to make a plunge cut to start with (see "Making a Plunge Cut," page 67). For wood siding, use a hammer and chisel to neatly finish the cutout at the corners. For vinyl siding, finish the corner cuts with a utility knife. Use snips for aluminum. When making a vertical cut across horizontal beveled siding, it helps to tack on a piece of 1x4, to provide a level surface for your circular saw to rest on.

Seal up the area you have just cut out with felt (tar paper) or house wrap, so that no bare wood sheathing is exposed.

**4** **Check for straightness.** Check the surface against which you will be placing the ledger by holding a string against its length. If, anywhere along the length, there is a gap of more than ½ inch between the string and the wall, tack shims to the house so that when you attach the ledger it will be straight. Remember that the front edge of your deck will follow the contours of your ledger. Remove or pound in any obstructions, such as nailheads or screws.

**4** Hold a string against the house and look for gaps that indicate the wall is not flat.

**5** **Install flashing.** If you have cut out a section of siding, install flashing that is the same length as the cutout. (It will cover the top of the outside joists as well, so snip the front edge to make it fit over them.) Tuck the flashing up under the siding. Before you slide it in, make sure you have a clear path for your flashing, prying the upper siding piece loose and removing all nails in the flashing's path. Handle the flashing carefully because it bends easily. Gently renail

the siding back into position to hold the flashing in place.

For noncutouts with flashing, it is possible to attach the flashing to the house simply by first installing the ledger, then setting the flashing on it and gluing it in place with roofing cement or caulk. But this will leave you with a problem spot: the cement will probably come loose in time, and it will be difficult to repair it because decking will be in the way. So it is best

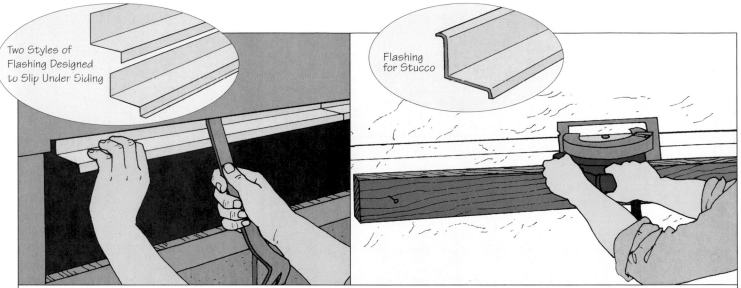

Two Styles of Flashing Designed to Slip Under Siding

Flashing for Stucco

**5** If you have cut out horizontal siding to make room for the ledger, slip flashing under the course of siding above. If your ledger will be attached to stucco, cut a groove to receive the flashing lip.

to find a way to tuck the upper flange in. For beveled horizontal siding or shingles, you may have to buy extra-wide flashing, depending on how far above your ledger the next piece of siding or row of shingles is located.

For stucco or masonry, buy or make flashing that has an extra bend so that a lip can be stuck straight into the side of the house. Using a masonry blade on your circular saw, cut a straight line into which the flashing can be inserted.

Depending on the hardness of your siding material, this may require several passes. Be sure to wear protective eyewear. For stucco or masonry, you won't actually put the flashing in place until after the ledger is installed.

A variety of ready-made flashings are available. Choose a "Z"-shaped flashing, one that bends twice—once to slide up under the siding and once to cover the face of your ledger. This last, front-most portion of the flashing need not be wide, as long as it is enough to keep water from wicking between the flashing and the top of the ledger. Remember the joists will be smashed up against it, so it is best if it comes down at a right angle.

**6** **Cut and mark the ledger and header.** Cut the ledger and the header joist to length. For a rectangular deck, they will be the same length;

## Ledger Installation Options

Here is one variation on the cutout method, if you will be installing flashing: Cut the siding wider than the ledger—2¼ inches if you will be using two-by decking or 1¾ inches for ¾ decking—and plan to install your decking into the cutout instead of up against the siding. This will leave you with a ¾-inch gap above the decking, which will reduce water collection and will make it easier for you to sweep out any dirt and leaves that collect. This method works best for decking that runs parallel to the house. You will need extra-wide flashing.

Here's another variation on the cutout method that will add protection against water accumulation: Cut a rabbet (a notch running the length of the board) along the bottom rear of the ledger, and make the cutout on the house narrower, so that the ledger overhangs the siding at the bottom by about ⅛ inch. The width of the rabbet depends on how thick the siding is along the edge that was cut for the ledger.

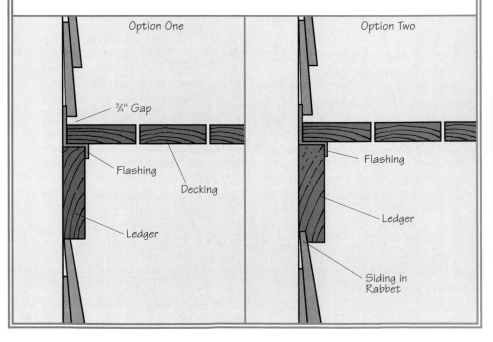

Option One

¾" Gap

Flashing

Decking

Ledger

Option Two

Flashing

Ledger

Siding in Rabbet

**6** Put the header and ledger against each other and mark them together for joist positions.

for other shapes, make adjustments according to your plans.

The ledger and header joist run parallel to each other, and the joists are perpendicular to them both, so it is often easiest to cut the header joist to length and hold them together to mark them both on top for joists before you install the ledger. After marking the tops, use a square to extend the lines down the faces of the ledger and header. Don't forget to make "X"s indicating which side of the line the joists will be installed on.

**Flashing an Outside Corner**

If your ledger will continue around an outside corner, allow 3 inches or so of extra flashing on the ends so that you can nip the pieces into this configuration after the ledger is installed.

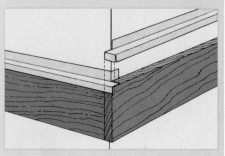

## ATTACHING THE LEDGER

Whether you are attaching to wood, masonry, or stucco, it is important to fasten the ledger securely. It must be as strong as a beam.

### Attaching the Ledger to Wood Framing

If your house is sided with wood, aluminum, vinyl, or stucco, you need to attach the ledger through the siding material into the wooden framing. You want to find the strongest structural member possible. Attaching a ledger to a frame house just below the interior flooring is simple, since there will be a rim joist behind the siding, running all along the area where you want to put the ledger. If you are putting the ledger elsewhere on a frame house, locate the wall studs and plan to put your screws into them. (Usually, when you see the head of a siding nail, that means there is something solid underneath.) If there is any doubt, test every spot where you will be installing a screw.

Use ⅜- or ½-inch lag screws. Select screws that are long enough to pass 1½-2 inches into the framing member. Use a washer for each—it will make

### Checking for Crown

Framing members should always be installed crown-side up. This way, the weight of the load will tend to straighten the lumber. If you install boards crown-side down you'll be giving sag a head start.

To check for crown, set one end of the board on the ground and sight down its length. If you see a slight hump, the crown side is up. If you see a slight valley, the crown is on the other side. If you see a severe crown, put the board aside to use later for smaller pieces such as blocking. If you see no crown at all, you might want to put that board aside too if you anticipate needing one later that is especially straight.

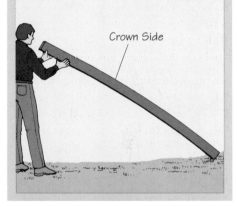
Crown Side

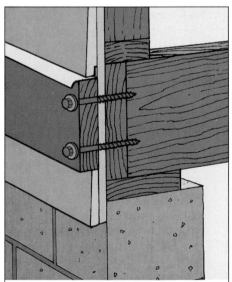

**Attaching the ledger to wood framing.** For house with wood, aluminum, vinyl or stucco siding, attach the ledger through the siding material into the house framing.

**Drilling lag screw holes.** Temporarily attach the ledger with a couple of nails or screws. Then drill pilot holes for lag screws through the ledger into the framing.

the screw hold more strongly because it keeps the head from sinking into the ledger.

If you have horizontal beveled siding and want to make a flat surface for your ledger, cut pieces of siding to the right width and length, and nail them in place. (See "Ledger Design Options", page 89.) It is a good idea to brush some water repellent/preservative on this piece, to make it just as rot resistant as the pressure-treated ledger.

**Drilling lag screw holes.** Position the ledger in place, and fasten it temporarily with screws or nails. Check again to see that it is in the correct position and is level. Drill pilot holes for all the lag screws. (Pilot holes actually make the screws hold better, since they prevent wood from splitting.) These should be sized so that the screws will slide through them yet fit snugly. A good spacing is to place a pair of them every 24 inches. Make sure you place lag screws so as to avoid both joist ends and joist hangers.

If you have a drill bit that is long enough, you don't have to remove the ledger at this point—just drill the pilot holes and install the screws. If your bit is not long enough—the holes should travel the entire length of the screw—remove the ledger to

drill the holes, taking care to go squarely into the house.

For a stucco house, you will probably not be able to simply drill right through the stucco into the framing. First, drill through the ledger and into the stucco just deeply enough to make a clear mark (doing this may dull your drill bit, so have plenty on hand). Then take the ledger down, and use a masonry bit to finish drilling all the way through the

stucco. Then switch back to a wood bit, and finish drilling into the house framing. Now you can put the ledger back up and attach it with the lag screws and washers.

Install the lag screws with washers using a ratchet wrench and socket. If any of the screws do not tighten down well (you should not be able to keep spinning it around after it is all the way in), remove it and install it in another spot.

## Attaching the Ledger to Concrete or Masonry

If you will be attaching to a concrete or masonry wall, first drill your pilot holes through the ledger before you put it up against the house. Then position the ledger correctly against the house; hold it in place temporarily with concrete nails, or prop it up with angled scraps of wood.

1 **Mark the wall.** Once the ledger is correctly in place, put a small masonry bit in your drill—one that can fit through your pilot holes—and use it to mark the location of your lag screws. After all the locations have been marked, take the ledger board down.

1 Position the ledger temporarily on the wall and drill through the holes in the ledger to mark lag shield positions on the wall.

2 Usually you'll need a heavy-duty hammer drill to make holes for the lag shields.

3 Tap the lag shield into their holes.

4 A ratchet wrench and socket makes short work of attaching the ledger.

ream out the hole in your ledger board to accommodate the new screw location.

**3 Install lag shields.** After the holes are drilled, install the lag shields by tapping them in. They should fit snugly, but you should not have to pound hard to make them go in.

**4 Attach the ledger.** Reposition the ledger and attach the lag screws and washers with a ratchet wrench and socket. You may have to give them a tap with your hammer to get them started.

If you are using the holdoff method (See "Ledger Design Options," page 89), insert every lag screw into the ledger so that it pokes through ½ inch or so, and place the washers or lumber spacers on the screws. With a helper or two, lift the ledger into place, taking care not to lose any spacers. Tap all the screws part way into place before you start to tighten.

## POSITIONING THE POSTS

The beams will either sit on top of the posts or get lag screwed or bolted to them. Both methods are strong. (The on-top method can be slightly more resistant to downward pressure on the deck, while the screwing or bolting method is better at keeping the beam from twisting.) If you are an accomplished carpenter, the on-top method is quicker, since it avoids a lot of drilling and fastening. However, it is less forgiving of mistakes because you must cut the top of posts accurately before you install the beam.

**1 Check for rough length.** You will cut the post to exact height later, but first make sure every post will be tall enough. Use a line level, water level, or long piece of lumber with a level atop it to find out how high each post needs to be. (It is best to slope your deck slightly down coming

**2 Drill holes for lag shields.** Choose a masonry bit that is the correct size for your lag shields. At each of the locations you marked, drill holes that are ¼ inch or so deeper than the length of the shields, and pound them into place carefully, to avoid mashing them. (A rubber mallet works well, but is not necessary.)

If you don't have many to drill or if you are going into a soft surface such as brick, a regular drill will do for this job; for a lot of holes in concrete, rent a hammer drill. Have plenty of bits on hand, and take it slow. Once a bit overheats, it very quickly becomes useless. Watch closely for smoke (sometimes hard to distinguish from concrete dust) and sniff for a burning smell; stop as soon as you sense either one. Sometimes a stone in the concrete will cause your drill bit to wander a somewhat, so that your hole will be up to ½ inch or so off. Avoid this if possible, but don't get too upset if it happens—you can

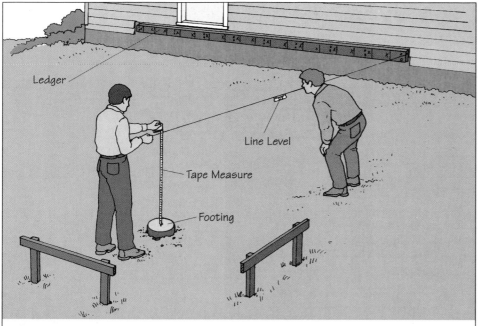

1 Check the length each post needs to be before cutting it to rough length.

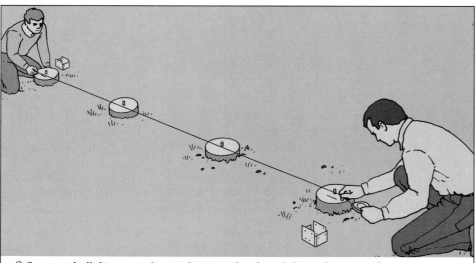

2 Snap a chalk line to indicate the outside of each line of post anchors.

away from the house, but this measurement is too small to worry about at this point.) Give yourself at least a few extra inches, and you won't have to worry.

**2 Locate and attach post anchors.** If you are using adjustable post anchors, now is the time to fine-tune their positions. Take two post anchor bases and hand one to your helper along with one end of your chalkline. Center one post anchor over the J-bolt on one end of a row of footings and mark its outside edge on the footing. Have your helper do the same at the other end. Snap a chalk line on all the footings in the row to indicate the outside edges of the anchors. Attach your post anchor according to the manufacturer's directions.

**3 Insert posts and put bracing in place.** Put each post into its anchor, and attach braces of 1x4 or 2x4. These should extend from near the top of the post to the ground at about a 45-degree angle. Attach each brace with a single screw or nail. When you have determined that the post is roughly plumb, firmly drive a stake (made of 2x2 or 1x4) up against each brace as shown.

**4 Plumb posts and attach bracing.** This is definitely a two-person operation: One person checks the level and, once the post is perfectly plumb, tells the other to drive in a screw attaching the brace to the

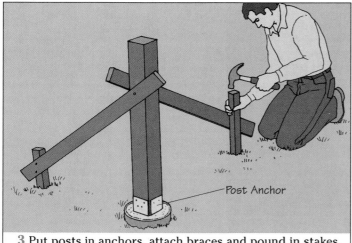

3 Put posts in anchors, attach braces and pound in stakes.

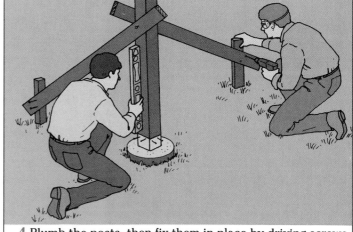

4 Plumb the posts, then fix them in place by driving screws through braces into anchors.

stake. Do the same for the other brace, and then recheck the first direction. Don't be surprised if you have to redo things once or twice. Once you have achieved perfect plumb, drive in more screws for stability—at least two for each attaching point. Drive in the nails to hold the post anchor to the post.

# MAKING AND INSTALLING BEAMS

There are four considerations when choosing the beam for your deck. First, think about space. If your deck is built close to the ground, you may not have room to put the beam on top of the posts or to put the joists on top of the beam. You can save room by using a bolted-on beam and/or by having the joists tie into the beam with joist hangers rather than sitting on top.

Next think about whether the beam will be visible, and if so, what it will look like. If your beam will be visible, choose the look you like best. Nicely installed bolts on a built-up beam can look good, but a massive timber has a classy yet rustic look. Be aware, however, of what sort of lumber is available to you—it may be that you can't get a good-looking 4x8, for instance.

If your deck is raised more than a few feet off the ground, there is another consideration: An on-top beam is more likely to need bracing than one that is bolted on.

Finally, consider weight. A 16-foot piece of 4x10, especially if it's still soaking from the pressure-treating, can be a real back-breaker. And things can get downright dangerous if you have to lift it high in the air. So in some cases, it is simply easier on your body to use a built-up beam.

## Types of Beams

Here are some common types of beams.

**A** A beam made of a solid piece of four-by lumber resting on top of 4x4 posts. If done correctly, this has a classic, clean look, but there is little leeway for correcting mistakes, and it can be difficult to find good-looking four-by lumber.

**B** A built-up beam made of two two-bys with pressure-treated plywood spacers sandwiched between. This is actually stronger than a solid beam, and usually less expensive, but it does take some extra time to build. And once built, it may be just as heavy and difficult to maneuver as a solid beam.

**C** A beam consisting of two pieces of two-by lumber attached to opposing sides of the posts. Though a bit time-consuming, this is often the best type of beam for the do-it-yourselfer, since it involves little heavy lifting and is correctable.

**D** A laminated beam, made of two two-bys that have been joined together with many screws or nails. This is also simple to build and gives you the option of either attaching the two pieces together on the ground or putting the second piece on after the first, thereby avoiding heavy lifting.

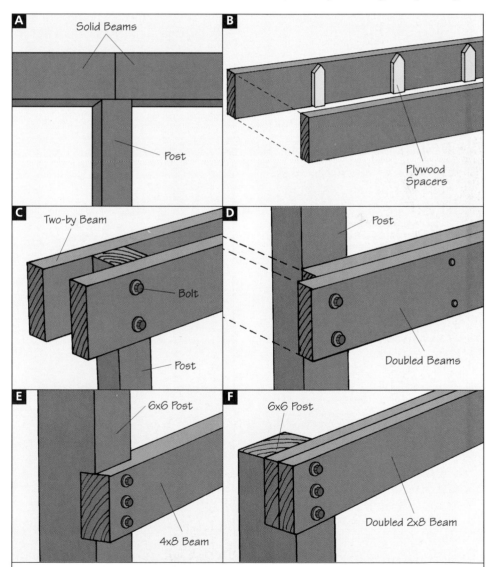

**Types of beams.** Here are five common types of beams used to build decks. (A) Solid beams set on top of posts. Any butt joints between beams fall on the center of a post. (B) Beams built of solid two-by lumber with plywood spacers are set on posts. (C) Two-by beams are bolted to opposing sides of posts. (D) Two-bys are nailed or screwed together to form four-by beams that are lag-screwed to posts. (E) A solid or doubled beam is set into a notch along the length or a 6x6 post or (F) at the top of a 6x6 post.

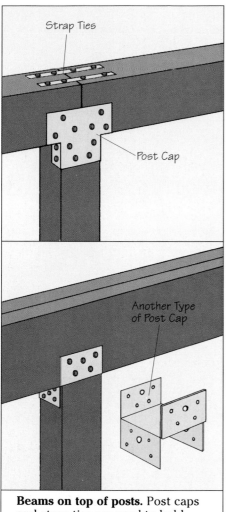

**Beams on top of posts.** Post caps and strap ties are used to hold beams in place.

**E and F** A beam set into a notched post. The notching adds some strength to the beam but takes away some for the post. So this is recommended only when you are using 6x6s for posts. The notches must be cut cleanly and accurately, with no gaps, or you will be inviting water to seep into newly cut lumber—always a bad idea.

Joists can either rest on top of your beam (usually the simplest solution because you can hide the beam by cantilevering the deck)—or joists can be attached to the side of the beam with joist hangers. All beams discussed above can accommodate either method.

**Beams on top of posts.** For attaching beams on top of posts, choose from a variety of specially designed hardware. This hardware work better than pieces of wood that you cut

and scab on, which always have exposed end grain and are prone to water damage.

**Attaching to the side.** Attaching the beams to the side of the posts gives you the option of bringing them to the same level as the joists. In fact, the beam takes the place of the header joist and so will be cut to exact length and marked for joists in conjunction with the ledger, as if it were the header joist. Make sure the beam is crown side up when you mark for the joists.

Lag screws are plenty strong, if you drill the correct pilot holes for them. But some people prefer to run bolts all the way through the members, and this adds a bit more strength in exchange for extra labor. For laminating two two-bys together, a lot of 2½-inch deck screws or 12d galvanized nails work much better than a few bolts.

## Installing a Beam

**1 Mark the corner posts.** Use a level and a long, straight piece of lumber, a line level, or a water level to mark the location of the beam on the post. Start at a corner post. First, find the spot that is level from the top of the ledger. (If you want the deck to slope slightly for drainage, measure down from that mark 1⁄16 inch for every foot of joist travel.) Make a mark; this shows where the top of the joists will be (as well as the top of the beam, if your joists will be on the same plane as the beam). From this mark, measure down the width of your joists. That is where the top of your beam will be located if the joists will rest on top of the beam. Do the same for the other corner post. If you have more than two corners, make these marks on other corner posts as well.

1 Mark each corner post for the height of the beam.

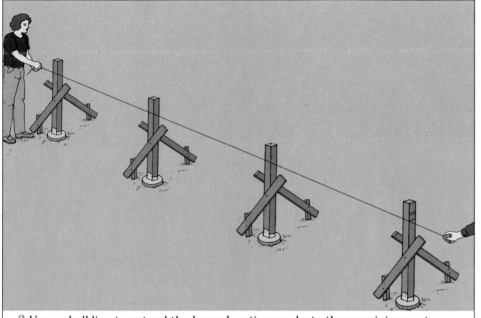

2 Use a chalkline to extend the beam location marks to the remaining posts.

3 Use your circular saw to cut the posts to height.

## 2 Mark the rest of the posts.
Use a chalkline to extend lines between the beam marks you made on the corner posts.

## 3 Cut off the posts.
Follow this step now, only if you will be supporting beams directly on top of posts. If posts are not cut accurately to height, you will have to use shims on top of some posts—not a great disaster, but something of an eyesore, and a potential rot spot. Your beam may be crowned (remember, always put the crown up), which means that the posts in the middle will need to be a bit taller than the posts on the end. If possible, hold the beam in place for final marking of the interior posts.

Double-check your circular saw to make sure it cuts at a perfect right angle, or your cut will look sloppy. (See "Squaring the Blade," page 62) Using a square, draw a line completely around the post. Get into a comfortable position, take a deep breath, and cut two opposite sides with a circular saw. For a 6x6 post, cut all four sides and then finish cutting the middle of the post with a hand saw or reciprocating saw.

## 4 Make and cut the beam.
This is one of the few cases where letting a board run wild is probably not

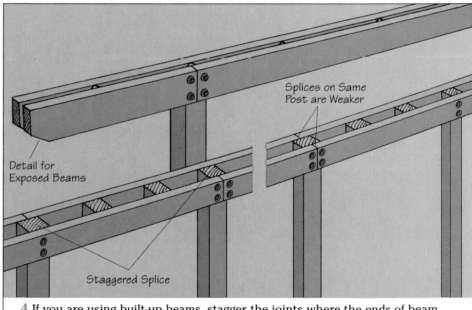

Detail for Exposed Beams

Splices on Same Post are Weaker

Staggered Splice

4 If you are using built-up beams, stagger the joints where the ends of beam boards butt.

a good idea because it may be difficult to cut the beam cleanly once it is in place. Double-check your measurements; a wrongly cut beam is rarely correctable.

If you are constructing a built-up beam on the ground, position your screws or nails so that they do not go through the same grain lines. This could cause splitting.

If you have splices in your beam, be sure they will fall in the middle of your posts. For built-up beams, stagger the splices, so that the splices on the two-bys fall on different posts. Cut the ends with a 45-degree notch (as shown in the illustration), for an attractive, finished-looking appearance. This cut will not lessen the strength of the beam.

## 5 Attach the beam.
If you have a heavy beam to wrestle into place, arrange for plenty of help and make sure that any ladders you use are extremely stable.

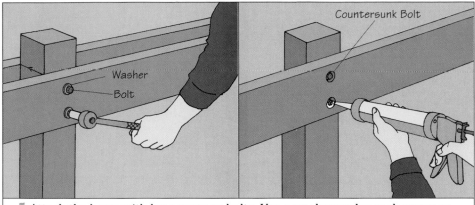

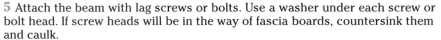

**5** Attach the beam with lag screws or bolts. Use a washer under each screw or bolt head. If screw heads will be in the way of fascia boards, countersink them and caulk.

**6** Use a hand saw or reciprocating saw to cut the posts flush to the top of the beam.

Put the beam in place, using screws to hold it temporarily. Measure to see the beam is properly located, so that your deck will be a rectangle, not a parallelogram.

Install lag screws or bolts, first predrilling pilot holes. For an on-top beam, slide the post cap into place and attach it with deck screws. Drill pilot holes, at least for the screws that go into the posts because these may split.

If your beam will get covered with fascia, countersink holes so that the bolt or lag screw head and washer can sit just beneath the surface of the board, and fill the countersink with caulk after the lag screw or bolt is installed. For beams that will be exposed to view, a more attractive alternative is to through-bolt with carriage bolts, if that is possible.

**6 Cut off the posts.** Unless your posts will rise up to become part of the railing or a bench, use a hand saw or reciprocating saw to cut the posts flush to the top of the beam. This is a trouble spot, susceptible to water damage, since it is newly cut open grain that will be difficult to reach once the deck is built, so brush on a good soaking of repellant-preservative.

# HANGING THE JOISTS

Joists are usually attached to the ledger on one end and a header joist or a beam on the other end. Where it is possible—at the header joist, for example—you can attach the joists by backnailing, that is, by nailing through the face of the header into the end grain of the joists. Use 3-inch deck screws or 16d galvanized nails, three per joint. But joist hangers are preferred in all locations by most building departments.

**1 Build the box.** It is usually easiest to start by assembling the outside members into a box. Assemble these carefully because they will probably be the most visible. Predrill for all screws or nails that come near the end of a board. If your outside joists sit on top of the beam, attach them flush to the ends of the beam. At the corners, attach the header and outside joists

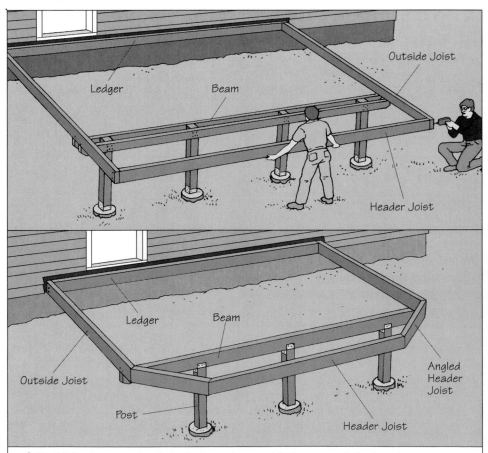

**1** Build the box, made of the ledger, the outside joists, and the header joist. It may take two helpers to hold the pieces for the deck at bottom while you screw it together.

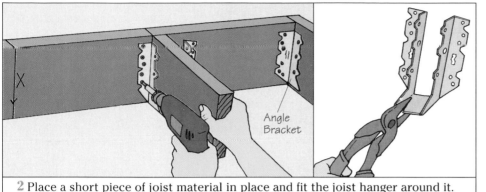

**2** Place a short piece of joist material in place and fit the joist hanger around it. Cut a joist hanger to make an angle bracket.

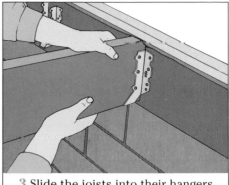

**3** Slide the joists into their hangers with the crown side facing up.

together with 16d galvanized nails or 3-inch deck screws, driven through pilot holes. Reinforce these joints with angle brackets attached to the joists with 1¼-inch deck screws.

Once again check for square (see "Establish the centers of the corner footings precisely," and "Check lengths and diagonals," pages 79-80. You are now for the first time testing the shape of your finished deck surface, and it is not too late to shift things around a bit. It doesn't have to be completely exact: for the 6-8-10 method of checking for square, it's O.K. to be off by ¼ inch.

**2 Install joist hangers.** At each joist location, install a joist hanger. You should use galvanized joist hanger nails, but we recommend first tack-ing the hanger in place with 1¼-inch deck screws. Lumber can vary in width as much as ¼ inch; if you have to move a joist hanger it is easier to remove a screw than a nail.

Take a short block of joist material and hold it in place: it should touch the line and cover the "X," but most importantly, its top edge must be flush with the top of the ledger or header. Slide the joist hanger up against it so that it touches on one side only. There are pointed tabs on the hanger; pound them in, and they *may* hold the hanger in place. Drive two nails in to hold the hanger in place. Double-check to make sure the block is still accurately in place, then close the hanger around it and fasten the other side with the recommended number of hanger nails.

At the inside corners of your "box," install angle brackets. You can make your own angle brackets by cutting joist hangers with tin snips.

**3 Slide the joists in place.** The joist ends must butt against the ledger or header tightly at all points. So before you measure for cutting

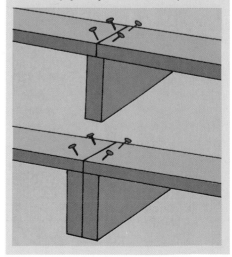

the joists, make sure the end you are measuring from is cut square. (Sometimes the lumberyard will give you ten that are square-cut and one that isn't, so look at them all.) Cut the joists to length.

Right now you're probably itching to make some real, visible progress in a hurry. But we recommend that you take a little time first to seal the open grain of the cut ends with some sealer/preservative.

Install each joist crown-side-up. This is a two-person operation. If things are tight you may have to slide both ends down at the same time. A little pounding is fine, but if a joist is so tight that it starts to bend, take it out and recut it.

If you have the kind of flashing that makes a 90-degree turn to cover the face of the ledger, just smash the joist into the flashing. But if your flashing makes only a slight downward turn (see illustration), there are two options: slide the joist under or smash it in and bend the flashing. Ask your inspector which is best.

**4 Finish fastening.** Eyeball the framing to see that everything looks straight and parallel. Finish installing the screws or nails in the joist hangers—put one in every hole. Where joists rest on a beam, toenail or drive a screw, to minimize twisting. Hurricane ties provide extra strength but are not usually required by code.

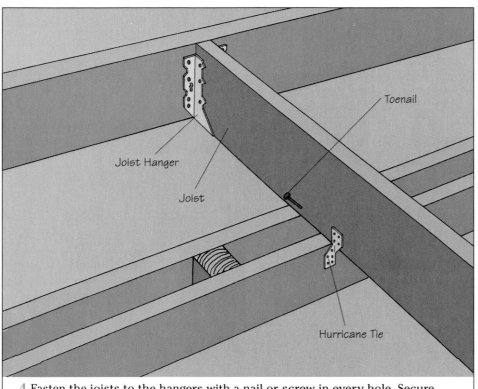

4 Fasten the joists to the hangers with a nail or screw in every hole. Secure joists to beams with toenails or hurricane ties.

### Splicing Joists

If your deck is too long for a single length of joist to span, you will need to join joists on a center beam. You can do it in one of two ways: you can let them overlap each other and join them together with 3-inch deck screws. The advantage of this system is that you do not have to cut the joists to length. Or you can cut them to exact length and butt their ends against each other, tying them together with straps.

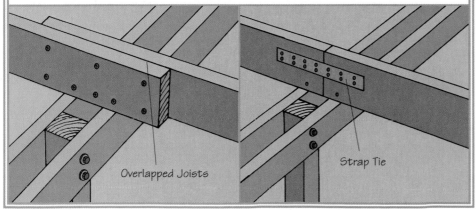

### Brace for the Rail Posts

If you will be attaching your rail posts later to a long outside joist, the post might wobble because the outside joist travels a long distance without attachment to another piece of framing to keep it from flexing. So attach extra blocking as shown.

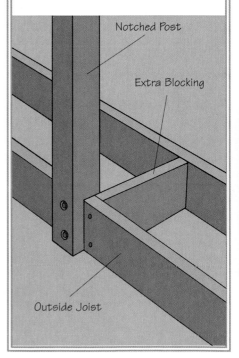

**Blocking.** Install blocking in an alternating pattern.

# BLOCKING

Blocking, also called solid bridging, is made of short pieces of joist material that are wedged between the joists and arranged in a staggered row. Blocking takes out bends in joists, keeps them from twisting over time, and adds some rigidity to the deck. If your joists span 12 feet or more, a row of blocking is a good idea, though it is something of a nuisance to install.

Chalk a line along the top of the joists to mark where the row of blocking will go. To begin with, cut four or five blocks to fit between your joists. For most of the spaces, this will be your joist spacing minus 1½ inches (so for joists spaced 16 inches apart, cut blocking at 14½ inches). Don't cut them all to begin with: As you proceed, you may find that you need to make them a little larger or a little smaller.

Install the blocks in a staggered manner on either side of your chalk line. This makes nailing or screwing a lot easier. The blocks should fit snugly enough to stay in place themselves but not so tightly that they cause your joists to bend. Check your joists for straightness—eyeballing is fine, though you can use a string line every third block or so.

# BRACING

Decks that are raised above the ground—more than 4 feet for 4x4s; more than 8 feet for 6x6s—need extra lateral support to keep them from swaying. An on-top solid beam has less lateral strength than a bolted-on beam and may need bracing even if it is lower.

If you will be installing solid skirting (siding panels that enclose your deck below the deck surface), that will provide a good deal of lateral support and can take the place of bracing. Lattice skirting, however, is much less effective. Guidelines on bracing vary greatly from area to area, so check with your inspector if you think you may need it. In most cases, bracing can be added after the deck is built.

Bracing can add a classic, hand-crafted look, and for less work than you might think. The only tricks are making accurate 45-degree cuts and making sure the braces which are in a symmetrical relation to each other are exactly the same size, for a uniform look.

**"Y" bracing.** In most cases, simple "Y" bracing is sufficient. To brace a post under a solid beam, cut pieces of post material (4x4 or 6x6) to go under the beam and against the sides of the post, or use 2x4s or 2x6s and attach them to the face of the post and beam. For beams attached to opposing sides of a post, sandwich the braces between the beams and secure with lag screws, bolts, or carriage bolts.

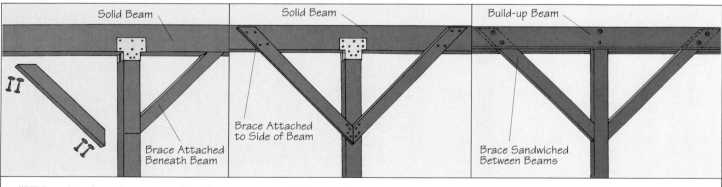

**"Y" bracing.** In most cases where bracing is needed, a simple "Y" configuration will do the job. For a solid beam, use braces underneath or attached to the side of the beam. For beams attached to opposing sides of a post, sandwich the brace between the beams.

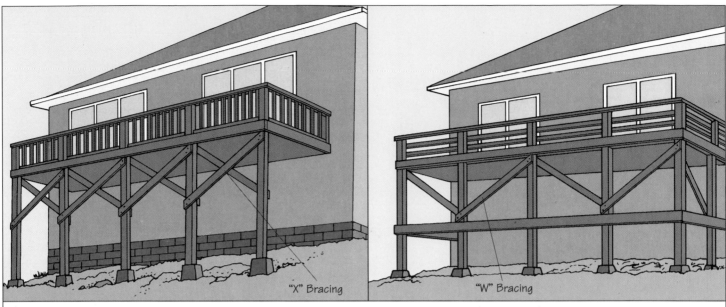

**Other bracing patterns.** "X" bracing and "W" bracing are two options when you need beefier support.

**Other bracing patterns.** Larger projects may require more elaborate bracing patterns. These are all best done with 2x4s or 2x6s on the face of the post and beam. When building these sorts of structures, first make marks on the posts and beams, and then hold up the braces for marking, rather than using a tape measure.

Braces that will span 6 feet or less can be made of 2x4s; for longer spans, use 2x6s. Consider traffic patterns when deciding on your bracing. If you need to walk under the deck, a simple Y may be the best way to go; if you need more elaborate bracing, you may be able to leave one section unbraced if you really beef up the other sections.

# SPECIAL SITUATIONS

Not all decks will be straightforward. Some decks may have to change levels to accommodate a sloping yard; others may need to be raised off the ground a few feet or more to meet a second-floor entrance. You may also have to build a deck around steps, trees, or other obstacles in the yard. Here are ways to deal with some common variations.

## Building Over Concrete Steps

Demolishing concrete steps with a sledge and hauling away the rubble is a lot of work. As long as the top step is lower than the top of the deck joists, it's usually easier to leave the step in place and frame around it. Before you do, make sure that there is no evidence that the step has heaved due to an improper footing.

If the step is sound, stop the ledger at both sides of the step. Notch the joists to fit over the top step and rest on the second step. If necessary insert cedar shims between the joists and second step. Block between the joist on the second step as shown.

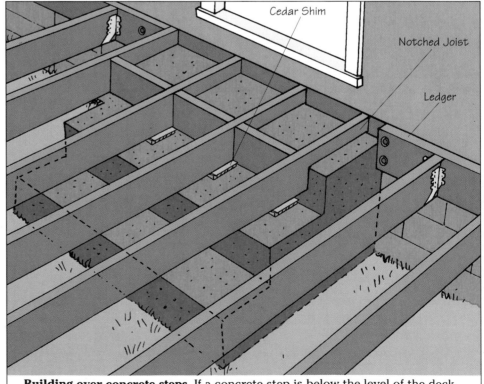

**Building over concrete steps.** If a concrete step is below the level of the decking, you can frame around it.

**Making a reference point for laying out the deck.** Check to see whether the side of your house is plumb. If it is, use it as a reference point. Otherwise, drop a plumb bob.

# Raised Decks

If you are building a deck that's 8 feet or more above the ground, most of the layout will be the same, but your work methods will differ dramatically. Most operations will take twice as long to perform, as you spend lots of time wrestling with ladders, carrying things up and down, and being extra careful.

Decking, ledgers, joists, and beams have all the same requirements as decks built low to the ground. Only the posts change: You will need 6x6s, possibly with bracing, and that means heavy lifting and extra-sturdy temporary bracing.

Follow the steps already discussed, with the following wrinkles:

**Making a reference point for laying out the deck.** To make sure that your footings and posts are in the right spots to support a deck high above, you need a reference point near the ground that is accurately located below a reference point at deck level.

Go to the corner of the house that is nearest the doorway for your deck. Check if the side of the corner adja-

cent to the deck is plumb as shown. Use a ladder to check in a couple of places in case the corner isn't straight. If the corner is plumb, you can use it to establish your reference point.

If the corner isn't plumb, drop a plumb line from a point marked on the doorway above. Have a helper place a framing square against the line and use it to make a mark near

**Bracing the posts.** Use 8- or 10-foot 2x4s for braces, and 2-foot-long 2x4 stakes driven deep in the ground for a heavy post like this.

the bottom of the foundation wall. Use this mark for your reference point.

**Bracing the posts.** Sink your posts into postholes rather than setting them on footings, if codes allow. This will make it a good deal easier to hold them in position and brace them. Apply plenty of preservative to the part of the posts that will be underground (especially the end grain), and drop 3-4 inches of gravel in the hole before inserting the post.

Use 2x4s or even 2x6s for temporary bracing. Pound the stakes deep in the ground. If you don't have a high step ladder, it will make building the deck much easier if you can confidently lean your ladder against a temporarily braced post—something you will have to do when you cut the posts to height, when you install the beam, and when you begin the framing. You may even want to use four rather than two braces.

If your inspector will allow it, wait until the framing or even the entire deck is completed before pouring the concrete around the posts. This will make your footing stronger, since it will not get banged around during the construction process—that could loosen the concrete's bond with the post or with the earth. Also, doing it this way gives you the luxury of being able to make small adjustments to the posts, if necessary.

**Notching the post.** Though not recommended elsewhere, notching the post for a beam is the best method when you have 6x6 posts. Unless your beam also is a 6-by, setting the beam on top of the post will leave open grain exposed on the post and will have a sloppy appearance.

After you have cut the post to height, use your angle square to mark for the beam; the best design is to notch it completely in, so that the face of the beam ends up flush with the face of the post. To do this, first set your circular saw cutting depth to equal the thickness of the beam—for example 3 inches for a beam made of doubled two-bys. Make the seat cut shown in the drawing. Now set your saw to maximum depth and, cutting from

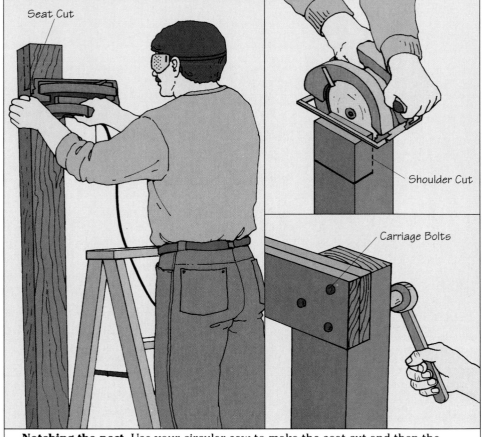

**Notching the post.** Use your circular saw to make the seat cut and then the shoulder cut. Finish the shoulder with a hand saw. Attach the beam with through-bolts.

top to bottom, make the shoulder cuts on the top and both sides. Finish the shoulder with a hand saw.

Attach the beam with through-bolts such as carriage bolts rather than lag screws. Apply siliconized latex caulk to the joints, and give the exposed end grains a healthy dose of preservative/sealer.

## Level Changes

Changes in levels should be comfortable. Each step should be no greater in height than a normal 7½-inch stair rise. Since the actual width of a 2x8 is 7¼ inches, often the easiest way to accomplish a level change is to place a 2x8 joist on top of the frame below.

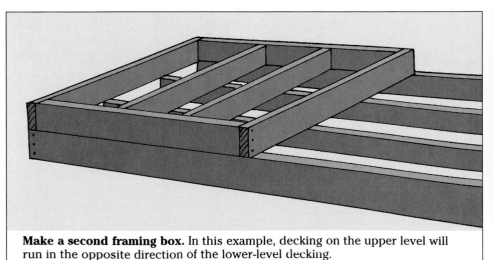

**Make a second framing box.** In this example, decking on the upper level will run in the opposite direction of the lower-level decking.

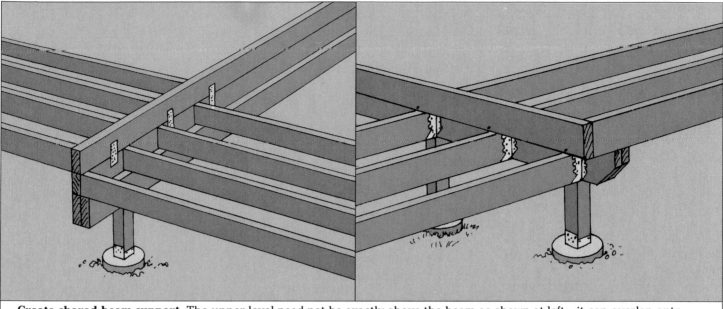

**Create shared beam support.** The upper level need not be exactly above the beam as shown at left—it can overlap onto the lower level a foot or so as shown at right.

When planning and building a change in level, take care that no decking pieces will be left unsupported at their ends. Here are two methods for making level changes:

**Make a second framing box.**
For small raised areas, the simplest method is to first build the main deck, and then construct a box of framing that sits on top of it. This is not cost-effective for larger raised areas, however, since there is double framing under the raised section.

**Create shared beam support.** The second method is to have the upper level partially overlap the lower, so that they share the support of the same beam on one end. The end joists of the upper platform can fall directly over the end joist and beam below or it can overlap the level below by about 12 inches. Each level will have its own support at its other end.

## Building Around Trees

Find out how quickly your tree will grow, and leave enough room for the next ten years or so. Either build a square block, or frame an octagonal shape, which will allow you to either cut out either an octagon or a circle. (To cut a circle in the decking, see "Decking Around a Tree," page 117.)

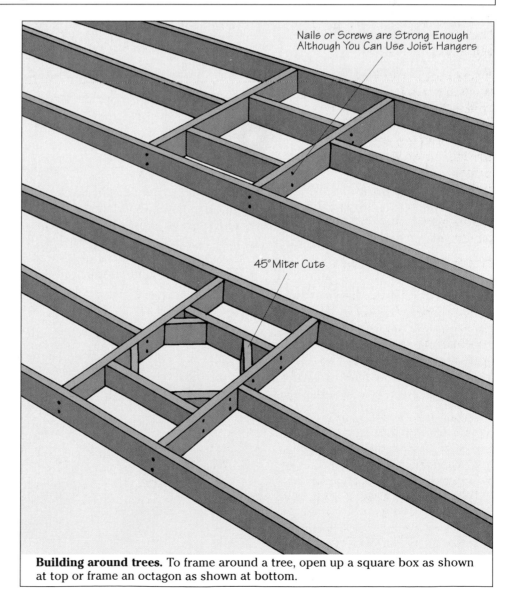

Nails or Screws are Strong Enough Although You Can Use Joist Hangers

45° Miter Cuts

**Building around trees.** To frame around a tree, open up a square box as shown at top or frame an octagon as shown at bottom.

# Chapter 9

# APPLYING DECKING, FASCIA, AND SKIRTS

Laying the decking is the most gratifying part of building a deck. The work proceeds quickly, because there is no heavy lifting and usually not a lot to figure out. With a helper or two, a fairly large deck can be covered in a day, even if it has some angles or pattern changes in it.

Similarly, installing fascia and/or a skirt can make a big difference in a short time. A couple of hours of careful cutting and installing will give your deck a well-crafted look.

There's no need to rush either the decking or the fascia. Here's where you want to take some pride in the way you straighten and join boards. If there's an unsightly board that needs to be replaced or recut, spend the extra ten minutes of labor now, and you won't have to look at that ugly spot for the next 20 years.

## Planning for the Railing

Choose your railing before you begin decking. See "Design Considerations," page 132 for possible designs. Then make sure your railing will go with your decking. If you want to install a permanent bench, see the designs in "Benches," page 145.

Most rail designs call for installing rail posts after the decking is laid. However, in some designs, especially those that incorporate benches, you must install posts or other supports before the decking.

For most designs, you have the choice: Either install the posts now and cut the decking to fit, or lay the deck and wait until later to notch for the posts while the deck boards are in place. In most cases, each method has equal number of drawbacks and advantages.

Another issue: Can you hang your decking over, past the joist (or fascia), or does your rail design demand that you cut it flush to the joists or fascia? If you are going to add a deck skirt that butts up under the decking and so takes the place of fascia, take this into account when you plan your decking overhang.

## DECKING OPTIONS

There are five decisions to make in choosing how to surface your deck. You'll have to choose a species of wood, its width and thickness, the decking pattern, how the decking will be fastened, and the fascia position.

## Type of Wood

The basic options for deck boards are green or brown pressure-treated, cedar, or redwood. Cedar and redwood are preferred for decking because they are much more attractive and less likely to split. But they are also more costly, and, unlike pressure-treated wood, are susceptible to rot if used in a situation where they will remain warm and damp for extended periods. So, if your deck is in a shady spot in a warm, wet climate, pressure-treated wood might be the better choice. See "Lumber Species," page 52 for a full discussion of your decking choices.

## Lumber Dimensions

For a description of decking board sizes, see "Size and Surfacing," page 50. Do not use boards wider than 6 inches (nominal), except as an occasional accent piece. The wider the

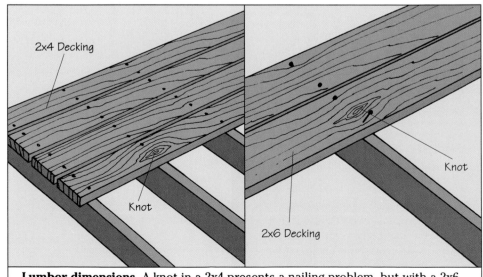

**Lumber dimensions.** A knot in a 2x4 presents a nailing problem, but with a 2x6, you can usually work around it.

board, the more it will expand and contract with the weather, causing cracks and working nails loose. So choose between 2x4, 2x6, or ⅝x6 deck boards.

The lumber easiest to work with is either 2x6 or ⅝x6. These two sizes will allow you to make progress faster and are less prone to twisting than 2x4s, which are often cut from smaller, younger trees. When you run into a knot in a 2x4 you've got a nailing problem, whereas a 2x6 is wide enough to give you room to work around a knot.

## Patterns

There's nothing substandard about simply running your decking parallel or at right angles to the house. Clean, straight lines of good lumber can look mighty fine. But if you want to liven things up a bit with a pattern, here are some options:

As a general rule, the more complicated it looks, the more work it will be. If there are a lot of angle cuts and if most boards are not of a uniform size (as with the simple or double 45-degree patterns), count on extra waste lumber. By contrast, the herringbone and especially the parquet designs may look complicated but actually have many square-cut boards of uniform length and so can be installed fairly quickly and with little waste. Keep in mind that on three sides of a typical deck—the sides that are not connected to the house—the decking will be "run wild" and cut off in a straight line after the boards are installed. So any angle cuts on those three sides will take no extra work.

If your deck is on different levels, the most natural way to develop a pattern is to run the decking on a different angle for each level.

**Alternating board sizes.** Another easy way to produce visual interest is to mix 2x6s with 2x4s. You can simply alternate the sizes, or you might follow every 2x6 with two 2x4s.

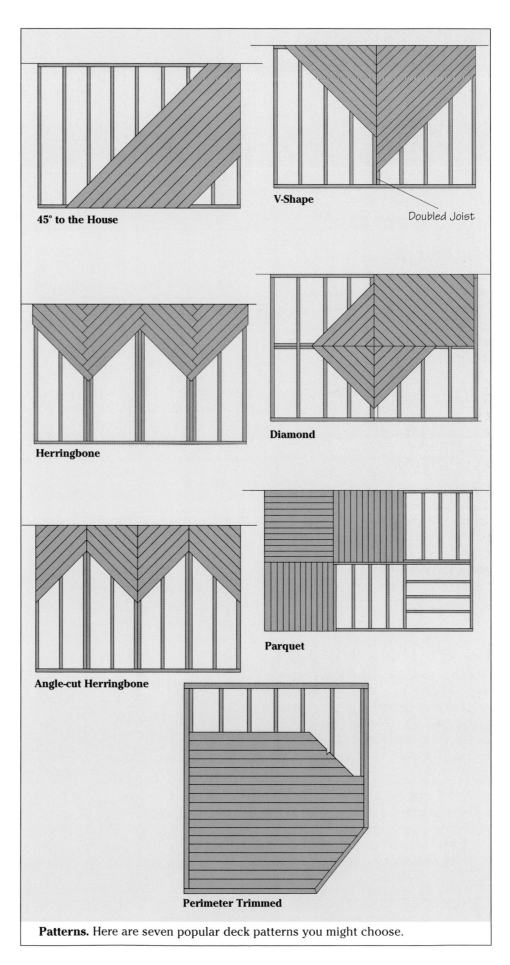

45° to the House

V-Shape

Doubled Joist

Herringbone

Diamond

Angle-cut Herringbone

Parquet

Perimeter Trimmed

**Patterns.** Here are seven popular deck patterns you might choose.

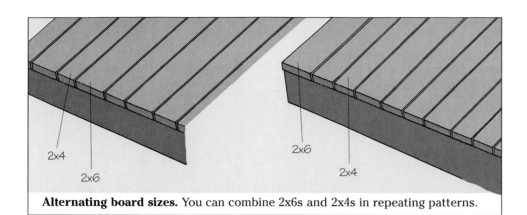

**Alternating board sizes.** You can combine 2x6s and 2x4s in repeating patterns.

## Method of Fastening

Good old nails work well—use galvanized deck nails, 16d for two-by lumber and 12d for ¾ lumber. However, screws hold better than nails and make it easier to correct mistakes and make future repairs. The extra cost of screws is a small price to pay for the extra performance you will get. However, some people will opt for nails because they don't like the look of a lot of screwheads. For a deluxe deck surface, you can go with fastening systems that have no visible nail or screwheads. For a full discussion of all these methods, see "Fasteners," page 57. Adhesives are not recommended for fastening decking.

## Fascia Position

The most common way to install fascia is to let the decking overhang the joists 2 inches or so, then tuck the fascia board under the decking. If you will be adding a skirt made of lattice or one-by lumber, it can be installed the same way. This method is easy, does not require precise finish carpentry, and is rot-resistant. (There are no places where water can be trapped against open grain.)

Another method calls for cutting the decking exactly flush to the edges of the joists, then using the fascia to cover both the joist and the decking. If you have good finish carpentry skills and are confident that your lumber won't twist or shrink over time, you may want to use this design. (Cutting the decking can be tricky here because your joists may bend a bit and not follow the chalk line you will make on top of the decking.) The place where the butt

ends of the decking meet the fascia can be trouble because water can sit here for days and seep into the open grain, leading to wood rot.

Fasten one-by fascia boards to the joists with 6d galvanized nails or 1⅝-inch deck screws. You can miter-cut the corners for a more finished look, but only if you have good carpentry skills and are sure about the stability of your wood. It only takes a small amount of shrinkage for a mitered joint to develop unsightly gaps. Butt joints are the safest method.

## CALCULATING HOW MUCH TO BUY

When figuring how much lumber to order, you could just figure out your square footage then order enough lumber to cover it, plus 15 percent for waste. And the lumberyard would love it if you did—they could unload the lengths that are overstocked. However, if you do that, you run the risk of getting many

boards of an inappropriate size, leading to waste and lots of butt joints. Though it may seem tedious, it is best to spend an hour or so making a drawing of your deck surface that shows every piece of decking. Then you can determine exactly how many boards of which length you will need.

To figure for decking that will be cut at a right angle, start with the width of the deck to find out how many deck boards (or rows of deck boards, if the deck is longer than the longest deck boards you can buy) will be needed. Divide the total width of your deck by 5.6 (for 2x6 or ¾x6 decking) or 3.6 (for 2x4 decking). This figure adds ⅒ inch for the space between boards. (Actually, the space will probably be ⅛ inch.) For example, a 12-foot-wide section of decking (144 inches) will require 26 2x6s (144÷5.6=25.71) or 40 2x4s (144÷3.6=40). Now that you know how many boards you will need, just order the correct lengths.

For angles, the matter is more difficult. Start by getting an estimate of how many total lineal feet of decking you will need: Divide the deck's square footage by 0.47 for 2x6 decking or 0.3 for 2x4. (One lineal foot of 2x6 with a ⅒-inch space covers 0.47 square feet; 1 foot of 2x4 with a space covers 0.3 square feet.) So, for example, a 12x14-foot deck will require 358 lineal feet of 2x6 (168 square feet ÷0.47) or 560 lineal feet of 2x4 (168÷0.3). Add 5 to 10 percent for waste, and you will have a good general figure. Now look at your drawing

**Fascia position.** Tuck the fascia under the decking (left), or bring it up flush to the deck surface (right).

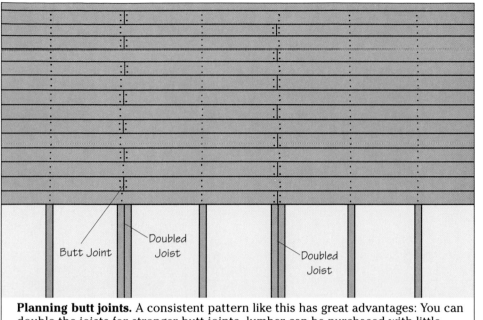

**Planning butt joints.** A consistent pattern like this has great advantages: You can double the joists for stronger butt joints, lumber can be purchased with little waste, and it has a pleasant, finished appearance.

Butt Joint

Doubled Joist

Doubled Joist

and at least estimate how many boards of which length you will need. When deciding on which lengths to buy, longer is usually better because cutoffs from long pieces can often be used for the shorter runs.

Sometimes it's possible to avoid making butt joints by buying extra long pieces of decking—18 feet or longer. These will probably cost more per foot, but they're worth it: You'll have fewer rot-prone butt joints, and the installation will be easier and quicker.

As we have mentioned before, the best way to get good lumber is to go to the yard and pick it out, piece by piece, yourself. This is especially true for decking.

**Planning butt joints.** If it's possible, plan the location of any butt joints. Unless it is part of a pattern, never place two butt joints right next to each other—it looks sloppy and unprofessional. In fact, it looks best to stagger joints at least two joists away.

# INSTALLING THE DECKING

Installing decking is most efficiently done in four stages. In the first stage, you sort through the boards and cut and seal ends that will be butted. The second task is to install starter boards. The methods for installing starter

boards vary according to the pattern you have chosen; we'll discuss each method. Once the starter boards are in place, you are ready for the third stage, laying down the decking. Finally, you'll make the final cuts, trimming overhanging boards and making any special cuts that might be necessary to fit your deck around posts or even a tree growing through your deck.

## Preparing the Boards

1 **Sort the boards.** Begin the installation process by getting organized and putting the boards where they'll be easily accessible. Sort through the stack of lumber and choose which side will be up for each piece. Weed out any boards with cracks, extreme crowns, or damaged visible surfaces. If you have a number of different lengths, stack them in piles according to length, so it will be easy to find the boards you want.

1 Organize and sort the boards.

## 2 Cut and seal ends that will be butted.

Where possible, you will run the boards wild — install them with their ends longer than they need to be, so you can cut them off later.

*THE PROS KNOW*

### Don't Worry About "Bark Side Up"

Some people — and books — will advise that deck boards be installed bark side up. (The "bark side" is the side of the board that faces toward the outside of the tree.) This is because if a *dry* board installed bark side up gets wet, it will swell into a shallow upside-down U shape. This shape will cause water to shed, which is good for the decking.

On the other hand, if boards are installed while still *wet* — either if the wood is "green" or if its pressure-treating liquid hasn't dried out — then the opposite can happen because the board will shrink as it dries out. A green board installed bark side up will dry into a U-shape, which means water will sit in a sort of shallow trough — meaning trouble for the deck.

But if you use good lumber — especially cedar, redwood, or Douglas fir — there is little chance of significant cupping. And a small cup is not really a problem especially because no end grain is exposed to the water. In fact, the U.S. Department of Agriculture has determined, after considerable testing, that it doesn't matter whether boards are laid bark side up or down. So unless you are using very wet or very dry pressure-treated lumber for your decking, just pick the side that looks the best, fasten it well, and treat it properly.

Board Installed Dry May Cup this Way

Board Installed Wet May Cup this Way

But wherever a board end needs to be butted — either against the house or against another board, you will, of course, need to make the cut before installing.

If the butted end requires a 90-degree cut, you may be able to just use the board as it comes from the lumberyard. But be careful here: check each end to make sure it is perfect, and watch out for those little cracks that often appear on the ends of boards.

Cuts to be butted will be either at 90 or 45 degrees. You'll save a lot of time by making as many of these cuts at one time as you can, rather than cutting a board to length and then nailing it in place before cutting the next

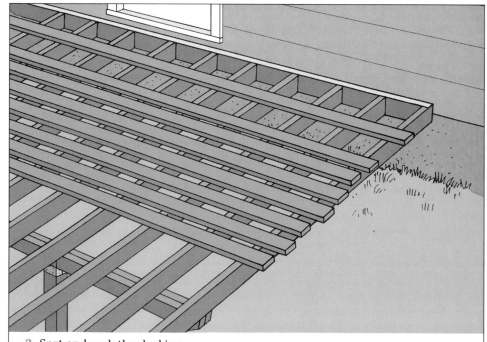

Sealer/Preservative

Angle Cutting Jig

2 Cut the ends that will be butted and coat them with clear sealer/preservative.

3 Sort and rack the decking.

board. A radial arm saw or a power miter saw will make this work a little easier but a circular saw will work just fine too. Use the techniques discussed in "Making Accurate Square Cuts" page 63, and "Cutting on an Angle," page 65.

While you've got them all cut and sitting there in a pile, it's a simple matter to give the cut ends a thorough coating of clear sealer/preservative. For a small amount of work, you will make your deck last longer.

**3 Rack some boards.** Carry the first ten boards or so to the deck and rack them, that is, arrange them on the deck in the order you will be using them. This not only makes them easy to reach, but also gives you a temporary surface to stand on while you install the decking.

## Installing Starter Boards

It's important the starter board or boards be correctly positioned. The way you do this depends on the pattern you are using. Here's how to position that important board for each of the various decking patterns:

**For decking parallel to the house.** Start at the house. Cut this piece exactly to length, making sure you

have the right amount of overhang, if any. (If you let it run wild and try to cut it later, your circular saw will bump into the house before it can complete the cut.)

The starter board should be perfectly straight. To make a guide line, measure out from the house, at both ends of the run, the width of the decking board plus ¼ inch, so that there will be a ¼-inch gap between the decking and the house to allow water to run past. Chalk a line on the joists. Attach the board flush up against this line.

If the side of your house bows in and out a bit, do not bend the board to follow the house and hope to straighten the decking out with later boards—that's a recipe for frustration. If a straight decking board looks bad up against the house, plane or cut the side of the board to make it fit better.

**For decking butted to the house.** If your decking runs at a 45-degree or 90-degree angle to the house, tack a spacer board — a piece of ¼-inch plywood works well — against the house, and butt the boards up to it.

**For decking parallel to the house.** Snap a chalk line for aligning the outside edge of the first deck board.

### THE PROS KNOW

#### Adjust Decking Spacing Near the End

You may be tempted to lay out your whole decking surface, to ensure that you don't end up with an awkwardly sized piece at the end. However, this is very difficult to do, because boards may vary slightly in width, and because it is difficult to know precisely what your gaps will be. Even if you could figure it out, it would be very difficult to, say, change your spacing by ⅟₁₆ of an inch so as to make things come out right. When you come to within three or 4 boards of finishing the decking, you can make adjustments in the spacing if necessary. Usually the last piece hangs over, so that you have room to play with.

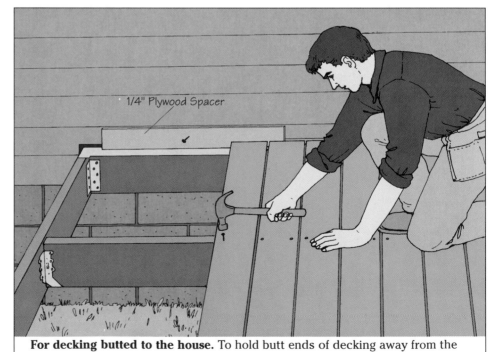

1/4" Plywood Spacer

**For decking butted to the house.** To hold butt ends of decking away from the house at a uniform distance, use a temporary spacer board.

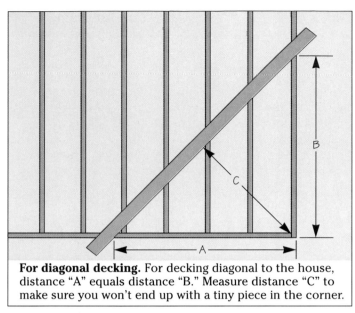

**For diagonal decking.** For decking diagonal to the house, distance "A" equals distance "B." Measure distance "C" to make sure you won't end up with a tiny piece in the corner.

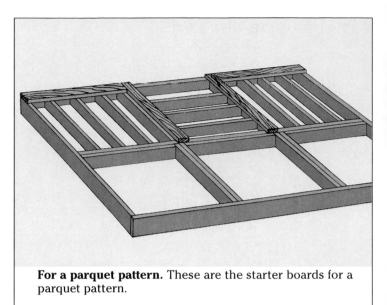

**For a parquet pattern.** These are the starter boards for a parquet pattern.

**For diagonal decking.** Don't start with a short piece in a corner. Instead, start with a straight board 72 inches long or more, and place it on a 45-degree angle by measuring equal distances from the corner of the joists (see illustration). Before you fasten it, measure from the center of the board to the corner of the joists, to make sure that your corner piece of decking will not be too small.

**For a parquet pattern.** Ideally, all the decking pieces for this design will be the same length; if you have to make one side of the deck longer than the other, this will be difficult. (Remember that you have boards going in both directions.) Tack at least four starter boards in place, as shown, and measure carefully to make sure that all your decking boards will come out right. Then drive the screws or nails home.

Or you can lay out all your decking boards, tacking some boards and just setting some in place with spacers, before you drive any nails or screws home.

**For a herringbone pattern.** If your herringbone pattern will be repeated twice, measure along both end joists a distance equal to one quarter the width of the deck as indicated on the drawing. Snap a chalk line across the joists at this point. Measure that same distance along the chalk line from the outside of both end joists. Mark those points to indicate the apex of your starter boards. For each section, cut two starter boards with a 45-degree angle on one end of each. One board will be a width's length longer than the other (5½ inches longer for 2x6 decking, 3½ inches longer for 2x4s).

**For a V-shape pattern.** Find the apex of a V-shape pattern in the same way as you would for a herringbone. The difference is, each pair of boards, including the starters, will be the same length with 45-degree angles cut on both ends.

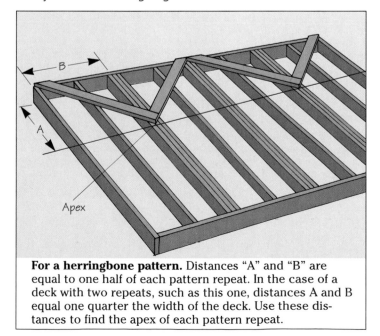

**For a herringbone pattern.** Distances "A" and "B" are equal to one half of each pattern repeat. In the case of a deck with two repeats, such as this one, distances A and B equal one quarter the width of the deck. Use these distances to find the apex of each pattern repeat.

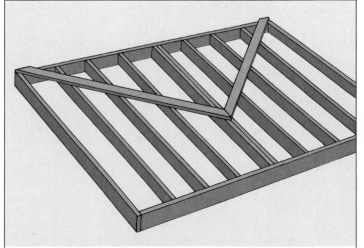

**For a V-shape pattern.** Starter boards for the V-shape pattern are of equal length and meet with a miter.

# Fastening the Decking

Now you're ready to make some visible progress. Deck fastening is best done on your knees, so you may want to get a kneeling pad or a pair of knee pads, if you tend to get sore.

**Position and cut the boards.** As you place each racked board into position, make sure the "wild" end hangs over far enough so that when you make your final cut you will be able to remove any little cracks at the ends of boards.

For angled, herringbone, and parquet designs, you will need to measure and cut at least some of the boards as you go. When possible, hold the boards in place and mark rather than using your measuring tape. For a true measurement, use spacers to give the board's true position as you hold it in place.

Think ahead to when you will make your final cut of the boards that are running wild, and make sure that your circular saw will be able to complete these cuts. This usually means that the one or two boards closest to the house need to be cut to exact length.

**Fasten with nails or screws.** Install only as many screws or nails as are necessary to keep each board firmly placed and straight. After all or a good chunk of the decking is in place, you can go back and install the rest of the fasteners . Doing it this way has advantages: If you discover that you have made a mistake or that a board has flaws, it will be easier to pull the board up before it is completely fastened. Doing most of the fastening at once can be easier on your back, because there is less getting up and down. And also, with all the boards in place, it will be easier to get your nail or screw lines straight.

Use nails as spacers. Aim for a gap of ⅛ to ³⁄₁₆ inch after the wood has dried out: If your decking is dry now, space with 16d nails; if it is wet, use 8d nails. In most cases you can just slip the nails in place, but wherever the boards are not tight, you will have to tack some down into joists — lightly, just enough so they stay put for a while. Some people find it simpler to tack all their spacer nails.

If you are fastening with nails, angle them towards each other for greater holding power. Make it only a slight angle, or your nail heads will not sit flat on the deck surface. Drive your screws or nails so that they barely break the surface of the board and their tops are flush with the top of the decking. If you are having trouble doing this without making indentations in the wood, use a nail set for the final whack or two. See "Nailing," page 68, and "Using a Power Drill or Screw Gun," page 70, for instructions on fastening without marring the wood.

Try to keep your nails or screws in a straight row, but don't worry about perfection. (Some people try to get straight lines by using a chalkline after the boards have been placed, but this usually makes things look worse, because those first nails or screws you put in will not be perfectly in line.)

**Predrilling to prevent splits.** Whether you are nailing or screwing, drill pilot holes wherever there is a chance that the decking will split: Usually, wherever the nail or screw comes within 3 inches or so of the end of a board. Take special care at the butt joints. Use a drill bit that is ⅔ to ¾ as thick as the shank of your nail or screw. Most of your predrilling can be done all at once, after all the boards are in place, so it really does not take much time.

At the butt joints, always drill pilot holes for all four nails or screw. Drill each at a slight angle toward the other board. Drive the fasteners with care, so as not to crack the boards with the head of the nails or screws.

Any small split that appears now will only get larger with time, so take care of it now. Remove the nail or screw and put it in a different location, drilling a pilot hole if necessary. Or

**Position and cut boards.** As you fasten boards, make sure there is enough overhang to allow you to cut off any imperfections on the ends of boards you run wild.

**Predrilling to prevent splits.** Always predrill where you will be installing screws or nails less than 3 in. from the ends of boards.

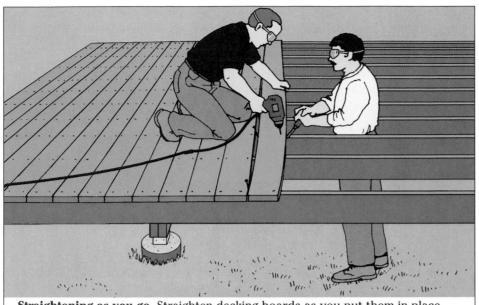

**Straightening as you go.** Straighten decking boards as you put them in place. Prying with a chisel often helps.

remove or move the board, if things look really bad.

**Installing with deck clips.** Deck clips or continuous deck fasteners allow you to install decking with no visible nailheads or screwheads. They are a bit more expensive than screws and take some extra time to install, but may be worth it if you have beautiful decking boards that you want to show off to their full advantage. Do not use deck clips if your decking is subject to substantial shrinkage or the boards will come loose.

There are several types of deck clips, each of which is installed a bit differently, and you should follow your manufacturer's instructions for correct installation. (See "Deck Fasteners," page 58.) Some require that you put nails into both the deck board and the joist, while others require nailing into the joist only. Some call for toenailing one side of each deck board; others do not. All of them automatically space the boards.

**Straightening as you go.** Every third or fourth board, test for straightness. You can do this by holding a taut string line along one edge of the board, or you can just sight down the board.

Inevitably, you will run into boards that are crowned and need to be bent into position. If you've got a really bad

piece, one that threatens to crack if straightened, don't mess with it — put it in the stack of boards to be returned to the lumberyard.

Most bends can be straightened just by pushing them into position; use a chisel or pry bar for the tougher ones. Start at one end and fasten as you proceed down the board — don't

nail both ends and then try to bend the middle in. Keep all your spacer nails in place until the whole board is straightened. Anchor the straightened parts of the board securely, with two fasteners at each joist if necessary, so the straight part doesn't get bent while you work. Sometimes it works to drive a toescrew through the edge of the decking board into the joist at an extreme angle. Don't do this with a toenail because if it doesn't work, you'll mar the decking when you remove the nail.

# MAKING THE FINAL CUTS

For the ends where you let your boards run wild, chalk a line for your final cut. Be sure to include the overhang, if any. Set your circular saw-blade about ¼ inch deeper than your decking thickness. If you feel confident about your skills, get into a comfortable position and make the cut freehand. See "Cutting with a Circular Saw," page 62.

Chalk Line

**Making the final cuts.** Snap a line and use your circular saw to cut the decking boards that you ran wild during installation.

To make extra sure the cut will be straight, tack a straight board onto the decking and use it as a guide. Be sure that It Is tacked well, so that the circular saw's bottom plate cannot slide under it.

## Cutouts for Through-Posts

If your posts continue upward to become part of your rail system, you will need to cut your decking to go around them. According to one school of thought, these cutouts should leave a ³⁄₁₆-inch gap between decking and post all around, so that water can run down the gap. Most would agree, however, that it is best to make these joints as tight as possible and then caulk them so they are water-tight. Tight fits certainly look better. For information about how to notch decking to fit around posts, see "Cutting Notches," page 66.

Hold the board in position up against the post to mark for the sides, and use your tape measure to mark for the depth. To make the cutouts with a circular saw, see "Cutting Notches," page 66.

## Decking Around a Tree

When installing the decking, run all the pieces as close to the tree as possible, even if this means cutting some boards at an angle. Once they are completely installed, it's time to figure how to make your final cut. For most trees you'll want to leave a gap of 2 or 3 inches between the tree and the decking boards.

There's no shame in making a square or octagonal hole—these can look quite charming. Cut the decking to slightly overlap the framing. See "Building Around Trees," page 107.

Figuring a circle is easy enough when there's nothing in the middle: Draw a circle with a compass made out of a nail, a string, and a pencil. (See "Laying Out and Cutting Curves," page 68.) But with that darn tree in the way, you can't establish a center point, and things get tricky. Common

sense, not mathematical methods, works best here. Use the framing (you can see it through the gaps in the decking) to establish four or eight equidistant points on the circumference of the circle. Perhaps a hula hoop will fit, or at least provide a frame of reference. You may have to use a garden hose or a piece of rope, and just take your time making *light* pencil marks until it looks right. Cut with a high-quality saber saw (see "Laying Out and Cutting Curves," page 68).

## INSTALLING SKIRTS

If you don't like being able to see under your deck, and if you don't want to plant and maintain shrubs,

cover it up with a deck skirt. Before you install the skirt, you must have something to attach it to, however.

## Framing for the Skirt

If you have already built your deck and now want to add a skirt, you may be in for a bit of extra work. The problem is to get a nailing surface for both the top and the bottom of the skirt. If your posts are tucked back under the deck, it will be difficult to attach skirt framing pieces to them. Essentially, you will have to construct a new frame and hang it from the deck.

**Framing for a skirt against posts.**
If your rim joists wrap around deck posts, you can frame for a skirt in two ways. The first way leaves the rim joists exposed. To do this, add

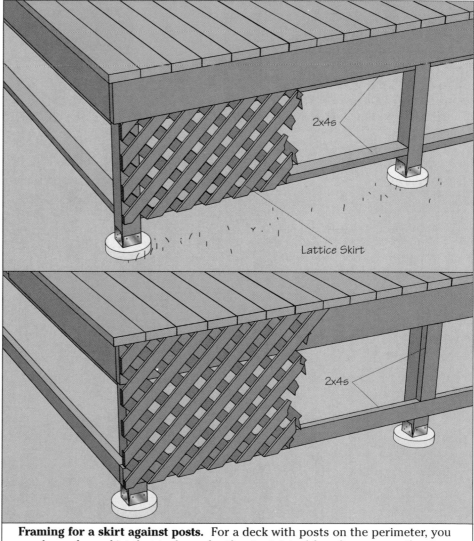

**Framing for a skirt against posts.** For a deck with posts on the perimeter, you can frame for a skirt that tucks under the rim joists (above) or covers the rim joists (below).

horizontal 2x4s that span between the inside edges of the posts. Tuck the skirt under the joists and attach it to the 2x4s ad the posts.

The second option covers the joists. Here you add a layer of 2x4 onto the outside of the posts and horizontal 2x4s spanning across the posts. (If your joists are covered with one-by fascia, you will also have to add 1x4 pieces, to come out flush.) Attach the skirt to the horizontal 2x4 at the bottom, to the vertical 2x4 pieces that are nailed to the post, and to the deck joist. This method works only when the railing is not attached to the side of the deck. The skirt will take the place of fascia because it covers the joist.

**Framing for a skirt when posts are recessed.** If your posts are recessed under the deck because the beam is cantilevered, you will need to hang a frame off of the deck. Nail lengths of 2x4 to the back side of the deck joists, so that half of the 2x4s width forms a lip below the joist. Attach vertical 2x4 pieces to this top 2x4 with 3x6-inch mending plates and 8d galvanized toenails or 2-inch angle-driven deck screws. Attach horizontal 2x4s to the bottom of the verticals, also using mending plates and screws. For stability, add support pieces that angle up from the bottom 2x4 piece to a structural element under the decking. Attach the skirt to the 2x4s.

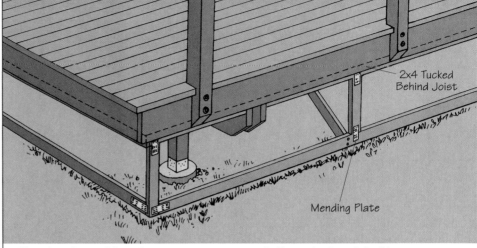

**Framing for a skirt when posts are recessed.** For a deck with hidden posts, hang a frame, using 2x4s and mending plates.

## Attaching the Skirt

Unless you live in a dry area, it is a good idea not to enclose the underside of your deck tightly: a skirt made of solid siding with no gaps could mean that the area under your deck will stay damp for long periods of time, which is not good for wood. So the best options are either lattice or vertical pieces of one-by with gaps between them.

To avoid rot, stop your skirting an inch or two above the ground. If you have dips or ridges in your yard, it looks best to straighten them out with a shovel and rake, rather than cutting the skirting to follow a wavy line.

**Lattice skirt.** You can make your own lattice, but it is much easier to purchase 4x8 foot sheets of ready-made

lattice. Unless you are sure that your skirt will not receive any abuse, choose heavy-duty lattice, the stuff that uses ⅜-inch slats for a total thickness of ¾ inch. Cut the lattice sections as you would sheets of plywood, and attach to the framing with 1¼-inch deck screws or 4d galvanized nails.

**Solid skirt.** The illustration shows 1x8 pieces, but you can use any size lumber — one-by or two-by — that looks good. In this configuration, the skirt pieces take the place of fascia.

Install the pieces much as you installed railing balusters, using a spacer (here the width of a one-by works well) to maintain consistent gaps between the boards and checking for plumb every four or five boards.

**Lattice skirt.** Here, a lattice skirt is tucked under the joists.

**Solid skirt.** Here, solid pieces are attached to the joists and are tucked under decking, taking the place of fascia.

# Chapter 10

# BUILDING STAIRS

Most decks need stairs, just so you can get to the yard from the deck without going through the house. But a stairway can add visual interest and usable space as well.

Unless it involves landings, the project of building a standard stairway is usually neatly separate from building the main deck; it can be added on after you have finished your decking and fascia. In fact, we recommend that you do not even dig the footings for your stairway posts until you have begun building the stairs. Descending deck levels that function as stairs, however, are framed along with the deck. (See "Level Changes," page 106.)

Stairs often present opportunities for dirt to sit in cracks and for water to seep into end grain, leading to rot. In this chapter, we will show you the strengths and weaknesses of various designs in avoiding water damage. Design carefully and choose very rot-resistant lumber.

**Parts of a deck stairway.** Figuring stairways takes a bit of calculating, but the elements of a stairway are few. *Stringers*, the angled-down pieces usually made of 2x12, support the *treads*, which are the boards you step on. *Risers*, pieces of one-by lumber that are laid on end to cover up the space between the treads, are optional for

exterior stairs. In fact, risers are often omitted from outdoor stairs because they inhibit drainage and create a joint where water can collect and cause rot.

## DESIGN OPTIONS

Once the deck is built, you may find yourself changing your mind about the stairway — how it should look and how you will use it.

If all you need is a way to get from the deck to the ground, a simple 36-inch-wide stairway with standard treads and risers will do just fine and can be built without much trouble, using only two stringers.

But a narrow stairway of standard steepness might look small and cramped next to your deck. And there are uses for a stairway other than going up and down: Kids play there; conversations take place there during parties; you can sit there and enjoy your lawn foliage. For these things to happen, it will help to have wider and/or deeper steps, and perhaps even a landing.

### Treads and Risers

Even if you have ¾ decking, it is best to use two-by lumber or thicker for the treads. Using ¾ lumber will require extra stringers, which is time-consuming and expensive. If you use 2x4s fasten them carefully; they sometimes have a tendency to wobble because their fasteners are close together.

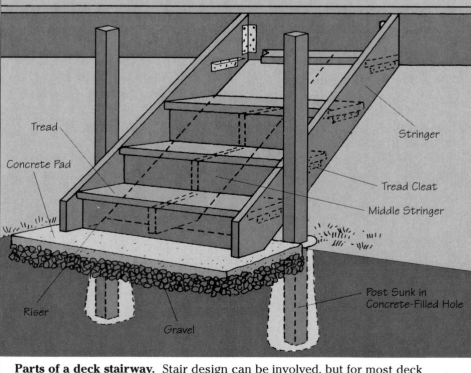

Labels: Tread, Concrete Pad, Riser, Gravel, Stringer, Tread Cleat, Middle Stringer, Post Sunk in Concrete-Filled Hole

**Parts of a deck stairway.** Stair design can be involved, but for most deck stairs, construction is quite simple.

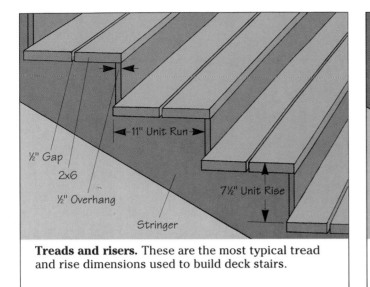

**Treads and risers.** These are the most typical tread and rise dimensions used to build deck stairs.

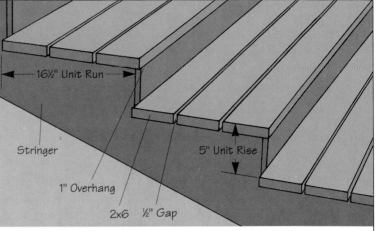

**A more gradual rise.** Adding a third 2x6 tread means that you will cut larger notches and the stringer will be more horizontal — two things that will weaken the stringer.

The most common tread for an exterior stairway is composed of two 2x6s or one 2x12. Typically, you'd leave a ½-inch gap between two 2x6s for a total tread depth of 11½. Then subtract about ½ inch for an overhang, and you get a typical step depth of 11 inches. The depth of one tread is known as the *unit run*. A typical vertical distance between steps, known as the *unit rise*, is 7½ inches. This configuration will satisfy nearly every local building department, will make for familiar and comfortable stair climbing, and won't take up a lot of space. This rise and run combination is very common for interior stairs.

**A more gradual rise.** But you're outside now, and chances are you have room to be expansive. By adding a third 2x6 to your tread, for instance, you will have 16½-inch unit runs (allowing ½ inch gaps between boards and a 1 inch overhang). This means you can successfully lounge on them, rather than sitting hunched over.

Steps with unit runs of more than 16½ inches need to be framed like a deck — a 2x12 stringer cannot support them. In fact, a stairway with 16½-inch treads will require extra bracing if it runs more than four steps.

If you want a more gradual stairway, you must decrease the unit rise as you increase the unit run. A general rule of thumb: twice the height of the rise plus the depth of the tread should equal between 25 and 27 inches. (On a normal stairway with a rise of 7½ inches and a run of 11 inches, 7½ times 2 equals 15; 15 plus 11 equals 26.) So with a unit run of 16½ inches, the unit rise should be about 5 inches (5 times 2 equals 10; 10 plus 16½ equals 26½.)

However, even if you follow these principles, be aware that deepening the treads and reducing the unit rise both make for an unnatural step pattern, one that people have to think about as they ascend and descend. This can be annoying if the steps get used a lot for normal business, such as back-door entry or taking the garbage out.

## Should You Add Risers?

Riser boards not only fill in the spaces between treads, but also add some support for the treads. However, think of this support only as a sort of bonus — it cannot take the place of a middle stringer. The front of the tread rests on the riser, but the rear of the tread is supported only by a nail or screw driven through the riser. If the stairway is built so that you rely on this nail to keep the tread from flexing, the riser will crack at this point — a common problem with underbuilt stairways. Risers make the steps harder to keep clean, and they create additional possibilities for rot, because water and dirt will collect and sit in the joints between riser and tread. So the main reason to add risers is appearance: If you want to block the view under your stairs or if you like the appearance of boxed-in stairs, then add them.

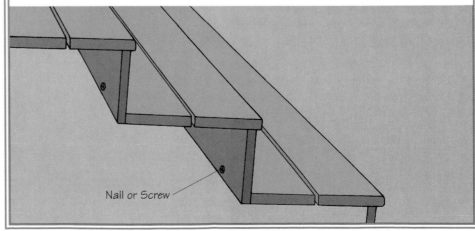

Nail or Screw

# Stringer Designs

Use 2x12s for your stringers. If you have two by treads that are longer than 36 inches, you will need a middle stringer. In choosing a stringer, you have three options: notched stringers, housed (solid) stringers, or for wider stairs, housed stringers with a notched middle stringer.

**Notched stringer.** The most commonly used type of stringer is notched, that is, cut out so that each tread can rest on top of it. However, there are disadvantages: Though cutting them does not require a great amount of work, any mistakes you make laying them out are difficult if not impossible to correct once the cuts are made. Notched stringers are prone to cracking, both while you are making them and in the years to come, because each "tooth" juts out on its own and can be easily broken off. And the entire top surface presents exposed end grain to the elements, making it very subject to rot.

However, there is a classic look to notched stringers and overhanging treads. And stairs that are wider than 36 inches will need a notched middle stringer anyway. With careful work, you can build a stairway with notched stringers that will last for decades.

Precut notched stringers are available at lumberyards. If the exact location of your bottom pad doesn't matter, you can adjust its position to accommodate store-bought stringers. Before buying, figure your rise and run, and make sure you won't end up with a bottom step that is more than ¾ inch different from the rest of the steps.

**Housed (solid) stringer.** A forgiving way to make a strong stringer is to attach tread cleats, also known as stair angles, to a solid piece of 2x12. This method actually takes about the same amount of work as does a notched stringer — you still must do all the figuring, and it does take time to install those cleats. But if you make a layout mistake with a solid stringer, it is easily corrected. And with no

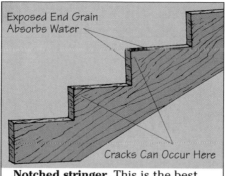

**Notched stringer.** This is the best design for preventing trapped water but notched stringers have their own weak spots.

notches sticking out, there is less chance that the stringer will crack.

However, there are disadvantages to a solid stringer. If the tread ends are not absolutely tight against the stringer, water can get trapped and seep into the end grain of the treads. If you use wood cleats (made of 2x4 or 2x2), they will also be subject to rot; metal cleats may rust if the galvanized finish is rubbed away.

If your stairway is wider than 36 inches, first cut a notched stringer, which will support the treads in the middle. Use it as a template for locating your tread cleats on the housed stringers: Just put it up against the housed stringer board and mark the positions for the cleats, as well as for the bottom plumb and level cuts.

If you want to install risers with solid stringers, attaching them will be a bit of a problem. You can screw through the solid stringer into the riser, but this joint will not be strong — a good kick will crack the riser. A better but more time-consuming method is to attach vertical 2x2 cleats to the inside

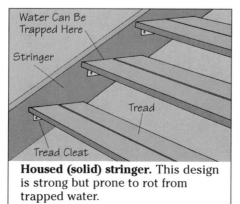

**Housed (solid) stringer.** This design is strong but prone to rot from trapped water.

of the stringers, and attach the risers to those.

**Stronger stringers.** For places where you need extra strength — for example, for stringers that are more than 8 feet long and have no underbracing — one solution is to laminate a notched stringer to a solid stringer.

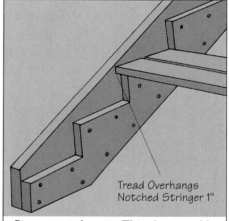

**Stronger stringers.** This design adds extra strength to the stringer. Here, a 2x10 is used for the notched stringer, so that the treads won't stick out past the solid stringer. If an interior notched stringer is needed, use 2x12.

# Bottom Landing Pad Designs

The stringers must have something solid to support them at the bottom and keep them from ground contact. This is usually provided by a pad that they rest on, made of concrete, masonry, or gravel. The pad can be a small area just under the bottom of the stringers or it can continue out to become a path.

This means that you must determine the location of your pad and construct it before you install the stairway. This will be time-consuming if you pour a concrete pad. A solidly constructed patio surface may be preferable to concrete: Not only does it look better in many situations; it can be installed relatively quickly, and you don't have to wait for the concrete to set.

In some areas, the building code may allow you simply to use a bed of gravel for the base. Though this is not as stable as concrete or masonry, it does drain water well.

Especially if you will not have rail posts attached to your stringers, it is a good idea to anchor the bottom of the stringers to the pad. If you are sure of where your steps will end, you can install J-bolts while the concrete is wet. But anchoring can also be done after the concrete is set and the stringers are in place. (See "Attach Stringers to Pad," page 128.)

## Railing Posts

If your stairway will have a railing, the railing posts should be installed in conjunction with the stairs. Whether set on top of footings or sunk into a concrete-filled hole, the posts add support to the stringers. In fact, if you have only two stringers, very solid posts can take the place of a pad, holding the stringers an inch or 2 above the ground. (Your inspector, however, may not accept this solution.)

On most decks, these posts will have the least amount of lateral support — they are braced only by the stringer. It is common to find stair rail posts that flop back and forth after a few years. For this reason, we recommend that

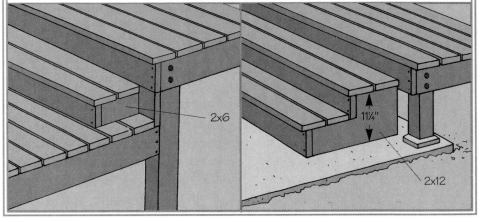

**Simple Box Steps**

If you only have one or two steps you can build simple box frames made of two-by lumber laid on edge. These designs work particularly well for transitions between deck levels. At left is a one-step design consisting of a three-sided 2x6 frame box. At right is a two-step design made from 2x12s. For an example of this type of step construction, see the "Low Rambler" deck plan on page 154.

rail posts be sunk into the ground, rather than resting on top of footings.

## Landings

If you have a long descent (say, more than 8 feet of stringer run), consider adding a landing, both for strength (you will shorten the stringer runs) and to break up a monotonous line. Landings usually require two or four footings with posts (depending on whether you can tie into the main deck or not).

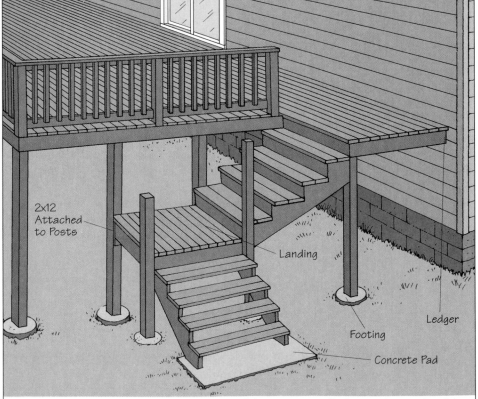

**Landings.** If your stairway must rise over 8 feet, it is usually best to have a landing.

## LAYING OUT THE STAIRWAY

When planning a stairway, your goal is to make the spacings of steps comfortable and make the space between each step the same as the space between every other step. Four measurements must be considered. You need to decide on a *unit rise*, which is the total vertical distance between the top of one tread and the top of the next tread, and the *unit run*, the horizontal distance traveled by each step. The unit run consists of the width of the tread minus any overhang or nosing. The *total run* is the horizontal distance traveled by the entire stairway; it is the sum of all the unit runs. Finally, the *total rise* is the horizontal distance from the deck to the ground. You'll usually have to experiment with rise and run

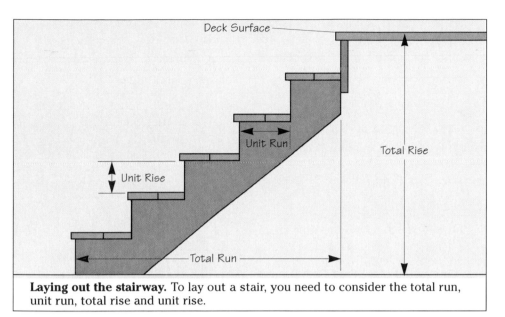

**Laying out the stairway.** To lay out a stair, you need to consider the total run, unit run, total rise and unit rise.

ratios to find the design that will give you safe, comfortable stairs. Here we'll walk through a typical case, to show you how to lay out your own deck stairs.

1 **Find the total rise.** If you knew that the ground below your deck is perfectly level you can find the total rise simply by measuring straight down from the top of the deck. But the ground may slope away from the deck. In addition, the ground may slope across the width of the stairs. So you need to determine where the steps will land and calculate the total rise from there.

The landing spot will determine the total run. You may have to engage in some trial-and-error before you find the exact total run that works with the unit run and unit rise you want. Here's a way to use your calculator to get a close idea of where the landing pad should be: Let's say you ideally would like a unit run of 11 inches and a unit rise of 7½ inches and your deck is 36 inches off the ground. Divide the total rise of 36 inches by the unit rise of 7½ inches to get 4.8. Round up to find that you will need five steps if the ground is level. One of those steps is the deck itself, so subtract it from the equation when figuring total run. Since you are shooting to make each step 11 inches deep, multiply 11 times 4 to find that your landing should be 44 inches from the

deck. (You might adjust the landing position later.)

Make two pencil marks on the edge of the deck to indicate the planned width of the landing pad. Let's say you want to build steps that are 36 inches wide, including the thickness of the stringers (but not including the overhang of the treads on either side of the stringers, if you are using notched stringers.) You'll probably want to make the landing pad a couple of inches wider on each side, so figure the pad will be 40 inches wide. From these marks, measure out the proposed total run, making

sure you are running your tape measure square to the deck edge. Drive a long stake into the ground at these points, making sure the stakes extend above the level of the deck. Plumb the stakes. (If these stakes are more than 60 or 72 inches tall, you will need to have a helper hold a level against them as you proceed, to make sure they are plumb.)

Have a helper hold one end of a string on one of the marks on the deck. Hang a line level on the string and run the other end to the corresponding stake. When the line is level, mark that level on the stake. Repeat the process to make a mark on the other stake.

Measure from the marks on the stake to the ground (or 1 inch above the ground, if you want your landing pad to be an inch higher than your yard). If the two measurements differ, use the shorter measurement as the total rise. You will make the landing pad level so that it rises above grade on the low side to compensate for the difference. Let's say for example you find the mark on the left stake as you face the deck is 40½ inches from the ground while the right stake 42 inches from the ground. The ground slopes away from the deck and down from left to right. Use 40½ inches as your total rise.

1 Because the ground near your deck may not be level, you need to use a line level and stakes to measure the total rise at the locations where both ends of the landing pad will be.

2 **Figure the unit rise and unit run.** Round the total rise off to the nearest whole number of inches and divide by 7. If you know you want short rises, you can start by dividing by 6 inches instead of 7. In our example, 40 divided by 7 equals 5.7. Round again to the nearest whole number. This tells you that to keep the unit rise and unit run you have in mind, you'll need six steps, including the one onto the deck, to cover the total rise.

You can adjust the unit rise or the unit run or both to accommodate your true total rise. In most cases, you will not want to change the planned unit run, because it is determined by the lumber you've chosen for stair treads. The easiest thing to adjust is the unit rise. Divide the total rise (40½ inches) by

six steps to get a unit rise of 6¾ inches. As mentioned earlier, two times the unit rise plus the unit run should equal between 25 and 27 inches. In our example, two times 6¾ inches plus 11 inches equals 24½ inches. Close enough.

Now it's easy to determine exactly where our stairs will land: Again, because one of the steps is the deck surface, your stringers will have five steps, each traveling 11 inches for a total run of 55 inches. Of course, because we have added a step since we figured our tentative total run, that's 11 inches further than our original total run of 44 inches. That's fine provided the ground is level where the stairs land; you can simply adjust the position of the landing pad. If the

ground continues to slope, you are better off increasing the unit rise, so you can stick with a four-step stringer. To do this, divide the total rise of 40½ inches by 5 (the rise includes the fifth step onto the deck). The calculator says that's 8.1, or for practical purposes, a unit rise of 8 inches. Two times 8 inches plus 11 inches equals 27 inches, also within the rule of thumb for stair design.

## INSTALLING THE LANDING PAD

A landing pad need only be a small slab, as thick as a piece of sidewalk. Extend your pad at least 2 inches to the front and rear of the bottom of the stringers, as well as at least 2 inches to each side. If you live in an area subject to frost, you need not go below the frost line; a small amount of movement due to frost heave will not damage the deck.

As mentioned, the landing pad can be concrete, a brick patio surface, or a gravel bed. If you choose concrete, you might prefer to postpone installing the landing pad until you lay out and cut the first stringer. Then you can put the stringer in position to test your calculations. (You can always cut a new stringer if you make a mistake, but a concrete pour in the wrong place is really tough to correct.)

**Concrete.** Concrete will make the strongest landing pad. The pad is small, so there isn't too much work involved, though waiting for the concrete to set may slow down your job.

First dig a hole deep enough to accommodate about 3 inches of gravel and 3 inches of concrete minus the elevation you have determined for your pad. Dig the hole wide enough to accommodate your 2x4 form and the stakes.

Construct a frame of 2x4 pieces laid on edge, reinforced with 2x4 or 1x4 stakes. This frame can be a permanent part of the pad (use pressure-treated lumber) or can be removed

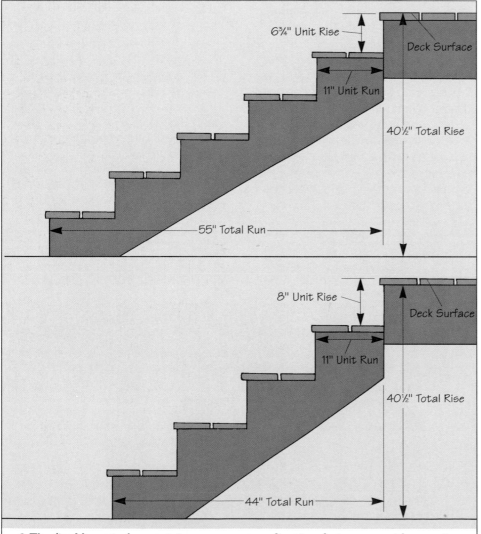

2 The final layout of your stair can vary according to what you consider most important in the design. Here are two designs for the same stair that use the same total rise and unit run while varying the unit rise and total run.

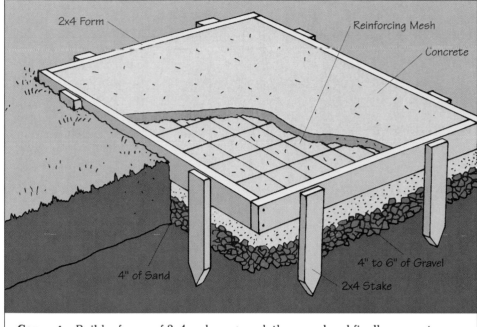

**Concrete.** Build a frame of 2x4s, place gravel, then sand and finally concrete.

are 2x6 pressure-treated lumber laid on edge or brick *soldiers* laid upright.

Fill with 6 inches of gravel, then 2 inches of sand, tamping each very firmly. You will have to tamp, then lay more, tamp again, until you have a surface that is nearly rock-solid and perfectly smooth and level.

Lay the bricks and pavers in the pattern of your choice. You can cut them using a circular saw with a masonry blade or with a brick set. Fill the joints by brushing in fine sand. Wet the surface with a fine mist from your hose, let it dry, and then fill again.

**Gravel bed.** The easiest landing pad is made with a simple bed of gravel. This is not as stable as concrete, but has excellent drainage, and if installed correctly can be surprisingly strong.

after the concrete has set. Make sure the frame is square and level.

Place the gravel and sand in the hole, tamping each down firmly with a piece of 4x4 or a hand tamper. If you will be using reinforcing wire mesh, cut it to fit loosely in the form (you don't want any wire sticking out after you've poured) and place it in the form, using four or five rocks to hold it up from the gravel a bit.

Pour the concrete and level it off with a piece of 2x4 that spans across your frame. Finish with a concrete finishing trowel, and use an edging tool where the concrete meets the frame. If you

like, give it a final brush stroke with a broom, for a skid-free surface (this can also hide some of the imperfections of your finishing job).

**Brick patio surface.** Before you install a brick surface, check with your inspector, who may require concrete. (Setting bricks or pavers in a bed of concrete is also an option.) Two tricks to getting a non-concrete patio surface that is strong enough: Tamp the gravel and the sand down extremely well and spread the load, so that the stringer rests on several pavers.

Choose a solid edging, so your bricks will not wander. Two common choices

Dig a hole 10 to 12 inches deep, fill part way with gravel, and install a frame made of pressure-treated 2x4 or 2x6 secured with stakes made of 2x4 or 1x4. Lay 3 to 4 inches of gravel, tamp it firm with a hand tamper or a piece of 4x4, and then lay the next layer. Don't lay the final 1½ inches until the stringers are in place.

When you build your stairs, spread the load, so your stringers will not dig into the gravel. Attach pressure-treated 2x4s to the bottom of the stringers, spanning from stringer to stringer. Rest this setup on the gravel, then fill in with the final 1½ inches of gravel.

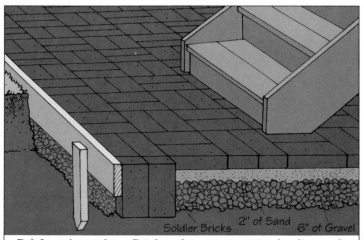

**Brick patio surface.** Brick makes an attractive landing pad and is easier to install than concrete.

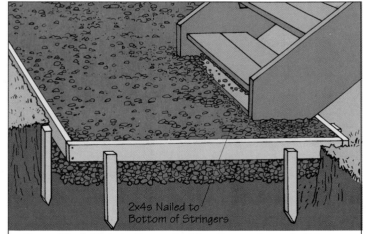

**Gravel bed.** This is the easiest landing surface of all to install. Gravel provides good drainage and is adequate in many situations.

# CONSTRUCTING THE STAIRS

**1 Estimate how long your stringer needs to be.** To buy the stock for your stringers, you'll need a rough estimate of how long they need to be. Here's a quick method: On a framing square, measure the distance between your unit rise on one side to the unit run on the other side. This will tell you how far the stringer has to travel per step. Multiply this number by the number of steps you will have, plus one (to be safe), and you will have a good rough estimate of how long your stringer needs to be. For example, a step with a unit rise of 7 inches and a unit run of 11 inches will travel 13 inches per step. If there are five steps, the stringers will need to be about 11 feet 3 inches long.

**2 Lay out the first stringer.** Using a framing square, transfer the rise and run to a 2x12 with the crown side up. It helps to mark your square with tape — one piece for the rise and one for the run. Mark the stringers lightly in pencil, because it's easy to get mixed up and have to start over again.

Start at the top of the stringer — the end that will meet the deck. When you come to the bottom-most step, shorten the rise by the thickness of the stock you are using for the treads.

Cut the top and bottom of this stringer — you don't have to cut the notches yet — and hold it up to the deck in the position where it will be attached when you build the stairs. Rest the bottom end of the stringer on the landing pad or a piece of lumber that simulates the height your landing pad will be. Check that the lines for the treads are level.

**3 Make the stringers.** For a notched stringer, cut first with a circular saw. Because you are entering the board at an angle, you may need to retract the circular sawblade guard at the start of each cut, to avoid making a wavy line. Be mindful of resting the bottom plate solidly and evenly on the surface of the board as you cut.

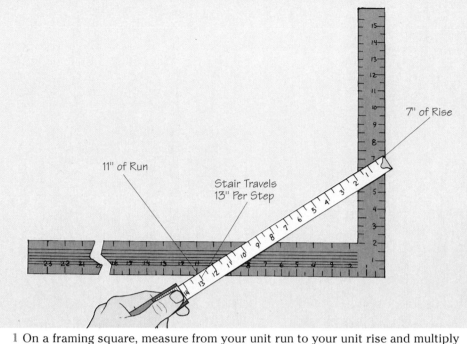

11" of Run
7" of Rise
Stair Travels 13" Per Step

1 On a framing square, measure from your unit run to your unit rise and multiply by the number of steps plus one to estimate how long your stringer will be.

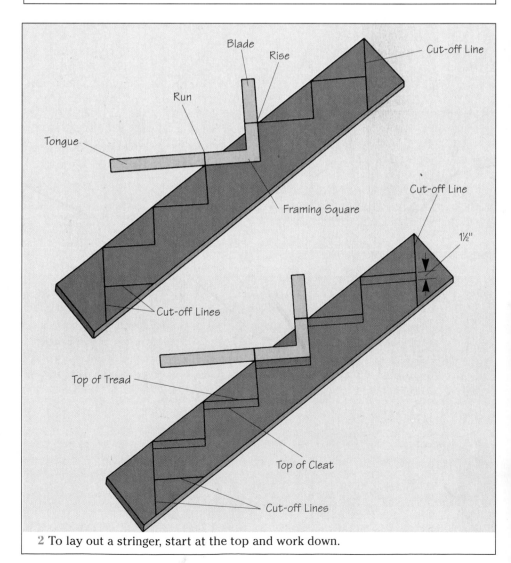

Blade
Rise
Run
Tongue
Cut-off Line
Framing Square
Cut-off Line
1½"
Cut-off Lines
Top of Tread
Top of Cleat
Cut-off Lines

2 To lay out a stringer, start at the top and work down.

It's okay to go past your lines a little (¾ inch or so), but only if the board face you are looking at will not be visible once the stairway is completed.

Finish the cuts with a hand saw, holding the blade at 90 degrees to the board, so that you don't get overlapping cut lines on the other side of the board.

Brush on a thorough coat of sealer/preservative at all your cuts — let plenty sink into all the end grain. Take care not to bump the "teeth" after cutting — they are very fragile until the treads get attached to them.

After you have cut the first stringer, use it as a template for the other(s). If you are going to have two housed stringers with a notched stringer in the middle, cut the notched one first and use it to mark the housed stringers.

For a housed stringer, first make the cuts at the top and the bottom. Position the tread cleats (also called stair angles), drill pilot holes, and fasten with 1¼-inch lag screws.

**4 Locate the posts and dig postholes.** Temporarily attach the top of the stringers to the deck, and rest the bottom on the landing pad or something that simulates the height

THE PROS KNOW

### Attach the Stringer Firmly to the Deck

You may have to make special preparations in order to have plenty of nailing surface for attaching your stringers to the deck. This is more often a problem with notched stringers than with housed stringers. One solution is to widen the deck framing by adding a piece of two-by lumber that spans from post to post. (See "Attach the top of the stringers to the deck," page 128.)

Another solution may be to attach under the deck, if there is a conveniently located joist running parallel to the stringer.

If you choose to do this, be sure to cut the stringer accordingly — don't cut off the upper end as you usually would. When you attach to the joist, pepper the joint with deck screws.

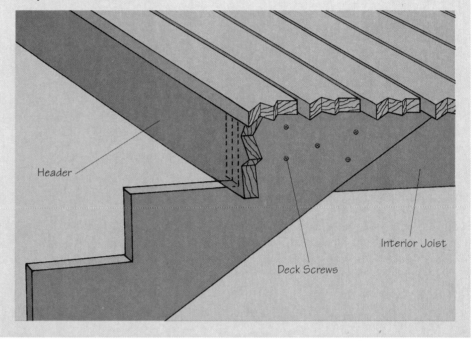

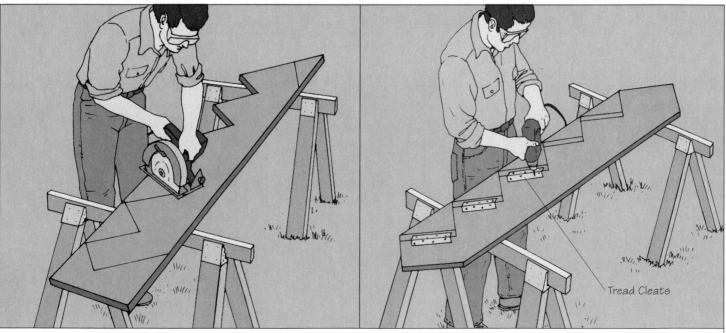

**3** Use a circular saw to cut the notches for a notched stringer, finishing with a hand saw. For housed stringers, predrill and attach the metal stair angles with screws.

of your landing pad — 1x4s will probably do fine.

Determine how far apart your stringers will be. If you have notched stringers, remember that the treads will overhang past them on both sides — 1½ inches is a good overhang. Use a framing square to make sure the stringers are square to the deck.

Mark for the post or footing hole. If you have notched stringers, align the front of the posts with the second or third rise cut on the stringers.

Move the stringers out of the way. Follow the instructions in Chapter 7 "Installing Footings," for digging post-holes or installing footings. If you are installing your posts directly in holes, do not pour the concrete yet — you can wait until the stairs are completed.

**5 Attach the top of the stringers to the deck.** For a firm connection, you may have to beef up the deck framing. Often there is not enough rim-joist surface, so the solution is to add a piece below the rim joist. Most often, this piece will span between two posts.

To attach a stringer to the face of a rim joist, drive nails or screws through the back of the joist into the stringer. If you are installing a notched stringer, you can also attach it with an angle bracket, as shown; it will be covered up by the treads. On a housed stringer, however, such a bracket would be visible, so it is best to do plenty of back-screwing through the joist into the stringer instead.

**6 Attach the bottom of the stringers to the pad.** There is not usually a need for great strength here, since the stairway itself will be quite stable. You can wait until most of the treads are installed before making this connection. There are several methods that work well. You can attach angle brackets to concrete or masonry using lag shields, set J-bolts in the concrete while it is wet and

4 Use stringers to locate the posts flush to the second or third rise cut on the stringers.

Framing Square

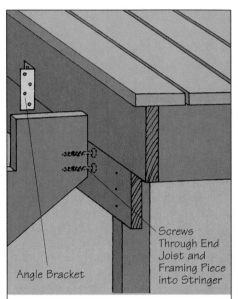

5 Attach the top of the stringers to the deck. One way is to add a framing piece below the joist.

Angle Bracket

Screws Through End Joist and Framing Piece into Stringer

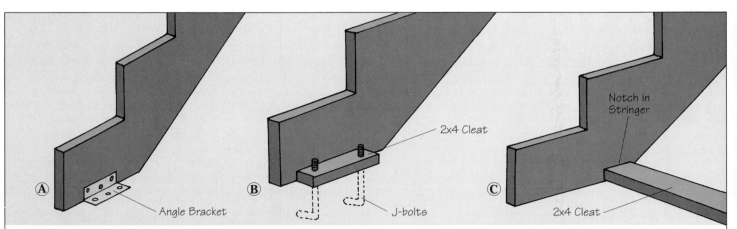

6 Here are three effective ways to attach the stringers to the landing pad. (A) An angle bracket can be installed on masonry, or after concrete has set, using lag shields. (B) J-bolts set in wet concrete support a 2x4 cleat. (C) Notching the stringer allows for installing a 2x4 cleat, which can be fastened to the pad with lag screws and shields.

Ⓐ Angle Bracket

Ⓑ 2x4 Cleat    J-bolts

Ⓒ Notch in Stringer    2x4 Cleat

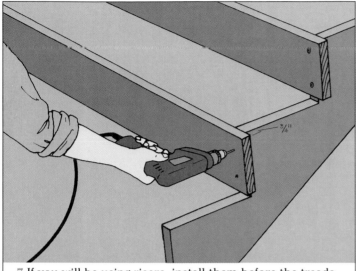

7 If you will be using risers, install them before the treads. It's a good idea to run the risers ¾-inch past the stringers on both sides.

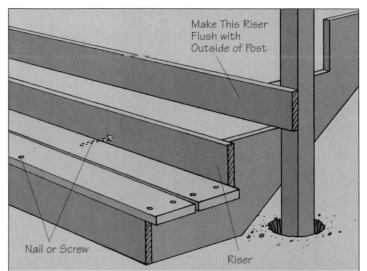

Make This Riser Flush with Outside of Post

Nail or Screw

Riser

8 Between the stringers, drive one nail or screw through the bottom of the riser and into the rear tread; drive another through the top of the front tread into the riser.

attach a wood cleat to them after the concrete has set, or notch the bottom of the stringers and install a 2x4 cleat attached to the pad with masonry nails or with lag screws and shields.

Make sure the stringers are square, and measure to see that they are exactly parallel. Unless you installed J-bolts while the concrete was wet, use a masonry bit to drill holes for lag shields.

7 **Install risers.** If you will be using risers, install them before the treads. The top of each riser must be flush with the horizontal stringer cut, but there can be as much as a ¾-inch gap at the bottom. (So if your rise is less than 7¼ inches, you will have to rip 1x8 to fit; for rises 7¼ to 8 inches, there is no need to rip.)

Risers are often installed flush to the outside of the stringers, but this design can lead to problems if your cuts are not perfect or if the boards shrink. If you let them overlap the stringers by ¾ inch or so, you will avoid these problems.

Drill pilot holes for your nails or screws. This is a very visible area that is quite susceptible to cracking.

8 **Attach rail posts and install treads.** Attach the rail posts to the stringers so they are plumb in both directions. Drive 3-inch screws or 16d

9 Plumb and brace the posts before pouring concrete into the postholes.

galvanized nails through the stringer into the post, or use carriage bolts.

For a housed stringer, cut the treads to fit exactly, drill pilot holes, and attach from underneath with 1¼-inch lag screws.

For a stairway with notched stringers, a good design is to have the treads run past the stringers 1½ inches. At least one of the treads will have to be notched to fit around the posts.

Attach the treads to the stringer with 3-inch deck screws or 16d galvanized nails. Drill pilot holes when you attach to the outside stringers.

If you have risers, attach the risers to the treads between the stringers, as shown.

9 **Pour concrete for rail posts.** Brace the post and check for plumb in both directions, and fill the hole with concrete.

# Chapter 11

# ADDING RAILINGS AND BENCHES

Whether you are standing on the deck or at a distance, the railing is the most visible part of most decks. The railing greatly influences the overall appearance of the deck, giving it either vertical or horizontal lines, an open or closed appearance, a polished or rustic look. Even more important than aesthetics, railings must be designed for safety. So choose your design carefully.

In this chapter we will present 11 railing designs. It is likely that you will run into another design you like. Chances are, it will be a variation on one of the designs presented here, and you will be able to adapt our instructions to fit your railing.

A built-in bench can take the place of a railing. This chapter will also show you some options for adding benches.

Because it is the last part of a deck job, you may approach your railing as something you just want to get over with. But if you give yourself time, you may find that railing work is the most enjoyable part of deck building. There's no heavy lifting, no messy digging; you are rarely on your knees or working in an awkward position. And with a few simple techniques you can produce a structure that looks professional and handcrafted, something you can point to with pride for years to come.

## MATERIALS

Railings can be made with factory-milled balusters and newels, cast metal, cables, plastic tubing, clear acrylic panels, and so on. In this book,

we will concentrate on the most popular and easiest-to-use railing materials—dimensional lumber. One-by, two-by, and four-by materials can be cut and assembled in a wide variety of combinations.

## Lumber

It is usually best to have the railing materials match the decking and fascia, but this is not a hard-and-fast rule. Sometimes it works best to think in terms of matching the railing with the house, since the railing is a vertical line that is seen with the house as a backdrop. On a Colonial or Victorian house, for instance, lathed spindles and fancy newels may look best, especially if they can mirror elements in the house.

And there's no rule that says you can't paint all or part of the railing. If you have an unpainted deck against a painted house, you already have wood and paint in combination, and there's no harm in continuing that pattern. You may want to paint your top cap, to protect it from the weather.

When choosing lumber, the railing is where you want to be the pickiest. Not only do these pieces get handled, they also provide nooks and crannies for water to sit and seep in. Splinters on a rail can be downright dangerous, especially for kids. And a railing that is rotting can be a hazard as well.

Cedar and redwood look best and splinter least. However, because they get handled and are very exposed to the weather, plan on treating railings made of these materials at least every

other year, unless you want them to "go gray."

Pressure-treated lumber of high quality—number one lumber that is brown pressure-treated may be a good choice—can also work, but choose carefully to avoid splinters and cracks. If you allow your pressure-treated lumber to go gray, you will almost certainly end up with splinters. See "Lumber Species" on page 52 for more information.

Precut 2x2 balusters are widely available. However, if you'd rather have different lengths, don't change your railing design just to accommodate their size—with a power miter box and an easily made jig, you can gang-cut 100 2x2s in an hour. It can sometimes be a problem to find good-looking 2x2s, because they often twist if not stacked well. If you don't like the ones you see, go to another lumberyard.

In some areas you can purchase lumber that has been milled to accommodate certain railing designs. Most commonly, you can purchase a top cap that has a 1½-inch-wide groove in the bottom to accommodate 2x2 balusters.

## Fasteners

When things come loose on a deck, it is usually at the railing. There's a lot of exposed joinery, and the railing gets leaned on and bumped against. So plan for a railing that is as strong as possible at all points.

Unfortunately, there are few specialized railing hardware pieces, and they

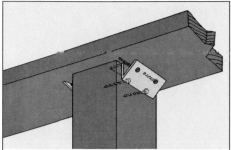

**Fasteners.** You can attach railings to posts with clips that are screwed through the side of the post before the rail is installed and then screwed at an angle through the bottom of the rail.

are not as effective as joist hangers are for the framing. Metal connectors for attaching rails to posts are unattractive, provide a place for moisture to collect, and may even rust. There is a post-to-railing clip which is more helpful; it allows you to connect the top cap to the post without visible nails. Wood cleats can be used to add extra nailing surface and better support than toenailing, but these also look unprofessional and may be susceptible to water damage.

So make the most of standard fasteners. If possible, through-bolt the posts to the joists, rather than using lag screws. Drill pilot holes for all nails or screws that are near the end of a board. Use 3-inch deck screws or 16d galvanized nails rather than anything smaller. And take extra care at those places where you have to fasten by toenailing or screwing at an angle.

# RAILING BASICS

All railings use some, but not necessarily all, of the following components. *Posts* are structural members, usually made of 4x4, that provide lateral strength (that is, they keep the railing from wobbling from side to side). *Balusters* are the numerous vertical pieces, often made of 2x2 or 1x4, that fill in spaces between the posts and provide a sort of fence. *Bottom rail* and *top rail* pieces run horizontally between the posts, and are either flat or on end; often the balusters are

## Designing Railings that Won't Rot

Here, as elsewhere on a deck, there are two considerations to designing a railing that won't be damaged by water: You want to minimize end-grain exposure and eliminate places where water can puddle.

The tops of posts and balusters will soak in plenty of water if they are exposed. The best solution is to cover the end grain with a top cap. A second-best technique is to cut the tops off at a 45-degree angle, so most of the water will run off.

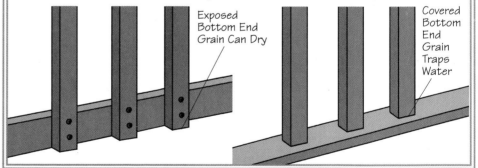

*Top Cap Protects End Grain*

*Angled Cuts Help Water Run Off*

*Horizontal End Grain Absorbs Water*

At the bottom of posts and balusters, it is best to leave the end grain exposed. Little water will seep upwards, and they will be able to dry out easily.

The most common location for standing water is on top of the bottom rail, especially if it is laid flat. If you choose a design that includes a flat-laid bottom rail, make sure your wood is rot-resistant.

*Exposed Bottom End Grain Can Dry*

*Covered Bottom End Grain Traps Water*

attached to them. Some railings do not have vertical balusters, and use several horizontal rails instead. The *top cap* is a horizontal piece of lumber laid flat on top of the post and top rail, covering the end grain of the post and providing a flat surface wide enough to set things on.

## Complying with Code

Since this is the thing that's easiest to check, your inspector will probably measure your railing to make sure it's up to local code. These codes are rarely unreasonable. In fact, to make

sure you have a safe rail, you may want to build your railing according to even stricter standards. Railings are usually required whenever the deck is 30 inches above the ground or higher.

You will probably be required to have a railing that is at least 36 inches high—some codes may go as high as 42 inches. If the deck is more than 8 feet high it is a good idea to build a 42-incher or so, since a 36-inch railing will only come up to an adult's beltline.

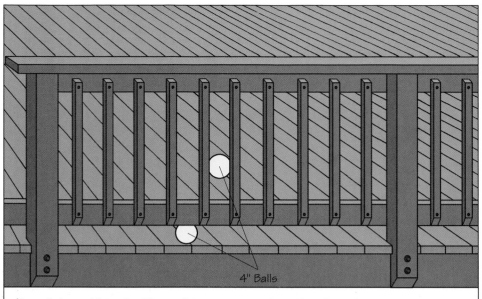

**Complying with code.** This railing meets a code calling for a 4-inch maximum opening.

Codes typically have a maximum allowable distance between railing members, to keep small children from falling through or getting their heads stuck between the rails or balusters. Most commonly the maximum distance is 4 inches. This means that there should be no place where a 4-inch ball will fit through the railing. Some codes call for a smaller maximum opening at the bottom of the railing.

There may be specific requirements about posts and fasteners, to ensure your railing is strong. This can get complicated with all the designs there are, but here's one good rule: If your railing is supported by solidly attached 4x4 posts, the posts should be spaced no more than 8 feet apart.

# DESIGN CONSIDERATIONS

**Matching decking overhang with railings.** The first thing to think about in selecting a railing design is how the railing will work with the decking. The basic rule is this: If you have balusters but no bottom rail, so that the balusters are attached to the joists or fascia boards, then the decking must be cut flush to the joists. Otherwise you would have to make hundreds of little cutouts to make room for all the balusters. But if you are using several rails instead of balusters or if you have a bottom rail to attach the balusters to, then the decking can overhang the joist (and you'll have to cut the decking out for the posts only).

**Choosing a cap width.** If your top cap will butt into the posts, it will be the same width as the post—which usually means it will be a 2x4. If you want a wider cap (for resting drinks or potted plants on), use a design that places the cap on top of the post.

A cap that sits on top of the posts should overhang the pieces it rests on by ¼ to 1½ inches on each side. Any more, and the cap could cup with time; any less looks unfinished. Most railing designs will allow you to choose either a 2x6 or a 2x8 for a top cap. The 2x8 may look a little clunky, especially on a small deck, but has lots of room for holding stuff.

Whatever design you choose, select the very best pieces of lumber for your top cap. Water sits on it, it gets looked at a lot, and you won't be able to straighten it out much during construction.

## Post Designs

**Notching posts.** It is possible to simply attach a rail post to the edge of the deck without notching the post; if done well it will be plenty strong. But

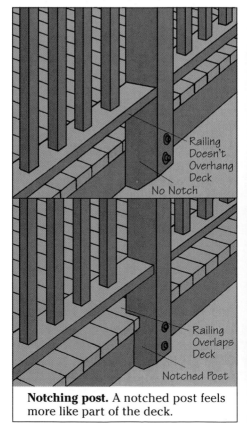

**Notching post.** A notched post feels more like part of the deck.

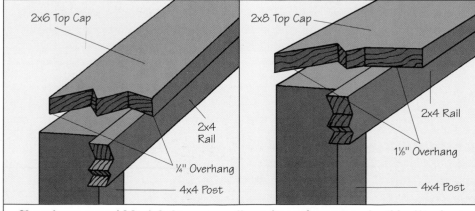

**Choosing a cap width.** A 2x6 top cap will overhang the post and rail by ¼ inch on each side while a 2x8 will create 1⅛ inches of overhang.

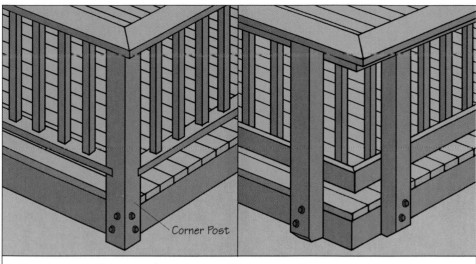

**Corner posts.** You can turn a corner with or without a corner post.

your design, follow the steps that apply to your railing, in the order recommended by your specific design instructions.

**Balusters and top rail only.** This is the simplest and least costly design. It is suitable for smaller railings only, because it lacks posts and a flat-laid top cap, both of which give lateral strength to other designs. Of course, the closer the balusters are to each other, the more strength you gain. If it is very long, this railing can have a monotonous appearance, since all the vertical lines are the same width.

Avoid having any butt joints in the top rail—a 2x2 is not wide enough to adequately nail both butted ends. You will not be able to set any drinks or potted plants on this railing.

To construct, install the balusters for each end of the rail, and attach the rail. Then fill in the middle balusters. Screws work better than nails, because the uncompleted railing will wobble quite a bit if you pound on it.

unless you have a generous deck overhang, the railing will look as if it is detached from the deck, and there will be an unsafe-looking opening at the bottom of the railing, since the railing won't be over the deck.

**Corner posts.** When the railing sections fit between the posts, you will probably need to set posts exactly on the corners, which means a double notch cut at the bottom if your other posts are notched. Other designs allow you to avoid making a corner post. For instructions on making a double notch cut on a post, see "Cut and Notch Posts," page 138.

**Through-post construction.** If you have posts that rise up through the deck to become part of the railing, you can't use designs that call for attaching balusters to the side of the deck. The other designs described below work just as well with through-posts as with added-on posts. Cut all the posts to the proper height before attaching the railing pieces.

# ELEVEN DESIGN CHOICES

From hundreds of possibilities, we present here 11 railing designs. Though some may appear elaborate, they are all within the reach of a capable homeowner. If you want to create your own design, you can mix things

up, combining aspects of several railings into something that is your own.

For each of the 11, we give some instructions that apply especially to that particular design. A section of step-by-step instructions follows this section on design. However, the designs do not all use all those steps, nor do they all follow the steps in the same order. So once you have chosen

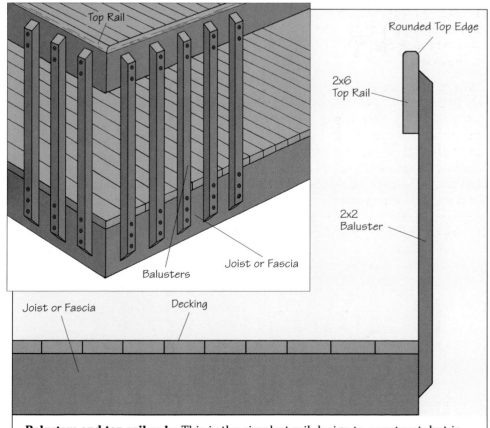

**Balusters and top rail only.** This is the simplest rail design to construct, but is suitable for small railings only.

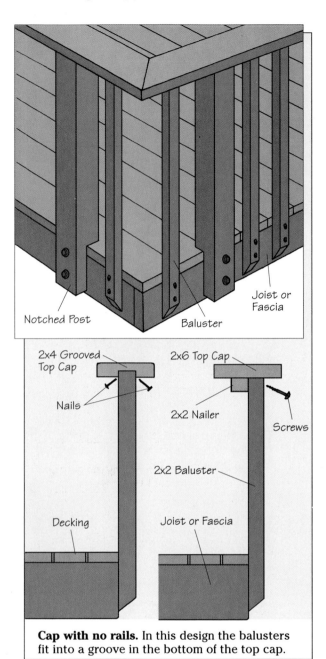

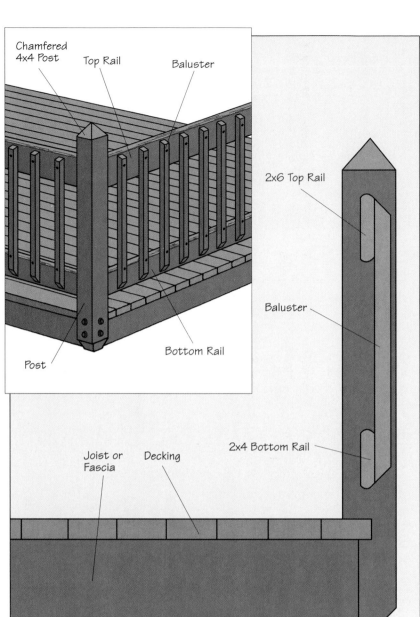

**Cap with no rails.** In this design the balusters fit into a groove in the bottom of the top cap.

**Two rails with no cap.** This design has a clean look but provides no place to set drinks.

**Cap with no rails.** This has the vertical feel of the first design, with the added strength of posts and the usefulness of a top cap. The easiest way to build this railing is to use a cap with a factory-milled groove for the 2x2 balusters to fit in. However, these caps come only in 3½-inch widths. If you want to set out some flower pots, use a 2x6 for the top cap, and attach a 2x2 nailer underneath it. Screw the balusters to the nailer.

Install the posts every 72 inches or so, and lay the top cap on them. Install the nailer between the posts (if you're not using the cap with a groove), and attach the balusters.

**Two rails with no cap.** Here horizontal lines are as strong as the vertical lines. The lack of a top cap gives a clean look, but affords no space for resting drinks.

For the chamfer, cut on the top of the posts, see "Post Top and Newels," page 140. Notch and attach the posts. Attach the top and bottom rails, then the balusters. Or build the baluster-and-rail sections ladder-style.

**Horizontal rails.** Horizontal lines dominate in this quickly constructed railing. You can square-cut and butt the ends of the rail, as shown, or miter them for a more finished look.

The top rail can be made of 1x6, if you want a large overhang on a 2x6 cap. Unless your posts are no more than 48 inches apart, the other rails should be made of two-by lumber. If local codes require spacing of less than 8 inches, either add a rail or make the lower rails of 2x6.

Install posts, then rails, then the cap.

**Two rails with balusters.** This has the look of ladder-style sections between posts, but the rails are continuous rather than butted to the posts. We show this one with posts that are not notched at the bottom—

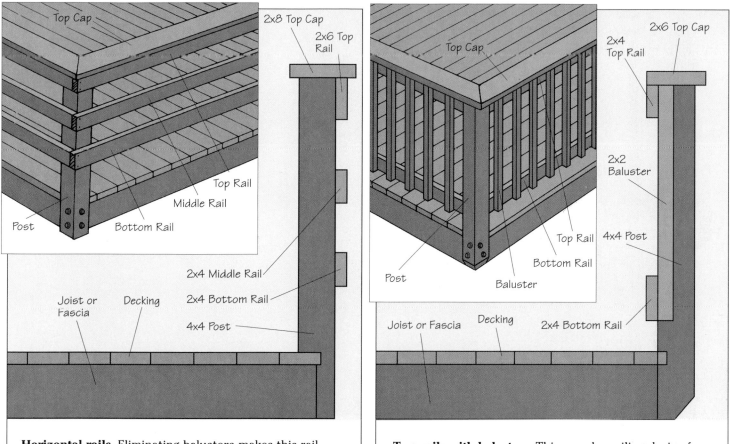

**Horizontal rails.** Eliminating balusters makes this rail quick to build.

**Two rails with balusters.** This popular railing design features ladder-style sections interrupted by posts.

do this only if your decking overhangs at least 2 inches, or the railing will not feel like it is part of the deck.

First attach posts, then run the rails, then the top cap. The balusters then can butt up against the bottom of the cap.

**Sandwiched 1x4 balusters.** Wider vertical pieces make this one look a bit like a fence. You can easily adjust the amount of privacy by moving the 1x4 balusters closer or farther apart. (Of course, keep code requirements in mind.) The top cap runs continuously, but the bottom rail and the 2x2 and 1x2 nailers run between the posts.

Install posts, then top cap. Next, you can install the bottom rail and 2x2 pieces and attach the balusters to them, or you can build sections ladder-style. Finish with the 1x2.

**Sandwiched panels.** The design is shown here with lattice panels, but you can use anything that will hold up to the weather: Plexiglas, safety

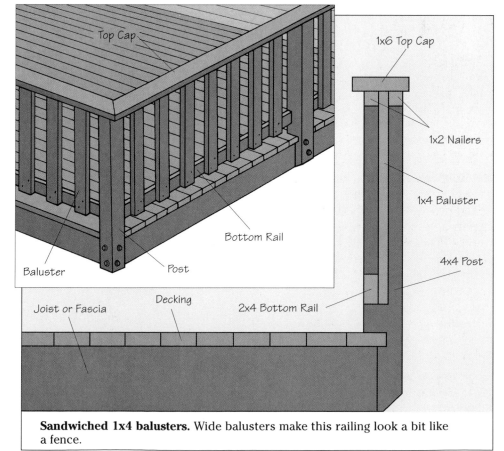

**Sandwiched 1x4 balusters.** Wide balusters make this railing look a bit like a fence.

glass, solid panels of siding material (make sure that both sides are weather-resistant). A drawback to this design is that on the bottom rail, water can collect and sit. So use very rot-resistant materials.

If you use lattice, get the heavy-duty stuff which uses ⅜-inch lattice pieces for a total thickness of ¾ inch. Plexiglas should be cut so it doesn't fit snugly. Leave an eighth of an inch or so for expansion and contraction. You'll probably have to make your own 1x1 nailer pieces—rip a 2x2 in half and give the cut edge a dose of sealer/preservative.

Install the posts, and attach bottom rail and top cap. Install one complete side of 1x1 nailer pieces, then the panel, then the rest of the nailers.

**Screen with lattice top.** This uses a combination of designs, providing lots of visual interest while increasing privacy and cutting down on wind. The potential weak spot is the slats: They can become loose over time and at the bottom they can soak up water that sits on the 2x4 bottom rail. So give the cuts some sealer/preservative, and attach the slats firmly with screws.

Cutting the top of the posts to a point will make them less susceptible to water damage (see "Post Top and Newels" on page 140 for the technique). The lattice section on top is constructed in much the same way as the sandwiched panels discussed above. Install the posts, then build the bottom sections ladder-style and install them between the posts. Add the topmost rail and one side of 1x1 nailer pieces, then the lattice, and finally the rest of the 1x1.

**Top rail of 4x6 on balusters.** This is an impressive, unusual railing that does not take a lot of extra work and is no more expensive than other railings. It is vital, however, that you have extremely straight, dry, and split-free 4x6 pieces for the top rail; there is absolutely no way to straighten them as you build.

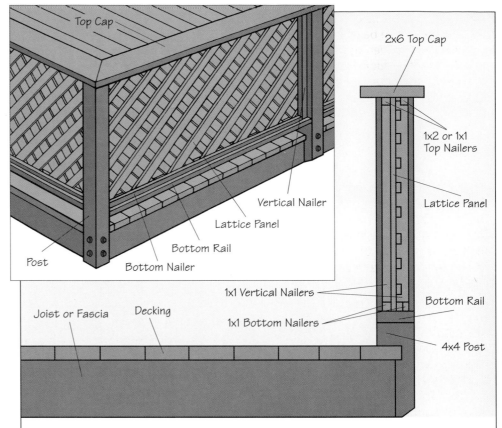

**Sandwiched panels.** This construction offers design flexibility. The panels could be lattice, Plexiglas or, for complete privacy, siding panels.

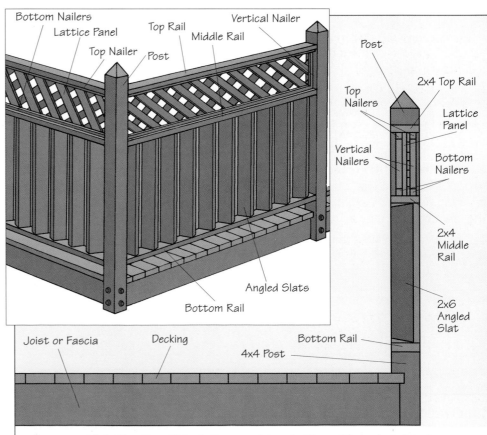

**Screen with lattice top.** This design combines lattice with angled slats to provide lots of visual interest.

The decking is cut flush to the joists. The bottom of the balusters are sandwiched between the joists, and the fascia is added after the balusters, creating a 1½-inch gap between the decking and the fascia. This is a good design for avoiding water damage.

Attach the balusters to the deck with two or three screws or nails. Then measure and cut the 4x6 pieces to fit (with a helper, you can set them on top of the balusters for measuring). Next, cut the groove in the 4x6 for the balusters. To do this, draw lines for a 1½-inch groove (make sure you do not cut all the way in places where the end of the 4x6 will be visible). Set your circular sawblade to a depth of about 2 inches. First cut to the lines, then make several passes between the lines, and clean out the groove with a chisel. Set the 4x6 pieces in place, and attach balusters with angle-driven screws or nails. Add the fascia board.

**Crisscross.** Achieving this grid-like pattern will take patience, both to lay it out and to install it. If you want the sections to be squares rather than rectangles, figure how far apart the horizontal pieces will be (the side view gives an example), and then space the vertical balusters in the same way. As shown here, the decking is notched for each 2x2 baluster—it is easier to install the balusters before the decking, if you want to do it that way. Of course, it would be simpler to cut the decking flush to the joists or fascia.

Use screws rather than nails, because all those 2x2s will flex if you pound on them.

Figure your grid carefully, laying out the position of all the balusters. (You may have to fudge a bit to make the balusters come out evenly spaced; if you end up with "squares" that are ¼ inch or so out of square, that will not be noticeable.) Install the balusters, then the 2x4 top rail and 2x6 cap. Finish with the 2x2 horizontal rails.

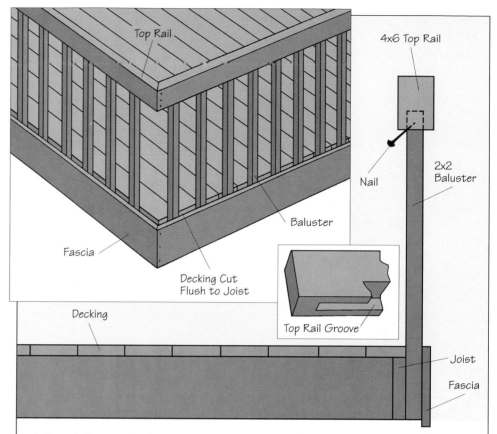

**4x6 on balusters.** In this clean-looking design the balusters are attached to a groove in the top rail and sandwiched behind the fascia.

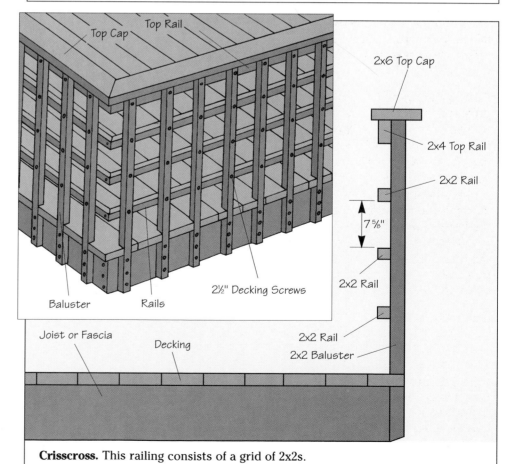

**Crisscross.** This railing consists of a grid of 2x2s.

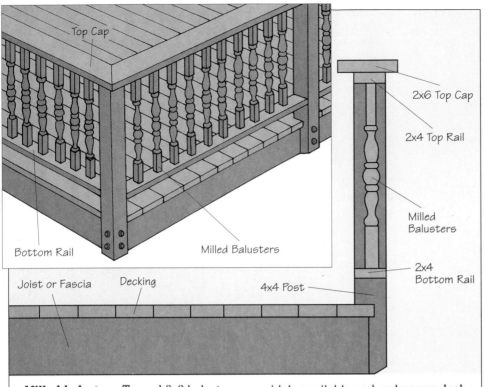

**Milled balusters.** Turned 2x2 balusters are widely available and make your deck railing reminiscent of one you might find on an old-fashioned porch.

**Milled balusters.** Factory-turned balusters, made of pressure-treated lumber, are widely available. These require no cutting, saving you some work. Inspect each carefully for cracks and gouges.

Here we show the easiest way to incorporate them into a railing system. Install the posts, then build sections of railing ladder style, fastening the balusters to the top and bottom rails with 3-inch screws driven through the rails into the balusters. Attach the rail sections to the posts, and add the top cap.

## INSTALLING THE RAILING

Construction methods vary a bit with railing designs, but most use the techniques we'll discuss here. Usually, you will first install the posts, then the top and bottom rails, then the top cap, and then the balusters. An alternate method calls for building rail sections ladder-style, and then installing them between the posts.

## Putting up the Posts

**1 Mark for posts and notch decking.** On the fascia or joists, mark the position of all your posts, making them evenly spaced whenever possible. Make square layout lines, so you will be able to install posts that need little straightening when you build the rest of the deck.

Use a saber saw to make any necessary decking cutouts for the posts.

**2 Cut and notch posts.** Determine the length of your posts, taking into account other railing members. (For instance, if you have 2x8 joists and want a railing 40 inches high, subtract 1½ inches for the thickness of the top cap that will sit on the post, and add 8¾ inches for the thickness of the decking plus the width of the joist, for a post length of 47¼ inches.) Cut all your posts to the same length.

To make a notch, mark for a cutout that is half the width of the 4x4 and as long as the width of your joist, plus the thickness of your decking. Cut carefully with a circular saw—don't go past the lines. Use a chisel to finish the corners and clean up the cuts.

For a corner post, the notch goes in two directions, but you actually remove less wood than with a regular

1 Mark for the post position and notch the decking.

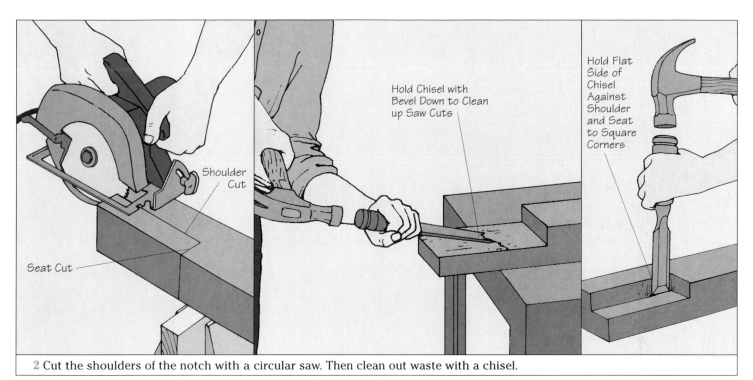

2 Cut the shoulders of the notch with a circular saw. Then clean out waste with a chisel.

post (see illustration). Cut with your circular saw as far as you can without going past the lines. Chisel out the remainder with a good, sharp chisel.

3 **Drill pilot or screw holes.** Mark your posts for carriage bolts or lag screws that make the most of your joists. They should not go into the decking and should be within 1½ inches of the top and the bottom of the joist, if possible.

Measure and mark all the posts for the screws or bolts, so that they will all look the same. Have a helper hold each post in position, checking for plumb, while you drive the drill bit through the post and into the joist. If you have a long bit, just keep boring all the way through. If your bit is shorter than your screw or bolt, drill as far as you can, remove the post, and finish the hole. If you are worried about getting the posts plumb, first drill the top

hole and temporarily insert the bolt or screw. Then hold the level to the post and drill the second hole.

4 **Attach the posts.** Secure the posts with carriage bolts or lag screws with washers. Some people prefer the appearance of bolt or screw heads that are recessed into countersunk holes. If you do this, fill the holes with a high-quality caulk, to protect the open grain that has been exposed by the counterbore.

3 Hold the post plumb while you drill pilot or bolt holes.

4 Attach the posts with lag screws or carriage bolts.

## Post Tops and Newels

If your post tops are uncovered, don't just leave them square-cut: Not only is that inviting water damage, but it looks unprofessional as well. Here are some ways to dress up and protect your post tops.

• Cut to a point. You can do this with a circular saw if you are confident with that tool; a power miter box makes it easier. Using a square, draw continuous lines around all four sides of the post so that the last line meets with the first. The line should be 2 inches or so down from the top of the 4x4. Set the power miter saw at 45 degrees, and make the first cut as shown. Rotate the post to the next side, and cut again in the same way. Do the same for the remaining two sides, and you will have cut the post to a point.

• Add an ornamental dado band. To dress up your post, cut an ornamental dado line around it. This is easy to do with a circular saw: Draw a set of two lines circling the post, set the saw to cut about ½ inch deep, and cut each line. You may have to make several

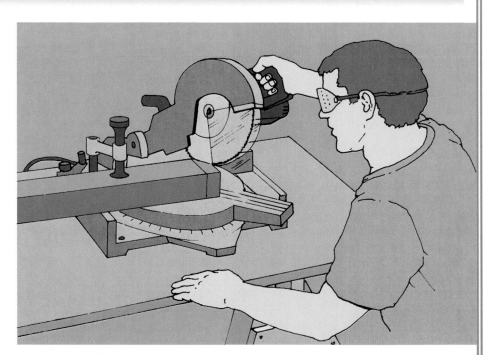

passes with the saw to clean out the interior of the dado—don't try to do it with a chisel, or you may split the wood.

• Install post caps or newels. There are a wide variety of decorative post caps that can be easily

installed on top of your posts. These may seem pricey, but considering the cost of all the materials that have gone into your deck, you may want to spend a bit more for this charming touch.

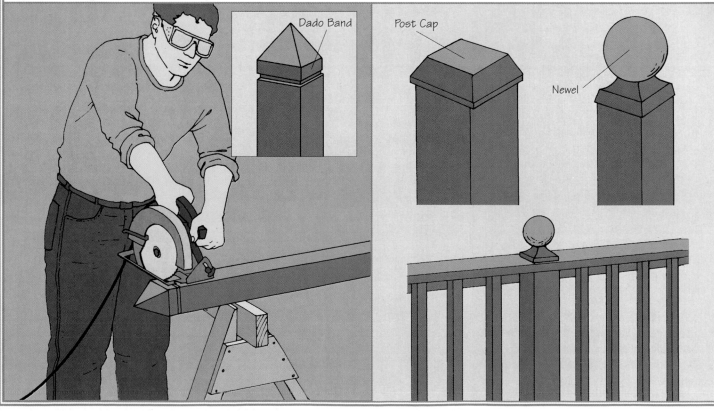

Dado Band

Post Cap

Newel

# Installing Top and Bottom Rails

**1 Mark and cut rails.** When installing rails, it's usually best to hold each piece in place, mark it for cutting, then install it before marking, cutting and installing the next piece. This is because installing a railing piece may nudge a post over a bit, changing the measurement for the next piece.

First, check your posts for plumb; you can probably still shift them a bit even after they are bolted or screwed on. Start with the top rails: Measure and install them before doing the bottom rails.

If you do not have a corner post, so that the rails must meet each other between posts, temporarily attach a rail that is too long in position. Hold the next rail piece up to it, and mark them both at once.

**2 Make beveled splices for long rails.** If your rails are not long enough to span the entire run, splice them on the posts. This looks much better than butt joints because splice joints won't leave a gap if the wood shrinks. Cut the pieces at 45 degrees, and drill pilot holes for your nails or screws.

**3 Install stair railings.** The easiest way to mark for cuts on the stair rail is to tack the rail in place and scribe the cuts. Check your posts for plumb, and then tack the stair rail piece to the rail so that it is parallel with the stringer, as shown. Mark the upper end for cuts in two directions, flush to the top and to the inside of the deck railing. Use a level to mark the lower end for a cut that is plumb with the end of the stairway. Mark the lower post to be cut off flush with the top edge of the top rail.

Cut the lower post and the rail with a circular saw, and attach the rail to the post with 3-inch decking screws or 16d galvanized nails, drilling pilot holes for all fasteners. Take special care to make these joints firm, because they will get handled often.

1 Hold rails in place for measuring. For angled cuts that meet between posts, tack one board in place to mark for the cuts.

2 To avoid unsightly gaps, miter-cut rails where you need to splice them together.

3 Tack the stair rails in place to mark where the rails and posts will be cut.

## Installing the Top Cap

**1 Measure and cut.** You will probably have to measure for most of the pieces, but hold and mark the pieces in place whenever possible. The corners require precise, splinter-free cuts, so do some practicing first if you are not sure of either your tools or your skills. Even if you have a power miter box, check that it cuts the angles exactly—if it is off even by one degree, you will end up with a poor-looking joint.

When possible, hang the top cap over an inch or so, rather than cutting it exactly flush to an edge. This makes it easier to achieve a finished appearance.

**2 Bevel-cut the splices.** Avoid splices if you can, because if the wood shrinks they will look bad and invite moisture into end grain. When splices are necessary, place them on top of posts, and bevel-cut the pieces at 45 degrees to meet on top of a rail.

**3 Install stair railing cap.** Use your angle square or sliding bevel gauge to find the angle of the upper plumb cut on the stair railing. Set your circular saw or power miter saw to cut both ends of the stair railing cap at this angle. Cut it a bit long at first, so

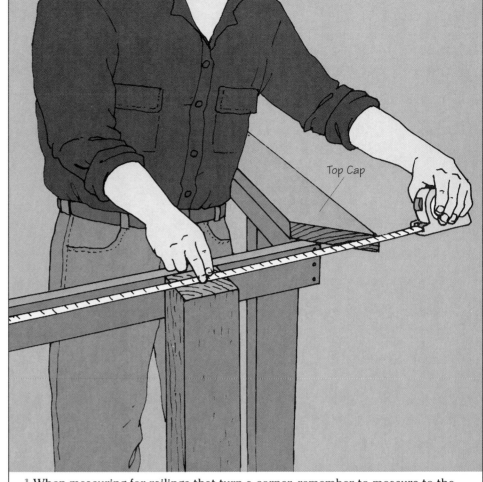

**1** When measuring for railings that turn a corner, remember to measure to the outside of the miter cut.

you can test fit the top end and adjust the angle a bit if you need to. Some end grain will be exposed on both

ends, so dab on some sealer/preservative. Install the stair railing cap in the same way as the other railing caps.

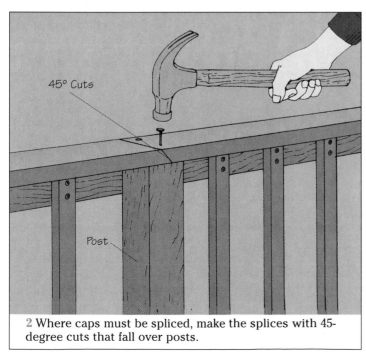

**2** Where caps must be spliced, make the splices with 45-degree cuts that fall over posts.

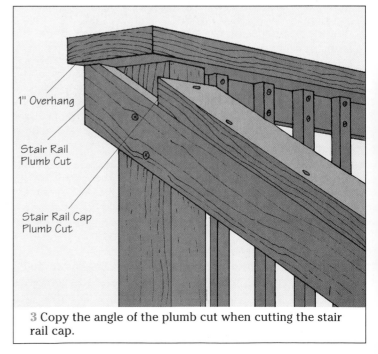

**3** Copy the angle of the plumb cut when cutting the stair rail cap.

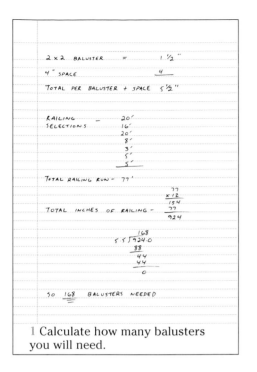

1 Calculate how many balusters you will need.

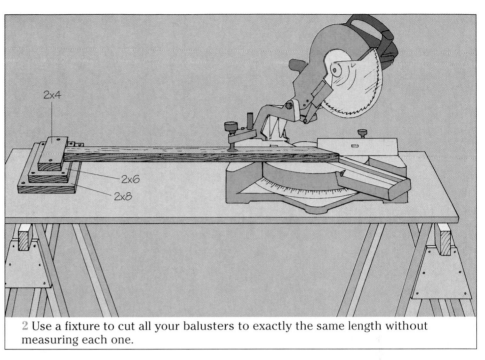

2 Use a fixture to cut all your balusters to exactly the same length without measuring each one.

## Balusters

1 **Figure materials.** If you will be installing a lot of balusters, it is probably not worth your while to figure out where they all will go so that you can make the last one come out the same distance from the post as the first one. It can be figured mathematically, but given the fact that 2x2s can vary in thickness by $\frac{1}{16}$, your figures will probably do you no good.

However, you do want to know how many balusters you'll need. Here's how to calculate that: Find the total amount of railing length taken up by a baluster plus a space. For instance, a 2x2 baluster (1½ inches wide) with a 4-inch space will take up 5½ inches. Then find the total amount of top rail length between the posts (don't forget both sides of the stair railing), and divide that number by your baluster-plus-space figure. If you have 77 feet of rail, that equals 924 inches; divide 924 by 5.5 and get 168 inches. You will need 168 balusters for your railing.

2 **Cut the balusters.** If you have a power miter box, construct a fixture for your saw like the one shown. Build it sturdy, so that neither the stop block nor the saw can move. If you will be cutting with a circular saw, cut

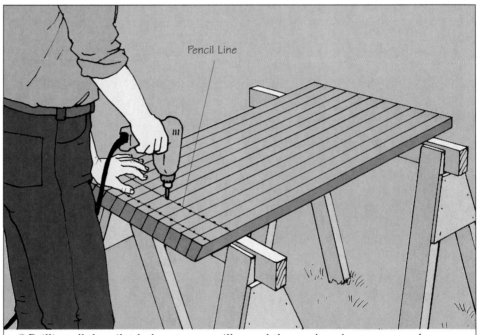

3 Drilling all the pilot holes at once will speed the work and ensure a professional-looking job.

one baluster to the correct length and use it as a template for all the others. Your stair railing balusters will probably be cut at a different angle than the rest of the balusters, so don't cut them yet.

3 **Drill pilot holes.** If you have soft material, you can probably get away without predrilling. But pilot holes ensure against splits and make the joints stronger, and it does not

take a lot of time to drill them if you do it in gang fashion. And by laying the balusters side by side and drilling straight lines of holes, you will add a touch of professionalism to your deck. Use a framing square to square up your bunch of balusters then draw pencil lines to align the holes.

4 **Install the balusters.** Cut a 2x6 spacer block to a length equal to the spaces between your balusters.

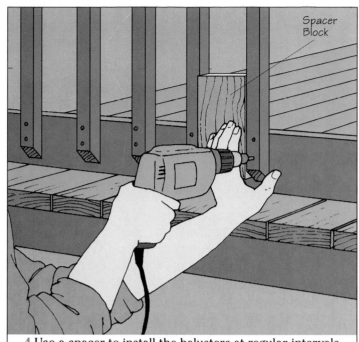

4 Use a spacer to install the balusters at regular intervals.

5 Get the angle for the top cut by holding a baluster plumb and using a scrap of 2x2 to space as you mark.

(Make sure the block is square.) Using the spacer, start next to a post and work outward. Every four balusters or so, make sure they are plumb, and make slight spacing adjustments as necessary.

**5 Install stair railing balusters.** If you will have stair rail balusters that butt up against the rail cap, find the angle for the top cut by holding a plumb baluster up against the top

rail and the top cap. Hold a 2x2 spacer on the baluster, and mark, as shown.

## Making Balustrades

An alternative method for building railings is to construct *balustrades*—sections of railing with balusters—on the ground, as if you were making a ladder. Once these sections are built, you will install them between the posts. If the

design calls for it, you will then install a top cap.

**1 Cut the rails.** Cut the top and bottom rails to fit between the posts. For a stronger railing—one people can sit on without worry—make a dado for the bottom rail as shown. If you dado, remember to make the bottom rail 3 inches longer than the top rail. Cut with a circular saw, and clean out with a chisel. (If you want to cut a

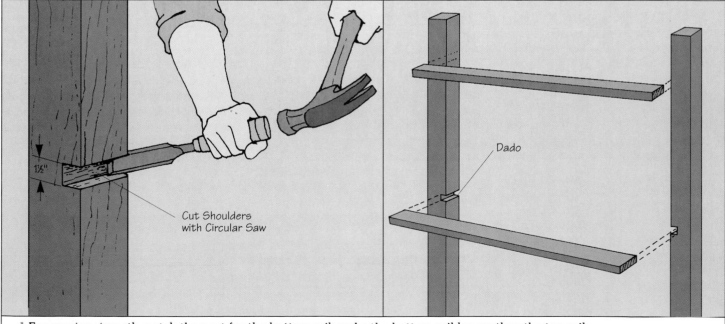

1 For greater strength, notch the post for the bottom rail; make the bottom rail longer than the top rail.

dado in the top rail as well, do not attempt to build ladder-style; it is difficult to get all the pieces to fit precisely.) See "Cutting Dadoes and Rabbets," page 67.

2 **Assemble the balustrade.** Lay the balustrade out on the deck, as shown. Lay down pieces of lumber to raise the balusters to the center of the rails, and use a spacer block to

lay out the balusters. Assemble with deck screws for a tight fit.

3 **Install the sections.** Set the railing section in place, propping it with pieces of 2x4 to hold it to the right height, if necessary. Here we have perhaps the most vulnerable place on your deck—the rails are usually held in place with toenails or

angle-driven screws only. So carefully drill pilot holes and install 3-inch screws or 16d galvanized nails.

# BENCHES

We present here a few of the many bench designs that are possible. On a small deck, it is often a good idea to harmonize benches with decking by using lumber pieces that match the decking. On a larger deck, it is often best to break up the monotony of the deck surface with different materials. Bench supports can have a massive look, using 4x4 or larger timbers, or you can tuck supports made of 2x6 under the seat, where they are barely visible.

Planning ahead and attaching the bench to your framing is a good idea if you are sure you know what you want. But attractive and sturdy benches can be added to a completed deck as well.

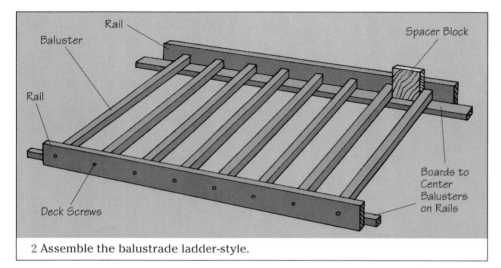

2 Assemble the balustrade ladder-style.

3 Install the balustrades with toenails or angle-driven screws.

**How Much Fixed Seating Do You Want?**

Attached seating can give your deck a comfortable, inviting feel. And often a bench can take the place of a railing.

However, fixed seating, especially if it takes the place of railing, could very well be wrong for your deck. Ask yourself: How much seating do you need? Will you really be comfortable with immovable seating in that location? Do you want to sit facing that direction, with your back to the scenery? And, will a large bench harmonize visually with your deck, or will it dominate and be clunky-looking?

You may want to limit your fixed seating to a well-chosen location or two. Or you may choose to make movable benches, which can harmonize with your deck just as well as fixed seating. And sometimes the best idea is to just buy some great-looking patio furniture.

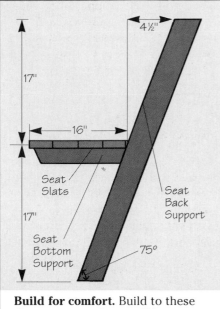

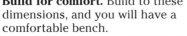

**Build for comfort.** Build to these dimensions, and you will have a comfortable bench.

## Build for Comfort

If you are building a bench with a back, it would be easiest to make one that has its back sticking straight up, at a 90-degree angle to the seat. However, this is uncomfortable and inappropriate for a deck, where people expect to relax and lounge. Slope the back a bit, for a more comfortable feel.

For a bench that takes the place of railing, watch that top cap: If it overhangs on the inside like most rail caps, you will get a nasty poke in the neck every time you sit down. Set it back a little.

The illustration gives standard dimensions for a bench that most adults will find comfortable.

## Railing Bench Attached to the Framing

This design calls for building the bench supports after the framing is complete and before you attach the decking. If your bench replaces a railing, the same code regulations as to height and size of openings will apply. (See "Complying with Code," page 131.)

**1** **Cut back supports.** The back support will be visible, so make it

pleasant-looking—a standard piece of lumber will look unprofessional. Two design options are pictured, both tilt the seat back at a comfortable 15 degrees from 90 degrees. For the first option, cut a piece of 2x6 to 36 inches plus the width of your joist, with parallel 75-degree cuts on each end. Then cut off the back of the top, as shown. For the second option, cut a piece of 2x12 to 36 inches plus the width of your joist, with parallel 75-degree cuts on each end. Then

make a long sloping rip cut, starting at 11¼ inches wide at the bottom and ending at 4½ inches wide at the top.

**2** **Construct supporting frames.** Tack each rear support to a joist; hold the bottom end of the support perfectly flush with the bottom of the joist. Attach the front 2x4 supports and the cross pieces in the same way. Check that the frames are parallel with each other and that the cross pieces are level (both individually and with each other), drill holes, and fas-

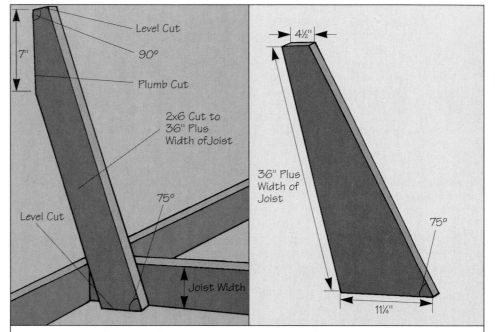

**1** Here are two options for cutting back supports.

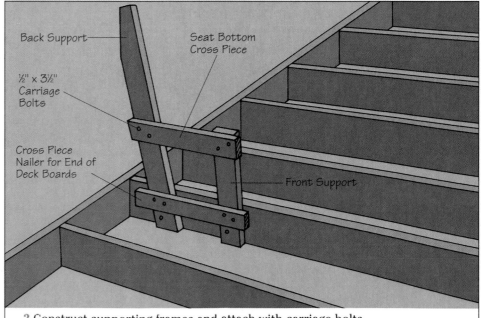

**2** Construct supporting frames and attach with carriage bolts.

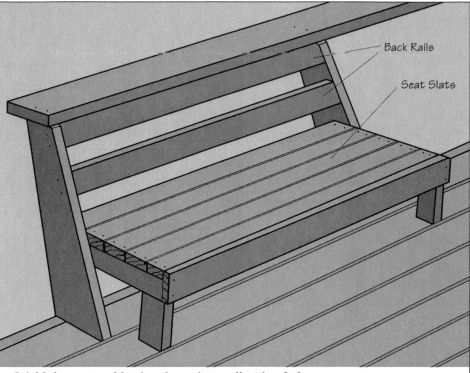

**3** Add the seat and back rails, and top off with a 2x6 cap.

between the back supports and atop the cross pieces with 3-inch decking screws or 16d galvanized nails. Set the top cap slightly back, so it will not dig into your neck when you lean back.

## Backless Bench, Attached to the Framing

This low, unobtrusive bench is an attractive way to provide built-in seating. Of course, without a back it won't substitute for a railing. But it's an easy addition to a ground-level deck.

**1** **Build supports.** Before laying the decking, construct T-shaped supports of 4x4 uprights and 2x8 crosspieces, as shown. Make the connections with contersunk 5-inch lag screws. Add 2x4 cleats to support the decking where needed. Locate supports every 4 feet or so.

**2** **Install the seat.** After the decking is completed, attach the seat pieces to the cross pieces. Install three 2x6 seat slats to the top of the cross pieces with 3-inch deck screws or 16d galvanized nails; make them flush

ten each joint with two ½x3½-inch carriage bolts with washers.

Provide support for the decking wherever it will butt into one of the vertical pieces you have just installed. To do this, run a 2x4 cleat across each pair

of front and rear supports with the top of the cleat flush to the top of the joists.

**3** **Add slats and back rails.** After the decking is laid, finish the bench. Attach 2x2s, 2x4s, or 2x6s

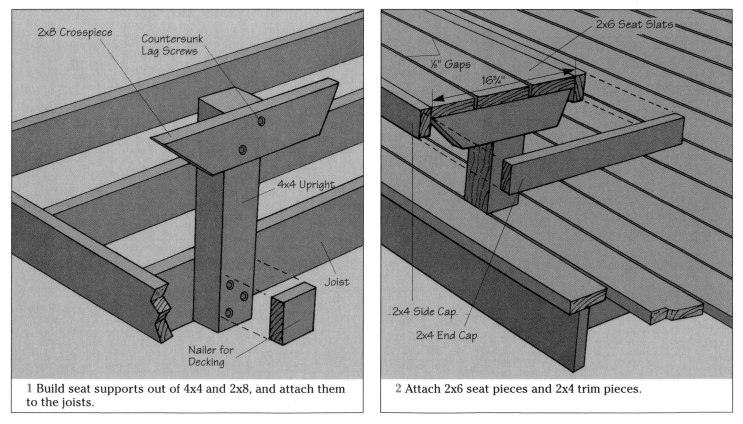

**1** Build seat supports out of 4x4 and 2x8, and attach them to the joists.

**2** Attach 2x6 seat pieces and 2x4 trim pieces.

to the sides of the cross pieces and flush to the ends of the end cross pieces as well. There will be about a ⅛-inch gap between each seat board. Cut 2x4 side caps and end caps to cover each edge, and attach it in the same way.

## Bench with Back Attached to a Finished Deck

You can add this one to a completed deck. It looks a bit complicated, but a careful handyman can pull it off, and it will give a great handcrafted touch to your deck.

**1 Cut back support and seat support.** Cut the 2x10 back support as shown, and use it as a template for the other supports. Be precise in your cutting—these pieces will be visible.

You will need two 2x4 seat supports for every back support. The little angle cut at the front of the seat supports is easy to do, and will make the seat significantly more comfortable.

**2 Assemble and install the supports.** The supports each require two more pieces of 2x4: a front leg square-cut to 15½ inches and a rear brace whose length is 10 inches, plus the thickness of your decking, plus the width of your joists. Attach each front 2x4 support, sandwiched between the two seat supports, with 3-inch deck screws. Drill pilot holes and use 3-inch deck screws to attach each rear brace to a back support.

Attach these assemblies to the deck with ½-inch carriage bolts long enough to go through the joist and fascia, if any. Attach the front with angle-driven screws, or use an angle bracket if you think this piece will receive some abuse.

**3 Install seat slats.** Attach six 2x4 seat slats, evenly spaced, with 3-inch galvanized deck screws. Attach the five 2x4 back slats in the same way. Cap it all off with a 2x6 that is placed so it will not dig into your back when you sit down.

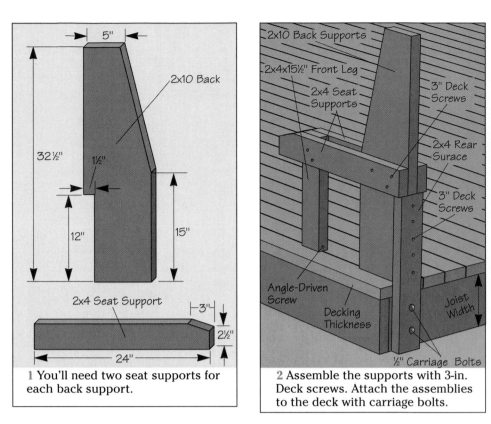

1 You'll need two seat supports for each back support.

2 Assemble the supports with 3-in. Deck screws. Attach the assemblies to the deck with carriage bolts.

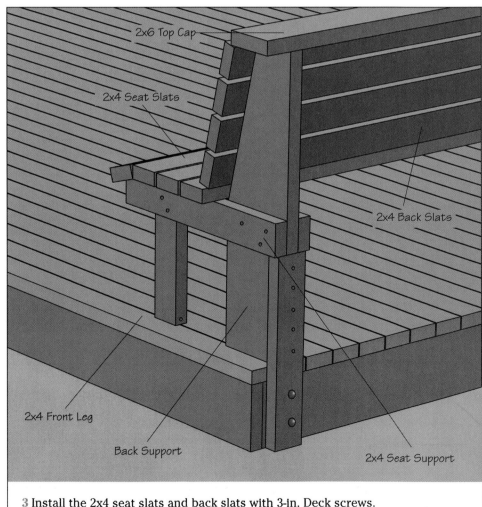

3 Install the 2x4 seat slats and back slats with 3-in. Deck screws.

# Chapter 12

# MAINTAINING YOUR DECK

How long your deck lasts and continues to look good depends to a great extent on how well it has been designed and built. If good dry boards are well fastened, if there are few places for dirt and moisture to sit and encourage rot, and if end grain is well protected or in a position to dry out, then you have a deck that can remain attractive and strong for many years.

However, even the best decks require maintenance. How much depends on your weather conditions and whether or not you want the wood to retain something close to its original color. But all decks require some maintainence, even decks that are in warm, dry climates and are owned by people who like the gray look.

## THE CAUSES OF DAMAGE

Decks are subject to damage from three sources: the sun, moisture, and insects.

## Sun

The sun's ultraviolet (UV) rays break down the lignin (the binding agent that holds the cells together) in exterior wood cells, but only penetrates to a depth of about $1/100$ of an inch. The damaged cells will actually block further degradation, unless the loose fibers are washed away by wind or rain. So except for contributing to cycles of wetting and drying that can cause wood to crack or distort, the sun will cause only cosmetic damage to your deck.

## Moisture

Water can cause damage in three ways: First, when wood absorbs moisture and then dries out, it expands and contracts, causing cupping, warping, and even splitting. This puts strain on your fasteners and can cause nails to pop out. If splitting occurs, new places for water to seep in will be created, leading to even more damage down the line. Second, moisture provides an environment where fungus and bacteria can cause rot and mildew. And third, in extreme conditions where boards cannot dry out for months, the result can be wet rot. (Wet rot results from the same oxidizing process as fire, so it takes on a charred-looking dark appearance.)

One simple and effective way to reduce water damage is to sweep your deck frequently and clean it occasionally, taking special care to get the crud out of every joint and cranny. Dirt and leaves make for wet spots that don't dry out easily.

Water-related problems are worsened by freezing temperatures. Boards that have soaked up water and then freeze can split. Spots where water seeps between boards and then freezes can cause fasteners to come loose.

## Insects

If wood-damaging insects are a problem in your area, expect them to attack your deck unless you use only high-quality pressure-treated lumber.

Cedar and redwood are to varying degrees bug-resistant, depending on how much heartwood they contain (See "Redwood" page 52 and "Cedar," page 53.), but are no guarantee. You can distinguish insect damage from rot by the long, thin tunnels they dig in the interior of boards.

Termites, carpenter ants, and wood-boring beetles usually live in the ground and come up to the wood only to drill for food, so don't expect to find actual insect bodies. And they can't stand the light, so nearly all their damage is done inside the lumber. This means you can't see the damage until the board has become so hollowed out that the surface cracks open.

---

### Beautiful Mildew?

Many people prefer the silvery gray color that often develops on a deck after a few years of exposure. Some even apply a gray stain (especially on pressure-treated lumber) to imitate the look. What most people don't know is that this mellow gray color is caused by a mildew that grows on the surface of the wood. You can remove this growth quite easily with either a fungicide or a bleach solution. However, since this natural graying affects only the top layer of the wood and does not affect the structural strength of your deck, there's really no reason to worry about it.

So if you are pretty sure you have a bug problem, the best solution for your deck is the same as for your house: Have an inspection, and have the ground around your deck treated to kill the bugs where they live. In addition, use a wood finish that contains pesticide.

# SEALERS, PRESERVATIVES, AND STAINS

There are many brands and types of deck finishes. None is perfect for all situations. Choose the best one by finding a deck in your area built of the same lumber as yours, that is three or more years old and still looks good. Find out what the owners of that deck have used and how often they have used it. Follow suit. Also learning about the ingredients will help you choose the right product for your deck.

## Ingredients

Though there are many products out there, the list of ingredients they use is fairly short. A deck finish can contain any of the following ingredients, in various combinations. (Usually, a less-expensive finish product means fewer and cheaper ingredients—and lower performance.)

**Water repellents.** A good deck finish will repel water while remaining flexible, so as not to crack. Most deck finishes contain paraffin and/or oil (either tung oil or linseed oil) for repelling water. You can tell that these products are working when you see water bead up after a rainfall. Depending on rainfall and traffic volume, paraffin and oil finishes will wear out and need to be reapplied fairly quickly.

**Resins.** A longer-lasting—and more costly—water repellent is resin, often called alkyd resin. Resin will soak into the wood and seal it from moisture without hardening on the surface like polyurethane or varnish. A heavy dose of resin will also give your deck a per-

**THE PROS KNOW**

### Use Film-Forming Finishes Only on Furniture

Though they are strong and long-lasting, polyurethane and varnish are not recommended for a deck surface. These products form a hard inflexible film on the surface of the lumber. When the wood moves due to moisture and temperature changes, the film cracks and sometimes even flakes. Once this happens, you will have to completely strip the old finish before reapplying a new one.

Polyurethane and varnish do not protect against the sun's UV rays. Not only does this mean that your wood will turn gray, but once the surface cells have been destroyed by the sun, the finish will flake off because it has nothing to adhere to.

However, for movable furniture, consider an exterior polyurethane, possibly one that contains powdered iron oxides for UV protection. Because of the smaller dimensions and (usually) higher density of furniture lumber pieces, there is less wood movement and therefore less chance of cracking — and the furniture can be moved indoors in the winter. A hard film surface works better than most deck finishes for objects on which you will sit or place food.

manent "wet look" that many people find attractive. However, it can also change your deck's color, turning it what some would call amber and others yellow.

**Preservatives.** Most preservatives contain fungicide, mildewcide, and insecticide in various combinations. All-purpose deck finishes usually contain a small amount of these, enough for a mild dose of protection. If you have serious problems in your area with either fungus, mildew, or insects, take other measures in addition to using a deck finish with a preservative.

**UV blockers, absorbers, and inhibitors.** If you want to maintain something like the original color of your deck and avoid having it turn gray, you will need some sort of

UV protection. Absorbers and blockers are solid particles—that is to say, pigment—which absorb or reflect UV rays to minimize its effect on the wood.

There is a tradeoff here, one that many people object to: In order to keep the sun from graying your wood, UV blockers and absorbers add some color to the wood. It doesn't take a lot of pigment to do the job, so if you choose carefully, this does not have to mean a drastic change in your wood's appearance. But your wood will not look exactly as it looked when you first installed it.

There is another solution, but it has serious drawbacks. Some expensive finishes contain UV inhibitors. These compounds are designed to disrupt the normal chemical action caused by UV light. The advantage here is that no pigment is required, so you can get something closer to the original look of your wood. But the chemical reactions that occur while UV inhibitors are doing their job cause them to break down and become less effective. So not only are they more expensive; they are significantly shorter-lived than pigmented UV blockers and absorbers. That means that if you don't reapply often, your wood will turn gray.

## Quality of Ingredients

Most products you can buy will need to be applied every year or two, depending on your climate and how much the deck gets used. However, there are some higher-end finishes that have proved themselves more durable that typically last four years even in regions with harsh weather.

This has to do not with the type of ingredient, but with how well they penetrate the wood. The best (and usually most expensive) products use solvents and pigments that soak well into the wood and therefore last longer. So although you may find it painful to pay for a pricey finish now, after you have spent so much on your deck, it is probably a good idea to get the better product. After all, finishing a deck is a pretty time-consuming and annoying job, and you don't want to have to do it every year.

## AVAILABLE PRODUCTS

The products you will see in the stores combine the ingredients discussed above in various combinations. You can choose a clear, semi-transparent or solid-color stain.

## Clear Finishes

Truly clear finishes will usually contain a water repellant plus preservative. Use these when you want your wood to go gray. It will have little visual impact (unless it contains resin) and will help your deck last significantly longer than it would if you didn't apply finish.

If you are going to use a stained finish for the surface of your deck, you may want to use a less-expensive clear sealer for the underside, where you don't have to worry about sun or discoloration. Just be careful none of the clear sealer gets sprayed up to the top, where it can affect the color of the stain.

Some products labeled "clear" actually contain some pigments for UV protection, and so are not really clear. This is fine, as long as you like the color. Others contain UV inhibitors and will keep your deck looking its natural color without pigment, but only if you reapply frequently.

## Semi-Transparent Stains

These contain varying amounts of pigment, but still allow the natural grain to show through. If they contain resin or a good deal of oil, they will make your deck look more or less wet—when looking at samples, pay attention to the sheen as well as the color to see if it's what you want. They will lighten over time and need to be reapplied. You can darken your deck by applying a second coat.

**Solid-color stains and paints.** Solid-color stains basically look like paint.

In fact they are essentially thinned paint that lets a bit of the wood grain show through. Solid-color stains are designed for siding and are not appropriate for surfaces that will get walked on—they will wear away quickly.

If you want a solid color on your deck surface, it is better to go with a porch-and-deck paint, but there are serious drawbacks to both solid-color stain and paint. Paint does not soak into the wood—it just forms a thin film on top. So as long as the surface is completely covered, you are fine. But on a deck, there will be uncovered places—the undersides and side edges of deck pieces, for instance—that are difficult to get at with a brush. And cracks can develop in the paint, due to expansion and contraction of the wood. Then water seeps into the wood and is

### THE PROS KNOW

#### Making Pressure-Treated Look Like Cedar or Redwood

If you choose a brown pressure-treated lumber, you will have a product that looks pretty much like stained redwood or cedar. If the color fades over the years, you can restain it using a semi-transparent deck finish. Experiment with a small, inconspicuous spot, waiting a few days for the color to settle in, before you do the whole deck.

If you have green pressure-treated wood, your best bet is to first wait a year or so to let it gray a bit. Then apply either wood bleach (oxalic acid) or a product specially made for cleaning pressure-treated lumber. Use a stiff broom or a scrub brush and really dig out the grime. Rinse thoroughly, and let it dry completely. You will now have a wood surface that has no gray and is somewhat less green than the original color.

To get the right color, experiment with semi-transparent stains, starting with very light coloration. There are products called toners, made for this purpose.

actually trapped there by the paint, which can lead to warping, cracking, and rot. (Paint works better on a porch with tongue-and-groove flooring, because there it can completely cover all the exposed wood.)

So it is best to use paint or solid stain only on vertical surfaces such as posts, balusters, and skirting that do not receive wear.

## APPLYING PENETRATING FINISH

Finishes should not be applied when the temperature is 40 degrees or colder. This is not a big problem. If it's too cold to finish your deck, leave it alone for the winter and then finish it in the spring. If some graying has occurred, you can wash with wood bleach first.

Be generous when applying a penetrating finish. You want the finish to saturate the wood fibers. In particular, the end grain of a dried piece (such as the ends of posts or decking pieces) will absorb finish almost as quickly as you can brush it on. Check these spots during application, and reapply until the wood stops absorbing the finish.

Avoid breathing vapors or spray mists. Wear rubber gloves and long-sleeved garments during application to reduce exposure and minimize the chance of skin irritation. Always wear goggles or safety glasses to protect yourself from any backspray or drips.

1 **Test the wood.** You don't want to wait too long before applying finish, or the deck will become dirty with use and you will have a heavy-duty cleaning problem. But it is also a mistake to apply finish to wood that is still green or wet with treatment. Your finish will not soak in and won't be effective.

For pressure-treated lumber, unless it is kiln-dried after treatment (marked KDAT), it is almost always necessary to wait a month or so before applying finish. Other woods may be ready as soon as you build. Test by sprinkling a little water on the deck. If it soaks in readily,

1 Sprinkle a little water on your deck at several locations. If water soaks in after about 30 seconds, the wood is ready to receive finish.

2 A universal pole sander, more commonly used for sanding drywall, is a handy tool for taking down rough spots or giving your deck a light sanding.

you are ready for the finish. If not, wait a week or so (depending on sun exposure) and test again.

2 **Prepare the wood.** Sand down any rough spots on your deck. Your deck should be completely clean—any dirt will be sealed in with the finish. A deck cleaner will both remove dirt and open up the grain of your deck to accept stain.

To further increase the finish's penetration and produce a cleaner-looking surface, you can sand the entire deck. A heavy-duty sanding job can be done with an orbital sander (use a belt sander only if you are experienced, and with great care—it's easy to make pits and valleys). Or use a universal pole sander, the kind with a swiveling pad that drywall finishers use. Use 60- or 80-grit sandpaper and sand with the grain. Vacuum thoroughly after sanding.

Do not sand pressure-treated wood. Sanding will release the toxins bonded to the wood cells. Instead, use a power washer, which you can rent. Experiment before you start, because some nozzles produce a spray powerful enough to dent the wood. Allow

3 Use a roller to apply finish to large decking areas. A brush works best for working the finish into joints.

the deck to dry thoroughly before applying finish.

3 **Apply the finish.** Horizontal decking boards can be coated with a roller or spray equipment. (Small pump-pressured sprayers can be purchased inexpensively at most hardware stores.) Follow the sprayer with a brush to spread out the finish. Apply finish to the underside of decking and to joists, beams, and posts. For posts, railings, and stair stringers,

brush application is best. Remember that visible end grain will absorb much more than flat surfaces. With a clean rag, wipe off excess finish that isn't absorbed after a half hour. Be sure to dispose of all rags properly. The heat generated from the evaporating finish can cause rags to burst into flames. Spread rags out and allow them to dry completely before disposing. If the rags will be reused, store them in an airtight container.

# LOW-TO-THE-GROUND RAMBLER

Various features combine to give this deck a rambling, spacious feel: the two deck levels, the generous single step, the decking running in three different directions, and the slightly non-symmetrical shape.

Because the deck is so low to the ground, there is no room to put a beam under the joists. So the joists are attached into the beams with joist hangers. All four beams are built-up, made simply by laminating two 2x6s together, and are bolted to the sides of 4x4 posts that rest on concrete footings.

There are 16 footings to lay out and install; this will be the most difficult

part of the job. On a smaller deck, we would suggest pouring all the footings level with each other, so you could just set the beams on top of the concrete—as in the Rectangular Deck on pages 159-162. But it is difficult to get 16 footings level with each other, so here we use short posts that are cut flush with the top of the beams. With this system, it is important that all the posts be cut off level. If you don't own a reservoir-type water level, we strongly suggest you get one before building this deck.

A final note before you build: The dimensions given on the drawings accompanying this project are for a particular deck built at a particular location. It's unlikely, for example, that you will locate posts exactly as shown. So, use the dimensions given as an example only. Measure and cut to fit as you build, adjusting dimensions as necessary.

## Parts List

| | Quantity | Lumber Size | Part |
|---|---|---|---|
| **Framing** | 2 | 2x6x10' | Ledger |
| | 2 | 4x4x8' | Posts (16 pieces at 2') |
| | 10 | 2x6x10' | Beams 1 and 2 |
| | 2 | 2x6x12' | Beam 3 |
| | 1 | 2x6x10' | Rear header |
| | 1 | 2x6x16' | Western Outside Joist |
| | 1 | 2x6x10' | Eastern Outside Joist |
| | 2 | 2x6x10' | Western and Eastern Headers Joists |
| | 1 | 2x6x6' | End Header Joist |
| | 48 | 2x6x8' | Joists |
| | 2 | 2x10x10' | Beam 4 (ripped to 8½") |
| | 2 | 2x4x8' | 2 Step Headers and 1 Step Joist |
| | 2 | 2x4x10' | 2 Step Headers and 2 Step Joists |
| | 1 | 2x4x12' | 11 Step Joists |
| **Decking** | 23 | 2x6x20' | |
| | 7 | 2x6x18' | |
| | 7 | 2x6x16' | |
| | 19 | 2x6x14' | |
| | 5 | 2x6x12' | |
| | 8 | 2x6x10' | |
| | 4 | 2x6x8' | |

**1 Install the ledger and footings.** Bolt the ledger to the house, 2¼ inches below the surface of the house floor at the threshold. Lay out the footings as shown in the *Framing Plan*. Dig the holes, install concrete tube forms, and pour the concrete. Insert J-bolts while the concrete is wet. Allow the concrete to set.

**2 Install the posts.** First, install post anchors. Attach the reservoir end of your water level to the ledger so that the water is level with the ledger top. For each post location, place a piece of 4x4 in the anchor, plumb it and then use the water level to mark the ledger height on the 4x4. If the 4x4 is for an upper level post location, (labeled Posts 3 through 7 on the Framing Plan), remove it and cut it to ledger height before fastening it to the post anchor. Cut all the remaining posts to 10 inches below the ledger height before fastening them to their anchors.

**3 Install the lower level beams.** There are three beams on the lower level, each made of doubled 2x6s. To locate the beam labeled Beam 1 on the Framing Plan, measure down 10 inches from the top of Posts 3 through 7 and strike a line on their southern faces. Cut three pieces of 2x6 to make the first layer of Beam 1 which will span from Post 1 to Post 7. Of these pieces, cut one to span from the west side of Post 1 to the middle

### Shopping List

**Lumber**
- [ ] 2 at 2x4x8'
- [ ] 2 at 2x4x10'
- [ ] 1 at 2x4x12'
- [ ] 52 at 2x6x8'
- [ ] 25 at 2x6x10'
- [ ] 7 at 2x6x12'
- [ ] 19 at 2x6x14'
- [ ] 8 at 2x6x16'
- [ ] 7 at 2x6x18'
- [ ] 23 at 2x6x20'
- [ ] 2 at 4x4x8'

**Hardware**
- [ ] 16 post anchors, with J-bolts, nuts, and washers
- [ ] 102 right angle joist hangers for 2x6
- [ ] 8 angled joist hangers for 2x6
- [ ] 5 angle brackets or clipped joist hangers
- [ ] 20 lag screws and washers, for attaching ledger to house
- [ ] 32 machine bolts, ½"x7", with washers and nuts
- [ ] 5 pounds of joist hanger nails or 1¼" decking screws
- [ ] 2 pounds of 2" decking screws
- [ ] 30 pounds of 3" decking screws

**Masonry**
- [ ] 16 concrete tube forms
- [ ] Gravel and concrete for 16 footings

# Framing Plan

of Post 3, a second to span from the middle of Post 3 to the middle of Post 5 and a third to span from the middle of Post 5 to the east side of Post 7. Use 3-inch screws to attach these pieces flush with the tops of Posts 1 and 2 and aligned with the marks you made on Posts 3 through 7. Then add the second layer of Beam 1, offsetting butt joints and using two machine bolts at each beam-to-post location.

As shown in the *Framing Plan*, Beams 2 and 3 are attached flush with the top of the lower level posts. Cut, assemble, and attach Beam 2 as you did Beam 1. Do the same for Beam 3, but let it run wild about a foot past each outside post.

**4 Install the rear header and outside joists.** The rear header will be attached to the house for part of its length. It doesn't matter how much of the rear header runs along the house, as long as you have at least 6 inches for attachment. To attach the rear header, take a 10-foot 2x6 and use a single 3-inch screw to attach it flush to the top and outside of Post 8 as shown in the *Framing Plan*. Level the rear header and then tack it to the house, letting it run wild under the ledger. Then bolt the rear header to the house, as you did the ledger, and add three more screws to the connection with Post 8.

Cut the western outside joist to length and attach it to beams and posts with 3-inch screws. Cut the eastern outside joist to length. Attach it to Beam 1 with a joist hanger and screw it to the post and the end of Beam 2.

**5 Cut Beam 3 and install header joists.** First, use a chalkline and angle squares as shown in *Marking the Beam* to mark the 45-degree cut on the western end of Beam 3. Extend the cutline down both faces of the beam. Then do the same to mark the 45-degree cut on the eastern end of Beam 3.

Cut off both ends of Beam 3 with a circular saw set to 45-degrees,

## Marking the Beam

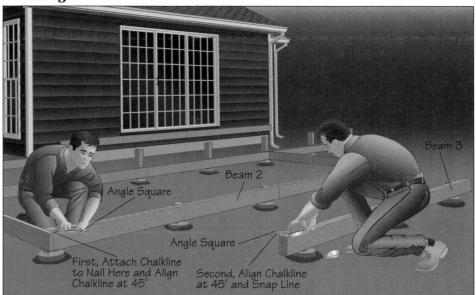

First, Attach Chalkline to Nail Here and Align Chalkline at 45°

Second, Align Chalkline at 45° and Snap Line

Angle Square

Angle Square

Beam 2

Beam 3

cutting from top to bottom on both beam faces.

Cut the western header joist to 9 feet 10¾ inches long and the eastern header joist to 8 feet 2¾ inches with miter cuts on both ends of each joist as shown in the *Framing Plan*. Attach these two header joists to Beam 3 with six 3-inch screws and to the outside joists with three 3-inch screws at each connection.

Cut the end header joist to fit between the other header joists.

**6 Install the lower level joists.** Lay out the lower level joists, 16 inches on center, and install them into joist hangers. Measure the length of the angle-cut joists by holding and marking them in place, using a framing square to make sure they are at right angles to the beam.

**7 Install the lower level decking.** Install the lower level decking with 3-inch deck screws running the boards diagonally as shown in the Decking Plan.

## Decking Plan

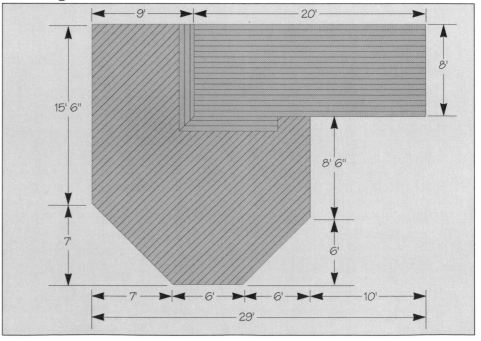

**8 Build the upper deck.** The upper beam, labeled Beam 4 on the *Framing Plan*, is made from 2x10s that are ripped to a width of 8½ inches to meet the top of the lower level decking. Before making these rip cuts, take a measurement from the top of Post 2 and Post 3 to the decking, in case your deck varies.

Beam 4 will be attached flush with the tops of Posts 3 through 7. Cut a piece of ripped lumber to span from the west side of Post 3 to the center of Post 5, and another to span from the center of Post 5 to the east side of Post 7. Together these pieces will be the same length as the ledger (19 feet 7½ inches in the deck shown). Temporarily tack these beam pieces to the ledger and mark the ledger and

the beam pieces at the same time for joists 16 inches on center.

Use 3-inch screws to attach these two beam pieces flush with the tops of Posts 3 through 7. Attach the upper level outside joists to the ends of the ledger and beam pieces. Then install the upper level interior joists, using joist hangers. Cut two pieces of ripped lumber to complete Beam 4, staggering the butt joint a few inches from the joint in the first part of the beam. Attach these pieces to the first part of the beam, driving a 3-inch screw every 12 inches. At every post, drill two ½-inch-diameter holes through the doubled beam and through the post. Install two machine bolts with washers and nuts.

Install upper level decking perpendicular to the joists as shown in the *Decking Plan*.

**9 Build the stairs.** Assemble a frame for the stairs on top of the decking, as shown in *Stair Framing*. Cut the 12 short square-ended joists and the inside and outside headers to the dimensions shown in *Stair Framing*. Assemble the frame with the joists 16 inches on center. With a helper, put the frame in place and attach it to Beam 4 with 3-inch screws. Miter one end of each of the mitered joists, and mark them in place for the cuts on the other end. Install 3-inch screws through the face of the outside headers into the mitered joists. Angle-screw the other end of the mitered joists into the inside headers. Angle-screw all the joists to the decking.

## Stair Framing

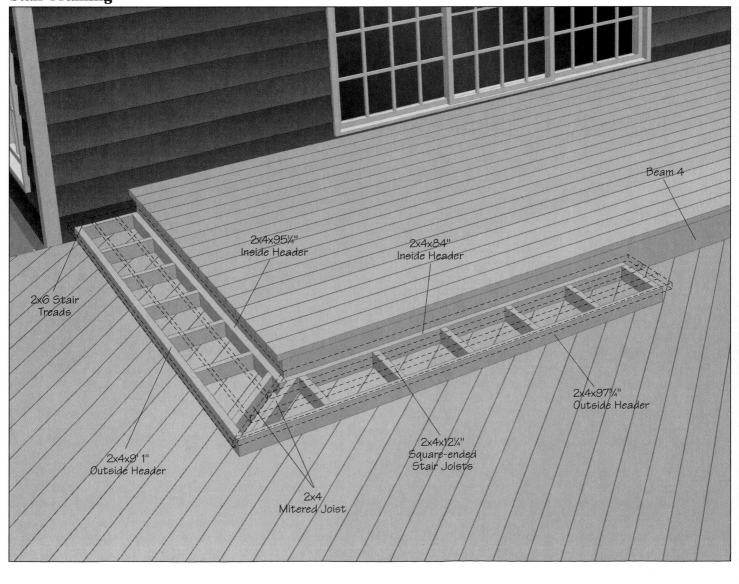

2x4x95¼" Inside Header

2x4x84" Inside Header

Beam 4

2x6 Stair Treads

2x4x97¾" Outside Header

2x4x9' 1" Outside Header

2x4x12¼" Square-ended Stair Joists

2x4 Mitered Joist

# SIMPLE RECTANGLE WITH BAYS

## Design

This handsome deck is straightforward to build and provides maximum space for the dollar. Its basic rectangular shape may not be flashy, but it provides plenty of room for cooking equipment, dining furniture, and a play area for the kids.

The railing has some simple touches that are easy to add. These include nipped corners on the ends of railing caps and bevel cuts on both ends of balusters and one end of posts. The entire deck is made of pressure-treated lumber, which will last for many years with minimal maintenance. The beam is tucked three feet under the deck to make the footings less visible.

Because the site is relatively flat, this deck was designed without posts: A built-up beam made of two 2x12s rests directly on top of the concrete footings. This means you must pour the footings level with each other, something you would not usually worry about if you used posts.

The two bays add a couple of wrinkles to the framing. The ledger must jog around them, and some joists will need to be angle-cut.

A final note before you build: The dimensions given on the drawings accompanying this project are for a particular deck built at a particular location. It is unlikely, for example, that your house has bays exactly like this one. So, use the dimensions given as an example only. Measure and cut to fit as you build, adjusting dimensions as necessary.

## Overall View

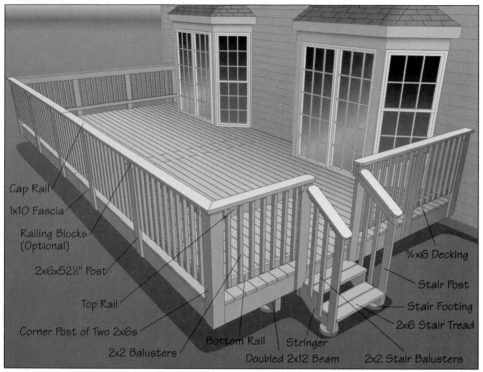

Cap Rail
1x10 Fascia
Railing Blocks (Optional)
2x6x52½" Post
Top Rail
Corner Post of Two 2x6s
2x2 Balusters
Bottom Rail
Stringer
Doubled 2x12 Beam
⁵⁄₄x6 Decking
Stair Post
Stair Footing
2x6 Stair Tread
2x2 Stair Balusters

## Parts List

|  | Quantity | Lumber Size | Part |
|---|---|---|---|
| **Framing** | 2 | 2x12x16' | Beams |
|  | 2 | 2x12x12' | Beams |
|  | 14 | 2x8x14' | Joists |
|  | 10 | 2x8x12' | Joists |
|  | 4 | 2x8x16' | Ledger, Header, and Stair Backing |
|  | 1 | 1x10x6' | Stair Backing |
| **Decking** | 26 | 5/4x6x16' |  |
|  | 30 | 5/4x6x14' |  |
| **Fascia** | 4 | 1x10x14' |  |
| **Railing** | 7 | 2x6x10' | 14 Posts, 52½" Long |
|  | 1 | 2x4x16' | Bottom Rail |
|  | 1 | 2x4x14' | Bottom Rail |
|  | 2 | 2x4x12' | Bottom Rails |
|  | 2 | 2x6x12' | Top Rail |
|  | 1 | 2x6x14' | Top Rail |
|  | 1 | 2x6x16' | Top Rail |
|  | 1 | 2x6x14' | Rail Cap |
|  | 3 | 2x6x16' | Rail Caps |
|  | 103 | 2x2x36" | Balusters |
|  | 22 | 2x3x5½" | Optional Railing Blocks |
| **Stairs** | 1 | 2x12x8' | Stringers |
|  | 1 | 2x6x12' | Treads |
|  | 2 | 2x4x8' | Posts and Top Rails |
|  | 1 | 2x6x8' | Stair Rail Cap |
|  | 2 | 2x2x8' | Balusters |

## Shopping List

### Lumber

- [ ] 1 at 1x10x6'
- [ ] 4 at 1x10x14'
- [ ] 30 at 5/4x6x14'
- [ ] 26 at 5/4x6c16'
- [ ] 103 at 2x2x36"
- [ ] 2 at 2x2x8'
- [ ] 2 at 2x4x8'
- [ ] 2 at 2x4x12'
- [ ] 1 at 2x4x14'
- [ ] 1 at 2x4x16'
- [ ] 7 at 2x6x10'
- [ ] 3 at 2x6x12'
- [ ] 2 at 2x6x14'
- [ ] 4 at 2x6x16'
- [ ] 10 at 2x6x12'
- [ ] 14 at 2x8x14'
- [ ] 4 at 2x8x16'
- [ ] 1 at 2x12x8'
- [ ] 2 at 2x12x12'
- [ ] 2 at 2x12x16'

### Hardware

- [ ] 4 J-bolts
- [ ] 35 lag screws and washers for installing ledger board pieces
- [ ] 32 joist hangers for 2x8
- [ ] 4 double joist hangers for 4x8
- [ ] 4 angled joist hangers for 2x8
- [ ] 4 angle brackets
- [ ] 5 pounds of 1¼-inch deck screws, for joist hangers
- [ ] 3 pounds of 2-inch deck screws
- [ ] 25 pounds of 2½-inch deck screws
- [ ] 3 pounds of 3-inch deck screws
- [ ] ½x3" lag screws with washers
- [ ] 3 mending or truss plates, 6"x12"

### Masonry

- [ ] Concrete for 6 footings
- [ ] 6 concrete tube forms

**1 Install ledger boards.** Mark for a ledger that is 1¾ inches below the surface of the interior floor at the threshold. Take care to make all the ledger pieces level with each other. Install the ledger, using a method appropriate to your house as described in "Installing the Ledger" page 89.

As shown in the *Framing Plan*, there is no need to miter the ends of the ledger board pieces for a perfect fit; the point is to provide continuous, adequate nailing surface for the decking.

**2 Dig and pour footings.** Lay out for the footings as shown in the *Framing Plan*, and install tube forms. Check to see that the four footings for the beam will all be level with each other, using a water or line level. The two footings for the stair should be just above grade, and should be level with each other. As soon as you have poured the concrete, place J-bolts in the center of each of the beam footings; use a string line to make sure they are lined up with each other.

**3 Install the beam.** The beam consists of doubled 2x12s. Build the beam by laminating the 2x12s together with 3-inch screws, two every 6 inches. Stagger the splices. Cut the beam to the length of the ledger, plus 3 inches.

Once the concrete is firmly set, have one or two people help you place the beam on top of the J-bolts, so that the bolts are in the center of the beam. Tap lightly with a hammer on top of the beam, so that the bolts make an impression on the beam. Remove the beam, and drill holes for each of the bolts. Place the beam on the footings, with the bolts slid into the holes.

**4 Attach the outside joists.** Attach the outside joists to the outside edges of the ledger, resting them on the beam. These joists are 3 inches longer than the other full-length joists will be.

**5 Lay out for the joists.** Cut the two pieces of 2x8 that will form

**Framing Plan**

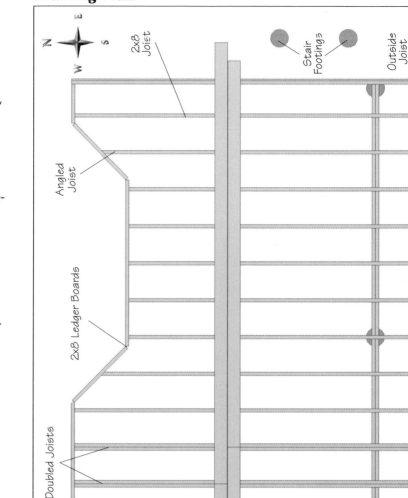

## Marking the Ledger

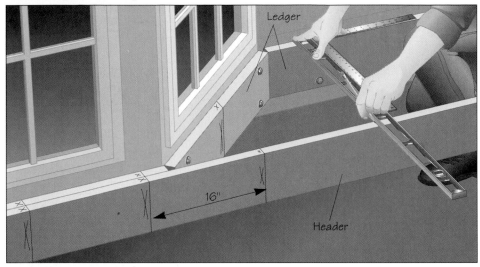

your header joist, so they will butt on a doubled joist as shown in the Framing Plan.

Temporarily attach the marked header joist to the ledger as shown in *Marking the Ledger*, and mark header and ledger together for joists. Use a framing square and level or other straightedge to mark on the sections of ledger that are set back.

**6** **Install the joists.** Attach joist hangers to both ledger and header. First, install the longest joists only, slipping them into the joist hangers on the ledger and resting them on the beam. These joists will be made from 14-foot 2x8s. Attach the header to these joists. Next, cut the two

## Stair Details

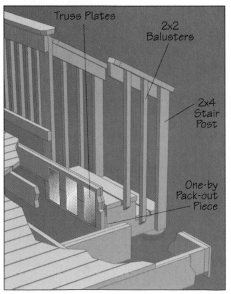

angled joists to fit, using 14-foot 2x8s. Now measure individually for the remaining joists, cut them from 12-foot 2x8s and install them.

**7** **Attach the fascia.** Cut the 1x10 fascia to cover the outside joists and header joist. Don't worry about getting the corners tight—they will be covered up by the railing posts. Attach with 2-inch deck screws.

**8** **Provide backing for stair stringers.** Cut a piece of 2x8 to 31½ inches. Rip a piece of one-by to 6½ inches wide and cut it to 31½ inches long. Use truss plates as shown in *Stair Details*, to attach the 2x8 under the rim joist. Attach the one-by pack-out piece under the fascia.

**9** **Lay the decking.** Begin with the first full piece of decking that touches the house. Place one end of each decking board over a doubled joist, staggering the butt joints by alternating the 14-foot decking boards with the 16-footers as shown in the *Framing Plan*. Allow the boards to run wild on both sides of the deck. Use 2½-inch deck screws, and drill pilot holes for all screws that will be 2 inches or less from the end of a board.

Once all the boards are laid, make a chalk line to cut boards flush to the fascia on all three sides.

**10** **Build the stairs.** The stair shown has a unit rise of 7 inches and a unit run of 11 inches.

However, since terrain varies, these dimensions will probably be useful only as an example. Read Chapter 10, "Building Stairs," to learn how to calculate and construct stairs. Add the treads, cut so that they come flush to the outside of the stringers. Attach the stringers to the backing you installed in Step 8, driving 2½-inch decking screws at an angle through the stringers into the backing.

**11** **Add the railing.** Cut the 14 2x6 posts to 52½ inches, with 45-degree cuts at both ends. Each of the two corner posts is made of two 2x6s. For these, make a 45-degree mitered rip-cut along one edge of four of the 2x6s. Cut all the rail balusters to 36 inches, with a 45-degree angle at both ends.

Position the bottom of each post flush with the bottom of the fascia. Drive four 3-inch screws, then install a lag screw with washers.

Attach the 2x6 top rail and the 2x4 bottom rail to the inside of the posts, using 2½-inch screws. Cut the rail cap pieces, nipping some of the corners with 45-degree cuts. Install the rail cap so that it overhangs the inside of the top rail by ¾ inch, and attach the balusters, using a 4-inch-wide piece of scrap lumber as a spacer.

This deck includes decorative railing blocks, which are optional. These are 22 pieces of 1½-inch-thick scrap stock ripped to 3 inches wide and cut to 5½ inches long. Attach one to each side of each post with 3-inch decking screws driven through the inside of the top rails.

**12** **Build the stair rail.** To construct the stair rail, first attach the two 2x4 stair posts to the stringers as shown in *Stair Details*. Do not cut the posts to height yet. Next, attach the 2x4 top rails that run parallel to the stair slope. Install the four 2x2 stair balusters, spacing them equidistant from the deck posts, stair posts, and each other. Cut the tops of the stair posts and balusters flush to the top of the top rail, then install the rail cap.

# JAPANESE-STYLE COVERED DECK

Here's a truly elegant free-standing deck. The deck itself is nothing spectacular—just a simple rectangle. What makes it special are the railings, benches, and the overhead structure. Generous and comfortable benches with attached tables provide plenty of room for reading, lounging, and conversing. The distinctive railings, inspired by Japanese architecture, will show off your craftsmanship. And the overhead structure filters midday light gracefully.

You may be able to buy the large timbers for the overhead in cedar. If not, brown pressure-treated wood is a good choice. It may take a lot of shopping around before you find pieces this large that look good.

The railings and benches are not as complicated as they look, but they do require accurate, clean cuts. If you have good basic carpentry skills and some patience, you will be able to do it. If you have a power miter saw or radial arm saw, a table saw, and a router, the work will be much easier. To build the top rails with those distinctive overhangs, you will need to make a lap joint (we'll show you how). The rail posts do not actually come up through the rail caps; the tops are actually separate post caps, which match the tops of the bench posts to complete the illusion. We'll show you how to make these yourself with a table saw or radial arm saw.

## Parts List

| | Quantity | Lumber Size | Part |
|---|---|---|---|
| **Deck Framing** | 2 | 4x6x14' | Beams |
| | 11 | 2x6x10' | Joists |
| **Fascia** | 2 | 1x8x14' | |
| | 2 | 1x8x10' | |
| **Decking** | 21 | 2x6x14' | |
| **Railings** | 3 | 4x4x10' | 9 Posts |
| | 4 | 2x4x10' | Rails |
| | 1 | 2x4x12' | Rails |
| | 1 | 4x4x8' | 1 Post and Post Caps |
| **Benches and Tables** | 2 | 4x4x8' | 4 Posts |
| | 1 | 2x4x8' | 4 Back Supports |
| | 1 | 2x6x8' | 4 Seat supports |
| | 1 | 2x2x6' | 4 Legs |
| | 2 | 2x4x8' | Back Bands |
| | 6 | 2x6x10' | 12 Seat and Back Slats |
| | 1 | 2x4x8' | Front Apron, Angled Apron, and Outside Apron |
| | 1 | 2x6x8' | Shaped Aprons |
| | 2 | 2x3x8' | Cleats |
| | 2 | 2x6x8' | Tabletop Slats |
| | 1 | 2x6x12' | 2 Seat Bands |
| **Nosing and Bottom Fascia Piece** | 2 | 1x4x14' | Nosing |
| | 4 | 1x3x12' | Bottom Fascia Piece |
| **Overhead Structure** | 4 | 6x6x12' | Posts |
| | 2 | 6x6x18' | Beams |
| | 3 | 4x6x16' | Cross Beams |
| | 5 | 2x4x18' | Rafters |
| | 9 | 16' Bamboo Poles | Top Pieces |
| | 4 | 18' Bamboo Poles | Cross Ties |
| | 3 | 6'x15' Reed Fencing | Lattice |

## Shopping List

### Lumber
- [ ] 4 at 1x3x12'
- [ ] 2 at 1x4x14'
- [ ] 2 at 1x8x10'
- [ ] 2 at 1x8x14'
- [ ] 1 at 2x2x6'
- [ ] 2 at 2x3x8'
- [ ] 4 at 2x4x8'
- [ ] 4 at 2x4x10'
- [ ] 1 at 2x4x12'
- [ ] 5 at 2x4x18'
- [ ] 4 at 2x6x8'
- [ ] 17 at 2x6x10'
- [ ] 1 at 2x6x12'
- [ ] 21 at 2x6x14'
- [ ] 3 at 4x4x8'
- [ ] 3 at 4x4x10'
- [ ] 2 at 4x6x14'
- [ ] 3 at 4x6x16'
- [ ] 4 at 6x6x12'
- [ ] 2 at 6x6x18'

### Bambo Poles and Reed Fencing
- [ ] 9 at 16'
- [ ] 4 at 18'
- [ ] 36'x15'

### Hardware
- [ ] 6 elevated post bases
- [ ] 18 joist hangers for 2x6
- [ ] 4 angle brackets
- [ ] 2 pounds of joist hanger nails or 1¼-inch deck screws
- [ ] 1 pound of 2¼-inch deck screws
- [ ] 5 pounds of 2-inch deck screws
- [ ] 15 pounds of 3-inch deck screws
- [ ] 26 pieces ¼-inch-diameter x 3½-inch lag screws
- [ ] 3 pieces ¼-inch diameter x 3-inch lag screws
- [ ] 1 pound of U-shaped stainless steel wire ties
- [ ] Copper wire

### Masonry
- [ ] Concrete and gravel for four large post holes and 6 footings
- [ ] 6 concrete tube forms

## Overall View

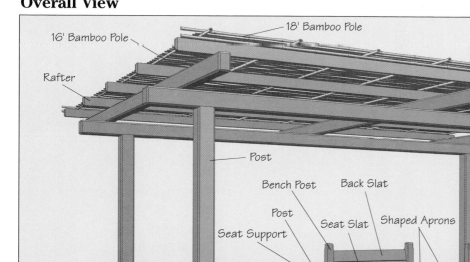

16' Bamboo Pole

18' Bamboo Pole

Rafter

Post

Bench Post

Back Slat

Post

Seat Slat

Shaped Aprons

Seat Support

Angled Apron

Tabletop Slats

Beam

Outside Apron

Cross Beam

Post Cap

Nosing

Bottom Fascia Piece

Fascia

Front Apron

Leg

Decking

Seat Band

Top Rail

Bottom Rail

## Framing Plan

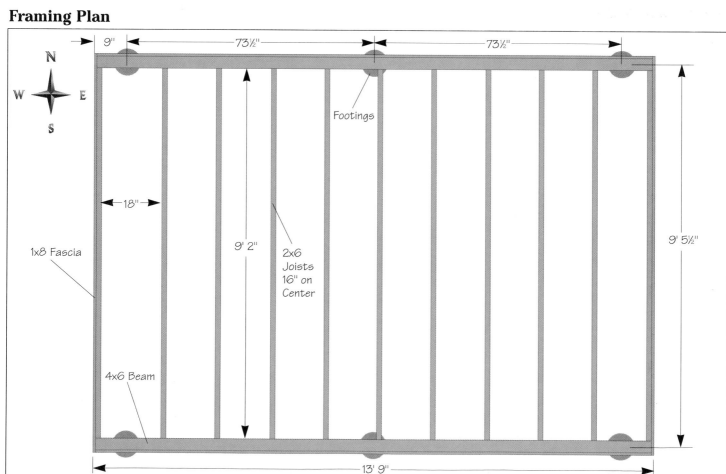

9"

73½"

73½"

N
W      E
S

Footings

18"

9' 5½"

9' 2"

2x6
Joists
16" on
Center

1x8 Fascia

4x6 Beam

13' 9"

**1 Install beams and footings.** Lay out for the footings, using the dimensions in the *Framing Plan*. Dig the holes and install concrete tube forms. Cut the two beams exactly to length. Place some scrap blocks of lumber on the ground near the tube forms and place the beams on top of them, so that they are above the tube forms and not resting on them.

Check for square, and make sure the beams are 9 feet 2 inches apart. Level the beams with each other, using the scrap blocks and some wood shims as shown in *Preparing to Pour Concrete*. Over each of the tube forms, install an elevated post base by screwing it onto the beam. The bottom of the post base will hang down into the tube form. Check again for square and distance between beams. Pour the concrete to fill the form around the anchor portion of the post bases and allow the concrete to harden before removing the blocks and shims.

**2 Install the joists.** On the beams, lay out joist positions 16 inches on center, starting at the east end. (The westernmost spacing will be further as shown on the framing plan.) Install joist hangers and joists. Use angle brackets at both ends of each end joist.

**3 Install fascia and lay the deck-ing.** Install fascia on the four sides, using 2-inch deck screws every 12 inches. Place the screws where they will be hidden by the nosing and fascia bottom trim. If your deck is very low, you may have to rip-cut the fascia, so it doesn't come into contact with the ground.

Install the 2x6 decking, using 3-inch deck screws. Allow the decking to run wild as you install, and finish with a chalkline cut, so that the decking is flush with the face of the fascia.

**4 Cut and notch the bench posts and railing posts.** Cut the posts to the dimensions shown in *Cutting Posts*. (See "Cutting Notches" on page 66 and "Cutting Dadoes and Rabbets," on page 67. There are four bench posts; two rail posts notched on the left; two rail posts notched on the

## Preparing to Pour Concrete

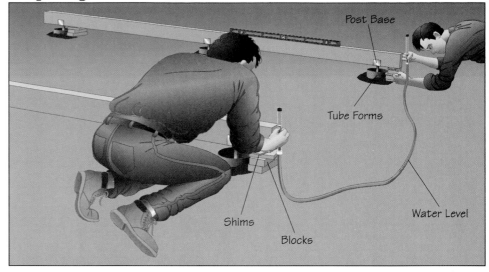

right; three rail posts notched on both sides; and three corner rail posts.

**5 Install posts and bottom rails.** Install the corner posts, then the middle posts, positioning them as shown on the *Decking/Seating Plan*. Attach each post to the deck with two countersunk 3½-inch lag screws. On the deck shown, the screws are covered with wood plugs made from pieces of dowel. Cut the bottom rail pieces to fit, making a rabbet cut at the end of each piece. Cut ¾-inch notches on the corner end of each front rail as shown in *Installing Posts and Rails*. Install the bottom rail rab-

bets into the rail dadoes. Secure each joint by driving two 3-inch deck screws at an angle from the bottom of the rails. Drill pilot holes for each screw, to avoid splitting the wood.

**6 Cut and install the top rails.** Cut the top rails to the lengths shown in the *Decking/Seating Plan*. Then chamfer all four sides of the rail ends as shown in *Installing Posts and Rails*. Lay out cut lines ½ inch from each end of the rails, on all four sides of the rails. Then tilt the blade on a power miter box or radial arm saw to 45 degrees and cut four chamfers on each rail end.

## Cutting Posts

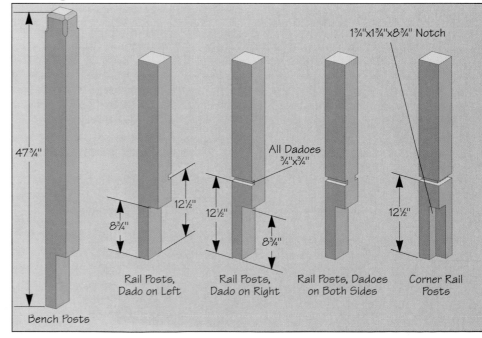

## Decking/Seating Plan

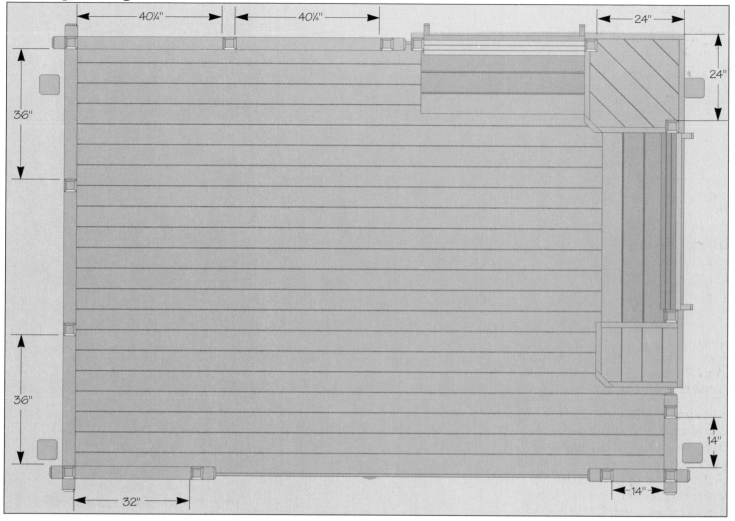

## Installing Posts and Rails

At the three corners, make ¾-inch-deep dadoes in both top rails to create half-lap joints, as shown in *Installing Posts and Rails*. Secure the rails to the posts with ¼-inch-diameter x 3-inch countersunk lag screws. Use one screw at each connection, driving it through both rails at the half-lap joints.

**7 Make post caps and complete the bench posts.** The post caps and the bench posts all get chamfered at their tops and all four sides. Because the post caps are only 4 inches long, for safety you need to make the decorative chamfer cuts before cutting the pieces to length.

Start with a piece of 4x4 about 8 inches long. Square one end and lay out stop lines on opposing faces, 3 inches from the end as shown in *Making Post Caps*. Set a chamfering bit in your router for a chamfer of about ½-inch.

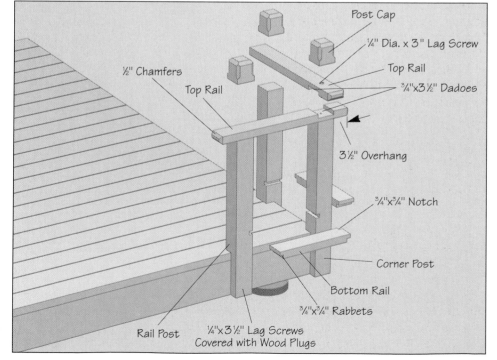

## Making Post Caps

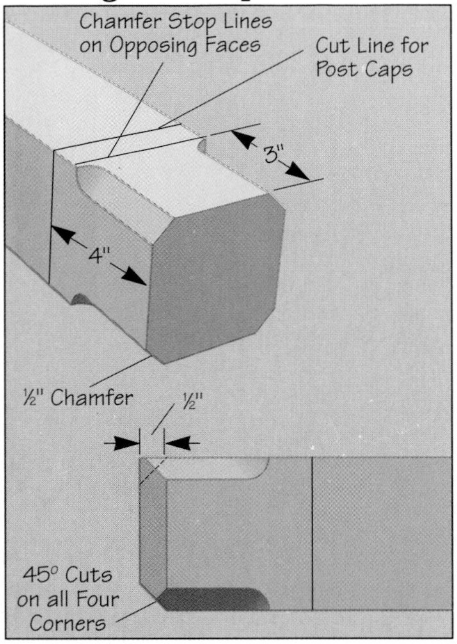

Chamfer Stop Lines on Opposing Faces
Cut Line for Post Caps
3"
4"
½" Chamfer
½"
45° Cuts on all Four Corners


## Back Support Layout

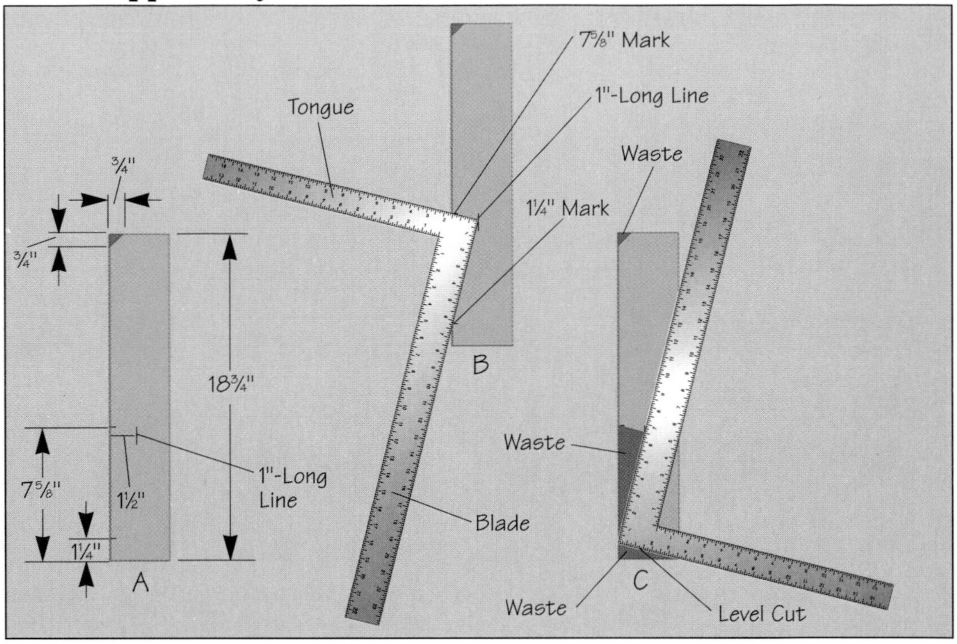

7⅝" Mark
1"-Long Line
Tongue
Waste
¾"
¾"
1¼" Mark
18¾"
B
Waste
7⅝"
1½"
1"-Long Line
Blade
1¼"
A
C
Waste
Level Cut


Clamp the 4x4 in place. Make a 3-inch-long chamfer on each edge of the 4x4 stopping at the stop line.

Now tilt the blade on your power miter box or radial arm saw to 45 degrees. Chamfer all four sides of the ends of the 4x4, just as you did the ends of the rails. Cut the 4x4 off at 4 inches and repeat the process six more times. Finally rout and cut the same chamfer details on the ends of the bench posts.

On the deck shown, a biscuit joiner was used to attach the post caps for a fastener-free finish. Dowel joints would be another approach. The simplest way to attach the caps is with 4d galvanized casing nails driven into pre-drilled angled holes on both sides of each cap. The procedure for chamfering the bench posts is the same as for the post caps except, of course, you won't cut off the chamfered part.

**8 Cut the back supports.** Cut four pieces of 2x4 to 18¾ inches long for the back supports. On one piece, lay out the angled cut as shown in "A" of *Back Support Layout*. Along one edge, make marks at 1¼ inches and 7⅝ inches from the bottom. From the 7⅝-inch mark, measure over 1½ inches as shown in "A" and strike a line down about 1 inch.

To lay out the notch, place your framing square on the board as shown in "B" of *Back Support Layout*, aligning the outside of the blade to the 1¼-inch mark, the outside of the tongue to the 7⅝-inch mark, and the corner to the 1-inch-long line.

To lay out the level cut, align the square to the notch and the bottom corner of the square as shown in "C" of *Back Support Layout*. Cut one back support and use it as a template to lay out the remaining four.

**9 Cut the seat supports.** Now cut four pieces of 2x6 to 18¾ inches long for the seat supports. Lay out a seat support as shown in *Seat Side View*. Make a mark along the top of

## Seat Side View

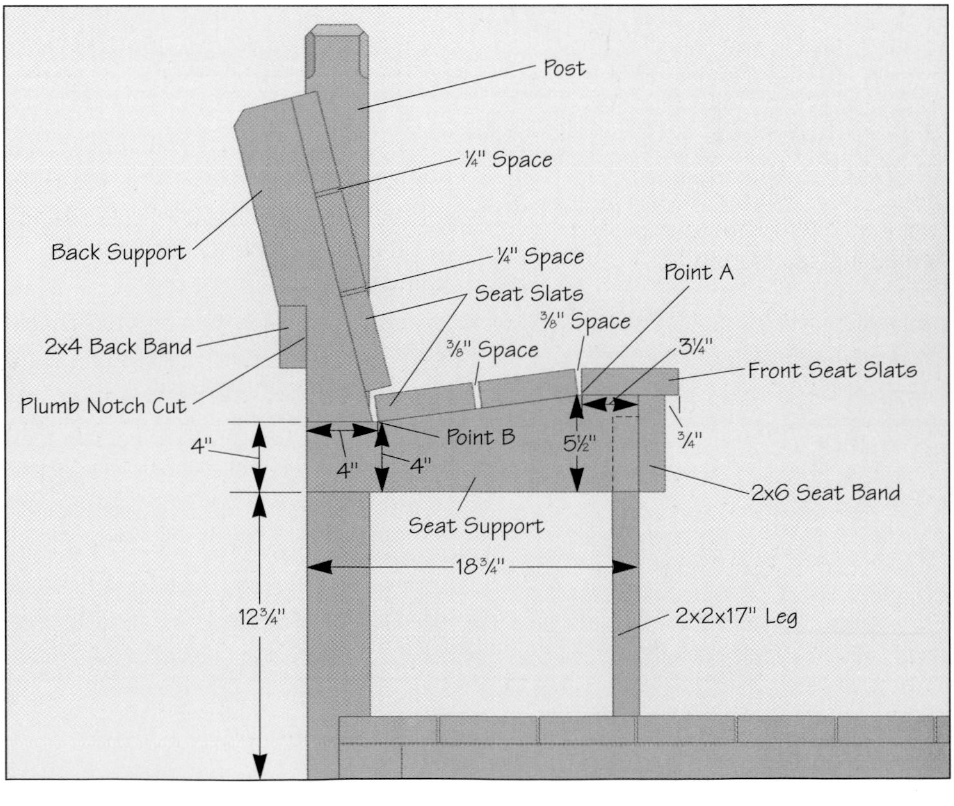

Post
¼" Space
Back Support
¼" Space
Seat Slats
Point A
⅜" Space
⅜" Space
2x4 Back Band
3¼"
Front Seat Slats
Plumb Notch Cut
4"
Point B
5½"
¾"
4"
4"
2x6 Seat Band
Seat Support
18¾"
12¾"
2x2x17" Leg

## Bench and Table Construction

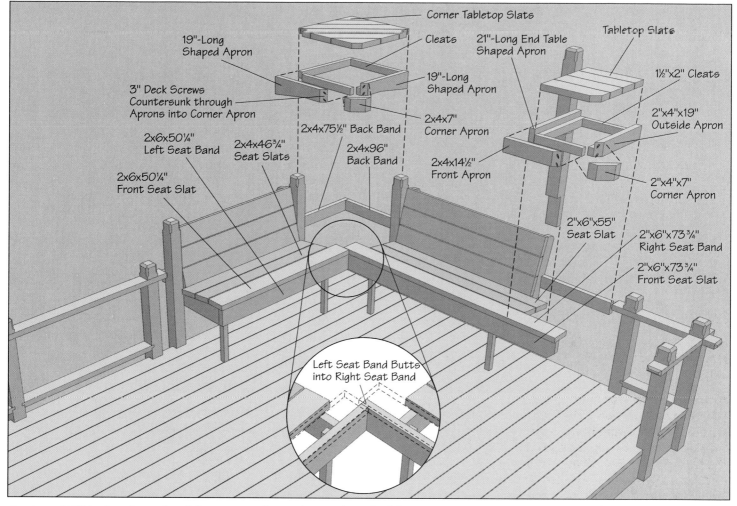

**Corner Tabletop Slats**

**Cleats**

**Tabletop Slats**

**19"-Long Shaped Apron**

**21"-Long End Table Shaped Apron**

**1½"x2" Cleats**

**3" Deck Screws Countersunk through Aprons into Corner Apron**

**19"-Long Shaped Apron**

**2"x4"x19" Outside Apron**

**2x6x50¼" Left Seat Band**

**2x4x46¾" Seat Slats**

**2x4x75½" Back Band**

**2x4x7" Corner Apron**

**2x4x96" Back Band**

**2"x4"x7" Corner Apron**

**2x6x50¼" Front Seat Slat**

**2x4x14½" Front Apron**

**2"x6"x55" Seat Slat**

**2"x6"x73¾" Right Seat Band**

**2"x6"x73¾" Front Seat Slat**

**Left Seat Band Butts into Right Seat Band**

the board 3¼ inches from the right side to locate Point A as shown. Then draw a 4-inch-long horizontal line located 4 inches from the bottom of the left corner to locate Point B. Draw a line from Point A to Point B to create the seat shape. Cut the board and use it as a template to make the remaining seat supports.

**10 Assemble the bench frames.** Cut the legs to 17 inches long. Measure up 12¾ inches from the deck along the seat posts to mark where the seat supports will go as shown in *Seat Side View*. Align the bottom of the seat supports to the line, check that they are level at the bottom and secure each support with three 3-inch deck screws.

Position the 2x2 legs as shown and secure each to the front inside edge of a seat support with two 3-inch screws. Cut the seat bands to the dimensions

shown in *Bench and Table Construction* and screw them to the front of the seat supports with three 3-inch screws at each connection.

Position the back supports with their plumb notch cuts flush to the outside of the posts and the level cuts sitting on the seat supports. Secure with 3-inch screws.

Cut 2x4 back bands to the lengths shown in *Bench and Table Construction*. Tuck them against the top of the back support notches and secure them to the posts with two 3-inch screws at each connection.

**11 Install seat and back slats.** For each bench back, cut three 2x6s to fit between the posts. Position the slats as shown in *Seat Side View* and attach them to the supports with three 3-inch deck screws at each connection.

The front seat slats on each bench are longer than the other slats because they continue under the tables. Cut these slats to the same length as the seat bands. Use 3-inch screws to fasten the longer slat to the right seat band flush at both ends with a ¾-inch overhang at front. Attach the shorter slat to the the left seat band butting it against the other slat with a ¾-inch overhang at front. (This will give you a ¾-inch overhang on the left end.) Cut two slats to 45¾ inches long and attach them to the left bench flush with the left end of the front slat. Cut two slats to 55 inches long. Attach them to the right seat supports with equal overhang on both ends. Rout a ½-inch roundover along the outside edges of the front slats.

**12 Cut the shaped table aprons.** The corner table is supported by both benches and the back band. The end table is support-

## Scribing Table Apron

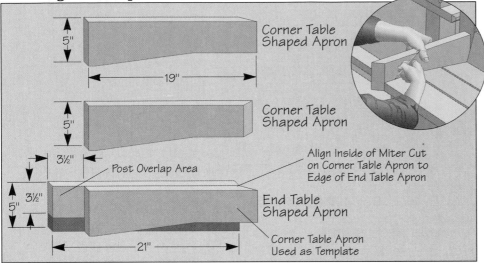

5"

19"

Corner Table
Shaped Apron

5"

Corner Table
Shaped Apron

3½"

Post Overlap Area

Align Inside of Miter Cut
on Corner Table Apron to
Edge of End Table Apron

3½"

5"

End Table
Shaped Apron

21"

Corner Table Apron
Used as Template

ed by the extended front bench slat and the back band. The distances between your posts and the dimensions of your bench may vary a bit, so the best way to construct the tables is to scribe and cut the pieces to fit. Also, rout a ½-inch roundover on the top outside edge of the table aprons before you install them. Otherwise the router base will hit the post before the chamfer is complete.

First rip a 6-foot 2x6 to 5 inches wide. Cut two pieces to 19 inches long with 45 degree angles on one end of each. These will make the shaped aprons for the corner bench. Cut a third piece to 21 inches long (square on both ends) to make the end table shaped apron.

To obtain the shape of the bottom cut on the three shaped aprons, butt one of the 19-inch pieces against the post at the left side of the left bench. Align the bottom of the piece to the bottom of the front seat slat as shown in *Scribing Table Aprons*. Run your pencil along the top of the seat slats. Cut the piece and use it as a template to make the other corner table shaped apron. Finally, use one of the corner table shaped aprons as a template for the end table shaped as shown. The 3½-inch-square area on the end table shaped apron will be screwed to a post.

**13** Install the shaped table aprons. Butt the longer shaped apron against the back band and

screw it to the side of the post with 3-inch deck screws. Make sure the apron is square to the bench, then fasten it to the bench with two 3-inch screws through the bottom of each seat slat. Drive two screws through the back band into the apron ends.

Butt both shorter shaped aprons against their posts and fasten them to the bottom of the seat slats with two screws each. Hold a piece of 2x4 against both 45-degree faces to make sure they are in the same plane. If not, shorten one before fastening with more screws. Put a length of 2x4 in the corner apron position and mark the position of the 45-degree cuts on both ends.

**14** Complete the tables. Cut the end table front apron and one corner apron to the dimensions shown in *Bench and Table Construction*. Fasten them together with two 3-inch screws as shown. Screw this assembly to the front of the end table shaped apron. Make sure the aprons are square, then measure for the length of the outside end table apron in case it varies from the 19 inches shown. Cut the outside apron to fit with a 45 degree angle on one end.

Rip 2x3s to 2 inches wide to make cleats to support the table top salts. Cut the cleats to fit around the inside perimeter of the table as shown in *Bench and Table Construction*. Use 2¼-inch deck screws to attach the cleats 1½ inches below the tops of the aprons.

Cut 2x6 tabletop slats to fit between the aprons as shown. Note that the corner table slats are positioned 45-degrees to the bench slats while the end table slats are parallel to the bench slats.

**15** Add nosing. Rip 1¾-inch-wide pieces for the nosing. Cut and attach the nosing and the 1x3 fascia trim around the perimeter of the decking with 2¼-inch deck screws. Also attach pieces at the bottom of the fascia, avoiding contact with the ground.

**16** Install 6x6 posts. The posts that support the overhead structure are butted against the nosing and bottom fascia trim. They are located 10½ inches from each corner as measured from the outside of the nosing. Dig 42-inch-deep post holes that are 10 inches in diameter. (Hole depth requirements may vary regionally; check with your building department.) Throw some gravel in the bottom.

Rout a ½-inch chamfer on all four sides of each post, stopping about 2 feet from what will be the top end of each post. Leave the bit in the router.

With a helper or two, place the posts in the holes. Check for square and plumb, and brace temporarily. Pour the concrete, and allow it to set.

The deck shown here has posts whose bottoms have been clad in copper sheet metal, attached with copper nails. This is a traditional oriental way of avoiding rot: As the copper oxidizes (and turns green), it protects the wood from rot and mildew. (Remember that copper is the main ingredient used for pressure-treating lumber.)

**17** Cut the posts and shape their tops. Cut the posts to 8 feet high, checking that the tops are level with each other. In the deck shown, the top of the roof posts are shaped to match the chamfered beams. This is a classy detail that you can skip, but it really isn't hard to do. The procedure is shown in *Shaping the Roof Post Tops*. First, lay out

## Shaping Roof Post Tops

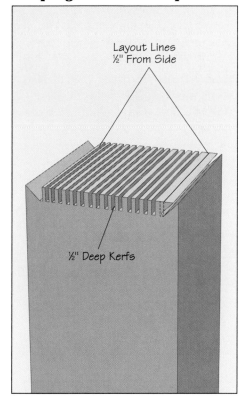

Layout Lines
½" From Side

½" Deep Kerfs

two lines along the top of the posts, ½-inch from parallel sides as shown. Set your circular saw to a 45-degree-angle. Then set the cutting depth to ½ inch. (Don't set the depth first, if you do it won't cut deep enough.) Make two angled cuts as shown.

Set the saw blade back to 90 degrees and reset the cutting depth to ½ inch. First cut along the layout lines. Then make repeated kerf cuts across the top of the posts, turning most of the waste area into sawdust. Use a chisel to knock out the rest of the waste and clean up the notch. Now, use the router to continue the chamfers to the top of the posts.

18 **Complete the roof.** Cut the 4x6 cross beams to 15 feet. Rout a 1/2-inch chamfer on all edges of the cross beams and the 6x6 beams including the ends.

With at least two helpers and two step ladders, raise the 6x6 beams in place, check that they overhang the posts equally on both sides, then fasten to the posts with angle-driven 3-inch screws. Set the three 4x6 cross beams on top of the 6x6 beams, and attach in the same way.

Lay out 2x4 rafters as shown in *Overhead Structure*, and fasten to the 4x6 cross beams with angle-driven 2-inch screws. Lay out for the bamboo poles and fasten these by driving 3-inch screws through the poles into the 2x4 rafters.

Finish by laying rolls of reed fencing on top of the bamboo poles or 2x2s. Fasten these with U-shaped stainless steel wire ties driven every 6 inches into the bamboo poles or 2x2s.

At the north and south ends of the roof, the 16-foot-long bamboo pieces are sandwiched between two 18-foot bamboo cross ties. With a helper, hold the pieces in place and tie them together with copper wire at each joint.

## Overhead Structure

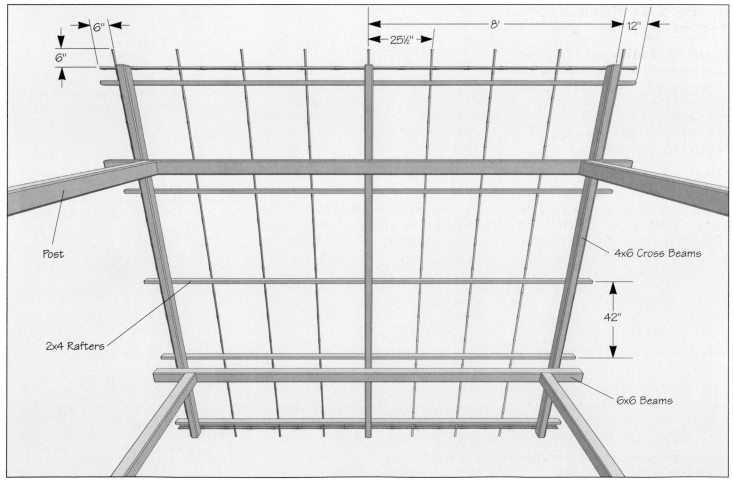

6"

6"

6"

25½"

8'

12"

Post

2x4 Rafters

4x6 Cross Beams

42"

6x6 Beams

# GLOSSARY

**Actual Dimensions** The exact measurements of a piece of lumber after it has been cut, surfaced, and dried. For example, a 2x4's actual dimensions are 1½x3½ inches.

**Architectural Scale Ruler** A tool which enables you to instantly convert to your scale: one side will give you numbers based on a ⅛-inch scale, another on a ¼-inch scale, and another on a ½-inch scale.

**Balusters** The numerous vertical pieces, often made of 2x2 or 1x4, that fill in spaces between rail posts and provide a fence-like structure.

**Beam** A large framing member, usually four-by material or doubled-up two bys, which is attached horizontally to the posts and used to support joists.

**Blocking** Usually solid pieces of lumber, the same dimensions as the joists, which are cut to fit snugly between the joists to prevent excessive warping. Also called bridging or bracing.

**Building Codes** Municipal rules regulating safe building practices and procedures. Generally, the codes encompass structural, electrical, plumbing, and mechanical remodeling and new construction. Confirmation of conformity to local codes by inspection may be required.

**Cantilever** Construction that extends out beyond its vertical support.

**Curing** The slow chemical action that hardens concrete.

**Dado** A type of groove that runs across the grain.

**Decking** Boards nailed to joists to form the deck surface.

**Dipping** A treatment where wood is immersed in a bath of sealant for several minutes, then allowed to air-dry.

**Fascia** Board facing that covers the exposed ends and sides of decking to provide a finished appearance.

**Footing** The concrete base that supports posts or steps.

**Frost Line** The maximum depth to which soil freezes. Your local building department can provide information on the frost line depth in your area.

**Grade** The ground level. On-grade means at or on the natural ground level.

**Joist** Structural member, usually two-by lumber, commonly placed perpendicularly across beams to support deck boards.

**Joist Hanger** Metal connector used to join a joist and beam so that the tops are in the same plane.

**Kickback** The action that happens when a saw suddenly jumps backward out of the cut.

**Knot** The high-density root of a limb that is very dense but is not connected to the surrounding wood.

**Lattice** A cross-pattern structure that is made of wood, metal, or plastic.

**Ledger** Horizontal board attached to the side of a house or wall to support a deck or an overhead cover.

**Lignin** The binding agent that holds the cells in wood together.

**Nominal Dimensions** The identifying dimensions of a piece of lumber (e.g. 2x4) which are larger than the actual dimensions (1½x3½).

**Penny (abbreviated "d")** Unit of measurement for nail length; e.g., a 10d nail is 3 inches long.

**Permanent Structure** Any structure that is anchored to the ground or a house.

**Permit** A license that authorizes permission to do work on your home. Minor repairs and remodeling work usually do not call for a permit, but if the job consists of extending the water supply and drain, waste, vent system, adding an electrical circuit, or making structural changes to a building, a permit may be necessary.

**Plan Drawing** A drawing which gives an overhead view of the deck showing where all footings and lumber pieces go.

**Plumb** Vertically straight, in relation to a horizontally level surface.

**Plunge Cut** A cut that can't begin from the outside of the board and must be made from the middle.

**Post** A vertical member, usually 4x4 or 6x6, that supports either the deck or railing.

**Post Anchor** A metal fastener designed to keep the post from wandering and also to inhibit rot by holding the post a bit above the concrete.

**Posthole Digger** A clamshell-type tool used to dig holes for posts.

**Power Auger** A tool that is powered by a gasoline engine and used for drilling into the ground. Often used in larger projects to dig postholes.

**Pressure-Treated Lumber** Wood that has had preservatives forced into it under pressure to make it repel rot and insects.

**On Center** A point of reference for measuring. For example, "16 inches on center" means 16 inches from the center of one framing member to the center of the next.

**Rabbet** A ledge cut along one edge of a workpiece.

**Rail** A horizontal member that is placed between posts and used for support or as a barrier.

**Recommended Span** The distance a piece of lumber can safely traverse without being supported underneath.

**Redwood** A straight-grain, weather-resistant wood used for outdoor building.

**Rip Cut** A cut made with the grain on a piece of wood.

**Riser** Vertical boards placed between stringers on stairs to support stair treads. They are optional on exterior stairs.

**Site Plan** A drawing which maps out your house and yard. Also called a base plan.

**Skewing** Driving two nails at opposing angles. This technique creates a sounder connection by "hooking" the boards together as well as by reducing the possibility of splitting.

**Skirt** Solid band of horizontal wood members (fascia) installed around the deck perimeter to conceal exposed ends of joists and deck boards.

**Stringer** On stairs, the diagonal boards that support the treads and risers; also called a stair horse.

**Tacknail** To nail one structural member to another temporarily with a minimal amount of nails.

**Toenail** Joining two boards together by nailing at an angle through the end, or toe, on one board and into the face of another.

**Top Cap** A horizontal piece of lumber laid flat on top of the post and top rail, covering the end grain of the post and providing a flat surface wide enough to set objects on.

**Tread** On stairs, the horizontal boards supported by the stringers.

# METRIC CONVERSION CHARTS

## Lumber

**Sizes:** Metric cross sections are so close to their nearest U.S. sizes, as noted at right, that for most purposes they may be considered equivalents.

**Lengths:** Metric lengths are based on a 300mm module, which is slightly shorter in length than an U.S. foot. It will, therefore, be important to check your requirements accurately to the nearest inch and consult the table below to find the metric length required.

**Areas:** The metric area is a square meter. Use the following conversion factor when converting from U.S. data: 100 sq. feet = 9.29 sq. meters.

## Metric Lengths

| Lengths Meters | Equivalent Feet and Inches |
|---|---|
| 1.8m | 5' 10⅞" |
| 2.1m | 6' 10⅝" |
| 2.4m | 7' 10½" |
| 2.7m | 8' 10¼" |
| 3.0m | 9' 10⅛" |
| 3.3m | 10' 9⅞" |
| 3.6m | 11' 9¾" |
| 3.9m | 12' 9½" |
| 4.2m | 13' 9⅜" |
| 4.5m | 14' 9⅓" |
| 4.8m | 15' 9" |
| 5.1m | 16' 8¾" |
| 5.4m | 17' 8⅝" |
| 5.7m | 18' 8⅜" |
| 6.0m | 19' 8¼" |
| 6.3m | 20' 8" |
| 6.6m | 21' 7⅞" |
| 6.9m | 22' 7⅝" |
| 7.2m | 23' 7½" |
| 7.5m | 24' 7¼" |
| 7.8m | 25' 7⅛" |

## Metric Sizes (Shown Before Nearest U.S. Equivalent)

| Millimeters | Inches | Millimeters | Inches |
|---|---|---|---|
| 16 x 75 | ⅝ x 3 | 44 x 150 | 1¾ x 6 |
| 16 x 100 | ⅝ x 4 | 44 x 175 | 1¾ x 7 |
| 16 x 125 | ⅝ x 5 | 44 x 200 | 1¾ x 8 |
| 16 x 150 | ⅝ x 6 | 44 x 225 | 1¾ x 9 |
| 19 x 75 | ¾ x 3 | 44 x 250 | 1¾ x 10 |
| 19 x 100 | ¾ x 4 | 44 x 300 | 1¾ x 12 |
| 19 x 125 | ¾ x 5 | 50 x 75 | 2 x 3 |
| 19 x 150 | ¾ x 6 | 50 x 100 | 2 x 4 |
| 22 x 75 | ⅞ x 3 | 50 x 125 | 2 x 5 |
| 22 x 100 | ⅞ x 4 | 50 x 150 | 2 x 6 |
| 22 x 125 | ⅞ x 5 | 50 x 175 | 2 x 7 |
| 22 x 150 | ⅞ x 6 | 50 x 200 | 2 x 8 |
| 25 x 75 | 1 x 3 | 50 x 225 | 2 x 9 |
| 25 x 100 | 1 x 4 | 50 x 250 | 2 x 10 |
| 25 x 125 | 1 x 5 | 50 x 300 | 2 x 12 |
| 25 x 150 | 1 x 6 | 63 x 100 | 2½ x 4 |
| 25 x 175 | 1 x 7 | 63 x 125 | 2½ x 5 |
| 25 x 200 | 1 x 8 | 63 x 150 | 2½ x 6 |
| 25 x 225 | 1 x 9 | 63 x 175 | 2½ x 7 |
| 25 x 250 | 1 x 10 | 63 x 200 | 2½ x 8 |
| 25 x 300 | 1 x 12 | 63 x 225 | 2½ x 9 |
| 32 x 75 | 1¼ x 3 | 75 x 100 | 3 x 4 |
| 32 x 100 | 1¼ x 4 | 75 x 125 | 3 x 5 |
| 32 x 125 | 1¼ x 5 | 75 x 150 | 3 x 6 |
| 32 x 150 | 1¼ x 6 | 75 x 175 | 3 x 7 |
| 32 x 175 | 1¼ x 7 | 75 x 200 | 3 x 8 |
| 32 x 200 | 1¼ x 8 | 75 x 225 | 3 x 9 |
| 32 x 225 | 1¼ x 9 | 75 x 250 | 3 x 10 |
| 32 x 250 | 1¼ x 10 | 75 x 300 | 3 x 12 |
| 32 x 300 | 1¼ x 12 | 100 x 100 | 4 x 4 |
| 38 x 75 | 1½ x 3 | 100 x 150 | 4 x 6 |
| 38 x 100 | 1½ x 4 | 100 x 200 | 4 x 8 |
| 38 x 125 | 1½ x 5 | 100 x 250 | 4 x 10 |
| 38 x 150 | 1½ x 6 | 100 x 300 | 4 x 12 |
| 38 x 175 | 1½ x 7 | 150 x 150 | 6 x 6 |
| 38 x 200 | 1½ x 8 | 150 x 200 | 6 x 8 |
| 38 x 225 | 1½ x 9 | 150 x 300 | 6 x 12 |
| 44 x 75 | 1¾ x 3 | 200 x 200 | 8 x 8 |
| 44 x 100 | 1¾ x 4 | 250 x 250 | 10 x 10 |
| 44 x 125 | 1¾ x 5 | 300 x 300 | 12 x 12 |

Dimensions are based on 1m = 3.28 feet, or 1 foot = 0.3048m

Dimensions are based on 1 inch = 25mm

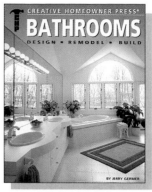
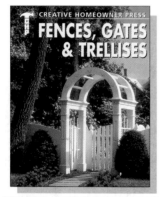
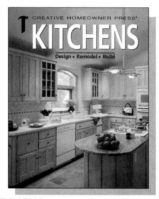

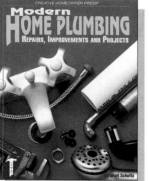
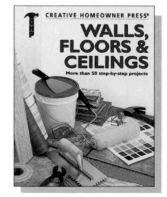